Religions of the West

NINIAN SMART

Religions of the West

PRENTICE HALL
Englewood Cliffs, N.J. 07632

Prentice Hall Inc
A Division of Simon & Schuster
Englewood Cliffs, New Jersey 07632

10 9 8 7 6 5 4 3 2 1

ISBN 0–13–156811–6

This book was designed and produced by
CALMANN & KING LTD., London

Designed by Andrew Shoolbred
Picture research by Donna Thynne
Maps by Hardlines, Oxford, and Tony Wilkins

Typeset by Tek-Art, Addiscombe, Croydon
Printed in Hong Kong

Cover: Unknown illustrator, *The Ascension of
Muhammad*, 1593–43, Persian manuscript. Oriental
Collection, the British Library, London.

Frontispiece: A father teaches his son how to put on
the *tefillin*, containing texts from the Torah. They
serve as a permanent reminder of God, and should be
worn by male Jews of thirteen years and above. They
are not worn on the Sabbath and festival days, for
these times are themselves special reminders of the
divine presence.

Contents

Preface

This book incorporates much material from my *The World's Religions* (1989). There I wrote of human religious history on a regional basis: here I tend to follow traditions. I have created two wholly new chapters, one the introduction and the other the concluding survey. These in turn are different from the corresponding parts of my parallel *Religions of Asia*. I have also expanded some treatments, for example of Sufism and Shi'a. I should like to thank Melanie White, Damian Thompson, and Rosemary Bradley for help in preparing this book for press, and Elaine Yastishock and Cybelle Shattuck for facilitations in Santa Barbara.

Ninian Smart
University of California, Santa Barbara
June 1993

Introduction:
The Importance of Understanding the Value Systems of the World

In trying to understand the wider world it is important, indeed in many ways imperative, to have some knowledge of the worldviews, both religious and secular, which underlie our various civilizations. This is as true of today's values as it is of ancient, medieval, and premodern cultures. The cultures of Europe, for instance, were intermingled with the ethos and beliefs of the Catholic and Orthodox faiths. Sometimes, however, people today have regarded the study of religions as a peripheral matter. They forget that what they themselves think – perhaps, for instance, that the days of religion are over and that religion is no longer intellectually compelling – is irrelevant to many of the societies of today's world. Moreover, in studying religions we also have to explore rival and alternative worldviews, such as Marxism and scientific humanism, which can also function as spiritual worldviews. There is no sharp line to be drawn between religion and non-religion.

Another reason why religious studies are vital is that today we are rapidly entering into and helping to construct a global civilization. The revolutions in telecommunications and airline travel have combined with political turbulence and consequent migrations to bring the peoples of the world into close relationships. In some areas this causes conflict; in other areas it promotes new harmonies between traditions. In either case mutual understanding is an important ingredient. The exploration of religions may itself help to soften some hostile and ignorant attitudes.

And so in this book I aim to present, briefly, the major traditions of the West and South. I mention the South because Christianity, one of our major traditions, has spread effectively into the South of our planet, notably in Africa, Latin America, and the Pacific region. Indeed the center of gravity of Christianity is moving southwards, though much of the leadership of the mainstream Churches remains northern. This book is thus a companion volume to my *Religions of Asia* (1992), which dealt with the faiths of South and East Asia, from Hinduism to Shinto.

If it is important to understand religions in order to grasp both ancient and modern world history, it is also interesting and even enlightening to explore the nature of religion as a quest in itself. By seeing the evolution and diversity of Christianity, the Christian can acquire greater insight into her or his background. This is also true in the case of the Jew or Muslim. And those who have no religion may come to have a better knowledge of traditions, influencing a greater depth to the rejection of traditions, or a greater illumination in the search for spiritual meaning. In such ways the study of religions is more than study: it is an exploration and a quest.

But how do we explore religions?

Judgment and Balance in the Exploration of Worldviews

Basically, studying religion needs both empathy (imagination) and information. Beyond these foundations lie various kinds of reflection on what we learn. You need empathy in human studies, whether straight history or the history of religions or anthropology or literature. You need to know what is the behavior and institutional expression of a religion: but you also need to enter into the actor's point of view. You must be able to imagine what it is like to be a Sunni Muslim or an Orthodox Jew or a Southern Baptist or whatever. This requires imagination, for which I use the word "empathy." As a Native American proverb has it: "Never judge a person till you have walked a mile in his moccasins." In order to do this effectively it is probably best to know an individual who belongs to a given religious tradition, or better to know many such individuals. It is useful to go to ceremonial occasions (Easter services, Passover meals, prayers at the mosque, and so on), and become what anthropologists sometimes call a "participant observer." But reading books can be a guide, if they are imaginative. For it is no doubt one of the main tasks of a teacher to be able to bring out the meanings of religious practices and experiences to believers. Obviously, films, dramas, and novels can give imaginative access to inner lives. The texts and memoirs of a tradition can help, too. In such ways we need to cultivate a sensitivity to the inner meanings and intentions of those who participate in a religion.

It is a platitude that believers differ greatly in the intensity and seriousness of their commitment. The depiction of a religion has to consider both the saint and the marginal adherent, the devoted follower and the hypocrite, the materially minded and the spiritually ambitious – and so forth. Although we will here err somewhat in describing religion "at its best," it is useful to bear in mind that we must imagine religions with a fair degree of realism.

Another way in which we can provide an even-handed treatment of religion is by adopting a framework which more or less dictates balance. What I have in mind is that there are various facets or dimensions shared by all religions, which must be examined in order to arrive at a rounded picture. So it is not enough, for instance, to depict Roman Catholic doctrines (important as they may be) in order to convey a picture of the Roman Catholic religion. It is necessary to say a lot about its practice – its rituals such as the Mass, its organization culminating in the Pope, its ethics, and so on. In this book I shall use a scheme incorporating seven dimensions of a religion (or of a secular worldview).

The Seven Dimensions of Religions

The seven dimensions or aspects of religion are a kind of checklist to ensure that in analyzing a religion we pay reasonably balanced attention to the diverse aspects of the tradition. The dimensions are: the ritual or practical dimension, the ethical or legal dimension, the experiential or emotional dimension, the narrative or mythic dimension, the doctrinal or philosophical dimension, the institutional or organizational dimension, and the material or artistic dimension.

Clearly some traditions at some times emphasize some of these dimensions more than at other times, and some traditions are more preoccupied by some than others. For instance, Roman Catholicism has always emphasized ritual – the rite of the Mass, baptism and so on. It also has typically regarded doctrines (such as traditional teaching about the nature of God as being a Trinity, three persons in one) as important. By contrast, the Society of Friends, known as Quakers, are much less concerned with ritual. Their meetings are very simple, and silence plays a meaningful part in them. Discourse is meant to come from the heart, when the spirit moves a person to utter. Moreover, they are not bound together by an elaborate system of doctrine or philosophy. Yet they put a great emphasis on ethics and the upright and peaceful conduct of life, in sober equality with their fellow human beings.

Given though that there are differing values placed on the dimensions they all usually play a significant part in the make-up of a religious tradition.

You will notice that although the existence of the dimensions represents a kind of definition of a religious tradition, I have not defined religion by its content of belief. It is true that the Western religions dealt with in this book tend to share a belief in God, and many scholars and legal systems in the past have thought of religion as involving such a belief. This view, however, is not altogether realistic, to put it mildly. Theravada Buddhism, in Sri Lanka, Thailand, and elsewhere, does not hold to a Creator God – and is in a sort of way atheistic. Early Taoism in China did not exactly hold to a belief in God. Indian Jains believe in saints and liberation, but not in God. And so we might continue. In short, it is more useful to define religion in a functional way, rather than in terms of some single focus of belief.

Secular Worldviews Seen Through the Dimensions

As well as being realistic, the dimensional mode also opens up the prospect of treating secular ideologies as kinds of religions. This is healthy, because secularists, in rejecting religion, sometimes try to claim that they should have more than equal treatment under the law, as if some worldviews (secular ones) are exempt from the provisions of Church–state separation. I mean, in effect, that Marxist regimes in East Germany and elsewhere (now defunct) worked very much as state religions used to. The dimensional analysis helps us to see such ideological systems through a non-partisan lens. Consider, too, the less formalized force of nationalism – which has reached a new ascendancy in the nineteenth and twentieth centuries. If you have a great-uncle or father who died violently, it is most probable that he died for his country. In a wartorn world, it is perhaps less surprising that states have induced national feeling and loyalty to such a remarkable degree. As a specific example, let us examine nationalism in the United States using our adopted framework. First, at the *doctrinal* level there is commitment to the concept of liberty and to the U.S. Constitution. The *mythic dimension* is expressed in the usual history of America, with its significant moments – the Puritans, the War of Independence, the founding of the new state, the Civil War, Lincoln's Gettysburg address, the absorption of migrants, World War I, the Depression, World War II, and so on. The *ethical dimension* is expressed in what it means to be an American. The *ritual* of the nation is clear; visits to Washington and the different memorials, saluting the flag, the President as high priest on national occasions, and so on. The *experiential dimension* comes through in *emotional* responses shown at such solemn occasions as Memorial

A scene during the old May Day parade in Moscow, discontinued in its full form after the collapse of the Soviet Union in 1990. The great icons of Communism were the figures of Lenin, Engels and Marx.

Day, with its grave evocation of the dead, and at national crises. *Organizationally*, the national religion is seen in the presidency, the army and other bodies – but above all, perhaps, in the school teachers, whose task it is to instil the national *myth* and *ethos*.

Nationalism, then, functions as a religion. Consequently, it is important to realize that in modern times Christianity, Judaism, Islam, and other religions have tended to blend with it and other so-called secular ideologies. So Christians are often nationalists, and Jews have loyalty to the nation of Israel. However, the chief message of this section is that a dimensional analysis is useful in describing and analyzing religious and other worldviews. That is the procedure we adopt here.

A final observation. As I have emphasized, the dimensional analysis is designed to foster a balanced view in the description of religious traditions. It is less able to deal with those individuals, who have always been there (I believe) but who are more prevalent now in the Western world, who manage to "choose" their own individual religions. Such people will increasingly make up an important constituency, as individualism spreads. People will more and more choose to take bits and pieces from here and there in world religions. And from an impartial point of view, as expressed in this book, there is nothing wrong with that.

In brief, religious and secular worldviews merge together. This is most obvious in the West, the subject-matter of this book, and we will analyze in greater detail the relationship between religious and so-called secular worldviews.

The Dimensions in Detail

The Ritual or Practical Dimension

Ritual involves patterns of action which typically are repeated and on the whole stereotyped. At a daily level we say such things as "Good morning" and "Hi" to one another. These greetings are a ritual, informal and uncomplicated, of everyday life. Though if someone did not respond to a "Hi," you would feel puzzled, maybe offended. What would such a response mean? So such gestures in everyday life are very important. At a more complex level, such ritual actions are part of the essential practice of many religions. Where would the Catholic be without the Mass, or the Hindu without the Brahmin sacrifice, or the Jew without Yom Kippur, or the Muslim without the pilgrimage to Mecca or daily prayer? I also include in this category practical action which might not be regarded strictly as ritual. These include the practice of abstinence (such as fasting in Lent or Ramadan) or yoga (such as Buddhist and Hindu methods of meditation, or Jewish, Christian, and Muslim methods of inner contemplation). In brief, the ritual dimension covers such activities as worship, individual devotion, prayer, the reading of scriptures in a devotional context, the Communion service, pilgrimages, confessions, hymn-singing, initiation rites, marriages, and so on.

Rituals run, as I have already noted, from the very formal to the informal. Modern times have seen the trend going from the former to the latter; on the other hand, there is a trend among conservatives in the other direction. Rituals nourish feelings and may reflect narratives and doctrines. For example, the Christian communion re-enacts the Last Supper. More accurately, it re-creates the crucial ritual initiated there by Christ. Rituals may also reflect and teach ethics and obedience to the law, as in the Jewish rite of bar-mitzvah, which initiates the growing boy into the life of the Torah. Islamic daily prayer instils into everyone a sense of absolute devotion to the Divine Being. In brief, ritual ties in with the other dimensions, but especially the ethical.

I would, as I have said, include under this head the practices which encourage the contemplative life – for example, those connected with the rigorous methods of yoga, which turn people inward, in the process inducing the purification of consciousness. Both yoga in India and Christian mysticism (not to mention analogous practices in Islam and Judaism) cause people to eliminate extraneous thoughts and concentrate on trying to reach purer and purer forms of consciousness. Some mystics in these theistic traditions – that is, those which believe in a personal God and Creator – see themselves as reaching inward to the Divine Being and to the attainment of some kind of unity with God. In order to attain this goal they adopt a rigorous discipline of inner meditation. Such practices are often considered as essential to religion as external rituals. I include them here under the ritual dimension.

The ritual dimension: a scene during the pilgrimage, or *Hajj*, to Mecca, where hundreds of thousands of tents shelter the pious pilgrims.

The Ethical or Legal Dimension

There is a recurrent thread in the great traditions of commitment to ethical and legal norms. The Jew owes allegiance to the Torah, and usually this Law is taken to impose a great number of injunctions – some of which are obviously ethical and others ritual. For instance, the observance of the Sabbath – from Friday sunset to Saturday sunset – is laid down to Jews. Orthodox Jews would not, for instance, answer or use the telephone during that period. But other commandments concern more obviously ethical attitudes and practice. The Ten Commandments, therefore, are a brief summary of ancient Jewish ethics. In Christianity, the nature of the Trinity is supposed to show, in the heart of the divine life, the centrality of love, the chief Christian virtue. In Islam, the merciful nature of Allah is supposed to require a merciful attitude among human beings, and the life of Muhammad is a standing and detailed example for ethical behavior.

The fact that religions may seek to implement a law can give them a strongly political role. Islam always hoped to establish a religious community in which religious and political power would be jointly exercised. It was remarkably successful in building up an Islamic civilization. There is often felt to be an incompleteness about a situation where practicing Muslims are in the minority. But law can, in effect, be practiced privately, as with minority Jews in the United States and elsewhere. Interestingly, issues about the Torah arise in Israel, which is a Jewish state, but where, however, the majority of Jews, paradoxically, do not practice the tradition. Whereas in the

The legal dimension: a rabbi reads the Torah or holy teaching from the scrolls, which are handwritten on parchment and are normally contained in the Ark, a focal point in the furnishing of a synagogue.

15

past many Christian countries imposed an orthodox version of the religious law, most now have secular or pluralistic constitutions which give a lot of latitude to individual choice.

The Experiential or Emotional Dimension

It is, of course, important that religions reflect and mobilize human feelings. A god or goddess is by turns awe-inspiring, loving, frightening, and fascinating. All this was summed up by Rudolf Otto in his famous book *The Idea of the Holy*, first published in 1917, in his description of what he called the *numinous* experience. This involves a vision of an Other Being seen as fearsome and awe-inducing. Another kind of spiritual experience is found in the inner realm, when a person pursuing the contemplative life purifies his or her consciousness and reaches a mystical state. This can be experienced as a direct vision of the divine within, or of the soul, or of nirvana. Another kind of religious perception is sometimes referred to as the *panenhenic* experience, in which a person feels herself in a state of union with nature or the universe. A further type of experience, widespread among the peoples of Africa, Latin America, and Native America, is the vision of the shaman, a figure credited with healing powers and clairvoyance. But in addition to these highly vivid kinds of experience, which recent research indicates are more common than often supposed (partly because in the modern world people are often shy about speaking of them), there are the varied emotions of religion. These include the sense of devotion and dependence, the exaltation at being at one with God, the calm which faith may inculcate or which may accrue from Buddhist or other teaching. We must be able to imagine such visions and emotions, if we are to penetrate religion.

The experiential dimension: Gypsies from Eastern and Western Europe gather for a convention of evangelical Protestants near the city of Tours in France.

It is altogether a different matter, of course, to account for the experiential dimension. Does it involve the genuine presence of a transcendent something? Is it only a projection of human feelings, which arises simply from the nature of the human psyche? In this book I will not be answering such questions, which relate to the truth or otherwise of religion. I am concerned with describing traditions. Mostly, of course, the adherents of such traditions believe in the reality of what their saints or leaders experience. And such visions and feelings are dynamic, in that they move men and women, often powerfully. In them lie the seeds of diverse spiritual movements which have helped to shape human civilizations. How very different the world would have been without the visions of a Moses, a Paul, a Muhammad, or a Simon Kimbangu.

The Narrative or Mythic Dimension
Every religion has its narratives. Sometimes these take the form of what is supposed to be history, like the story of the life and career, then death and resurrection of Jesus, or the story of the people of Israel, or the recounting of the life and mission of the Prophet Muhammad. Sometimes the stories are more fanciful and symbolic, such as the many myths of ancient Greece,

The mythic dimension: Tzazolteotl, a fertility goddess of rather fierce expression, here gives birth; she dealt with sexual transgressions.

17

which typically deal with the actions of the gods toward each other and toward humans. Often, too, the stories concern the origins of the universe – such narratives of creation set the scene for describing the later predicament of the human race.

Such stories are sometimes closely integrated into ritual. The Passover celebration in Judaism re-enacts the events which saw the people of Israel escaping, with divine help, out of Egypt. The Shi'i festival during the month of Muharram recalls the death of Husayn at Karbala and vividly re-presents the sorrow of that event. So there is often a close relationship between narrative and practice.

Very often such sacred and value-laden stories are referred to by scholars and others as myths. This is all right if we do not mean that they are false – for the word "myth" in English is often used to mean "false narrative." In trying to depict and analyze a religious tradition we should not impose our own views of what is true and false. Myths are true for those who hold them, and we must, as noted before, start from the believer's viewpoint and experience. Which religion is true, if any, is a subject for faith and philosophy, and that is a stage lying beyond the history of religions.

The Doctrinal or Philosophical Dimension

Religions do not express their beliefs merely through the medium of stories, but also through claims about the Ultimate or God and the cosmos. In some phases of religious history these doctrines may be unimportant, but at others there may be much more emphasis upon them. Challenges may appear when separate traditions and cultures come into contact. This may entail a more abstract or philosophical response. For instance, when Christianity was shaping up to become the official religion of the Roman Empire, the council called at Nicaea in 325 C.E. formulated the central Trinity doctrine: God was declared to be three persons in one. This was necessitated by the facts that Christianity arose from the strongly monotheistic Jewish tradition and that Christians in their ritual worshiped Christ and by implication the Holy Spirit. God was three in manifestation and yet one in essence.

While Judaism has at certain times been concrete in its ideas, relying heavily upon stories which elaborated the Torah teaching, at other times it has given a strongly philosophical expression to its beliefs, as in the writings of the famous Jewish philosopher and theologian, Maimonides (twelfth century C.E.). Islam very soon encountered the world of Greek philosophy and Christian doctrine, and this stimulated a whole range of philosophical and doctrinal formulations.

It may be noted that certain philosophies in the ancient world, such as Neoplatonism and Stoicism, functioned as religious worldviews, and so the gap between philosophy and religion did not exist in the way it does now. Today much of philosophy is technical and analytical: but in ancient Greece and Rome it was seen more as a vehicle for wisdom and for the delineation of a spiritual or other kind of worldview.

The complaint is often made that histories of religions have typically devoted too much attention to credos and doctrines, and have spent too little time dealing with religion *on the ground*, as it is lived out by the mass of people. The complaint about abstraction is justified. We should not, however, swing to the other extreme and ignore doctrines altogether. With a larger number of the world's population being educated, *written* doctrines are becoming more important. The schema of the seven dimensions is designed to give balance to our explorations, and so we must acknowledge that a somewhat abstract set of beliefs is one ingredient of most religions. Briefly, to function in an educated world, religions have to set out their philosophies.

The Institutional or Organizational Dimension
While we have seen above that some religious belief and practice is purely individual, it is usual for religious traditions to be embodied in social structures. In some areas the religious aspect of life may be mingled with the fabric of a group. It is often the case with small-scale peoples – so Nuer religion is just the religious aspect of Nuer life. But more often a religious tradition is embodied in a *social* organization. Even where in theory Judaism is the religion of a whole people, in practice it is divided into separate subtraditions with their distinctive organizations and social patterns. Some organizations are hierarchical, as in Eastern Orthodoxy, but without a high degree of centralization. On the other hand, the Catholic Church is united under a single Pope and a central administration, the Vatican. Other Christian subtraditions such as the Baptists and Congregationalists are much more loosely held together. Clustering around the major denominations are smaller and newer movements, each expressed through its own organization.

The material dimension: here an Islamic artisan is decorating a mosque. Note that the designs are abstract in accordance with Muslim teaching against the use of human representations.

The social fabric of a society will influence the way a religion develops. So American Catholicism has put much effort into developing its own educational system, while at the same time expressing its loyal adherence to mainstream American values. It was facing a problem in the United States it did not have to face in, say, Italy.

The organization of religion may be profoundly affected by persecution – as exhibited in Judaism during the last two centuries particularly, and in Christianity and Islam during much of the history of the former Soviet Union. It was persecution, for instance, which helped to reinforce the drive for a Jewish state in Israel. This tying of universal Judaism to the particular fate of Israel has had a profound effect on Jewish behavior and organization.

The Material or Artistic Dimension
Finally, religions tend to express themselves concretely in buildings, statues, texts, memorials, clothes, etc. In building St Peter's Basilica in Rome with all its overwhelming grandeur Catholicism sought to express the power and glory of the papacy. In creating plain undecorated churches in Scotland Calvinists sought to express the sobriety of their faith and their radical rejection of what they saw as Catholic encumbrances to the Christian

religion. In fashioning spectacularly colored ikons the Eastern Orthodox try to create a mood of adoration through these "windows on to heaven." In rejecting images of God, Judaism seeks to express the pure and elevated conception they have of YHWH, and their synagogues reflect the ikonless nature of their worship. The elegance of much mosque architecture testifies to the lofty nature of Allah. Material objects can therefore themselves be read like texts, which convey various powerful messages.

Sometimes those traditions which stress inwardness and are not so tied to outer material display can have a good chance of surviving persecution. The Eastern Orthodox Church, tied to monasteries and churches, could be more easily controlled by outsiders than the Sufis of Central Asia, who could meet as fraternities in a more or less private manner (they were thereby significant in preserving Muslim faith during the Soviet period).

History's Unfolding – and the Sequence of this Book

The story to be told in the following chapters begins with the rise of civilization in the Western world (as distinguished from its emergence in South Asia, India, China and elsewhere). Actually, although this flowering was a Western phenomenon in that it gave rise to the three more or less Western religions of Judaism, Christianity, and Islam, it took place in what is usually now classified as the ancient Near East. The two major centers were Mesopotamia and Egypt. These cultures formed the ambience of Israelite religion, the forerunner both of developed Judaism and Christianity. The Persian Empire, forming the culture which nourished both Zoroastrianism and Manichaeism, important once in themselves and for their influences on Judaism, Christianity, and Islam, will be the topic of Chapter 2. Chapter 3 also helps to set the scene, as it deals with the religions of Greece and Rome and more generally of the Roman Empire, including the Hellenistic period.

We will then look at the Israelite religion and the roots and formation of Judaism (Chapter 4) as it developed into a religion parallel to, but very different from, classical Christianity. Chapter 5 continues the story of the Jews from the late medieval period onward, concentrating in detail on themes of migration, the Holocaust and the foundation of the state of Israel. Early and medieval Christianity (Chapter 6) precedes a description of Christianity (focussing mainly on Europe) in the modern era. This chapter (7) will include a treatment of the Reformation, the Enlightenment, and the challenge of secular worldviews in the nineteenth and twentieth centuries. Missionary activity, colonialism, and the worldwide spread of Christianity are also discussed. In this connection, Chapter 8 deals with the extraordinary plurality of Christianities in North America.

Islam is the most recently established of the three most enduring and influential faiths in the Western world, and in Chapters 9 and 10 we chart the rise of this glittering civilization and its setbacks and revivals in the colonial period and beyond. Then our attention will turn, in Chapter 11, to the classical religions of the Americas, the South Pacific, and Africa, and we will show how these have blended with European philosophies to engender exciting new forms of faith. A concluding chapter (12) will deal with current developments; as new religions proliferate, old ideologies crumble, and we try to predict whether a global worldview will ever emerge to unite the human race.

In presenting a balanced picture we will not only make use of the seven-dimensional analysis mentioned earlier but also take stock of the varieties of each faith. Christianity, for instance, consists in four main varieties: the Orthodox world, largely in Eastern Europe and Russia; Catholicism, in Southern Europe, Eastern Europe, Latin America and elsewhere; the varieties of Protestantism, in Europe, America, the world's South and elsewhere; and finally new varieties of Christianity on the margin of the older groupings, such as the Mormons, new independent African churches, etc. In other words, each great tradition is a family of subtraditions, and that makes it a good deal less wise to generalize about a religion than we sometimes think.

Roots and the Formation of Religions

Finally we have to see how changes occur. In particular it is important to see how a tradition or subtradition gets to be formed. In this analysis, I will distinguish between the formation of a given religion or subreligion and the roots which it has. For example, Israelite religion is not yet Judaism as we know it – the latter came into existence in roughly the first three centuries C.E. It formed itself as rabbinical Judaism, which brought together various strands of practice and thought. This included the creation of the Talmud and the codification of oral Torah or Teaching, and the substitution of commentary and holy living for the practice of sacrifice. Focussed on the Temple in Jerusalem, sacrifice had perished with that institution in the stormy events of 70 C.E. Behind this foreground we can see the roots of the religion in ancient Israel. Similar remarks can be made about Christianity, which emerged into its recognizable classical forms (both Catholic and Orthodox) in the third and fourth centuries. But the roots of the religion lay in early Jewish culture and the life and times of Jesus.

But, naturally, traditions continue to evolve. This is not only because cultures change, but because in order to adapt the message to differing contexts the keepers and followers of the tradition must change its outward form. In a sense, a tradition, in order to stay the same, needs to change. What does it mean to say that Christ is King when kings now are largely figureheads? The message has to alter to convey its original point.

One aspect of the story of religion is left out: I do not here discuss how it all began. That is speculative and obscure. What we do know is that it took powerful forms when it did emerge out of the mists of prehistory. These strong religions became dynamic in both East and West. Here, we embark on the Western side of the story.

CHAPTER 1

The Dawn of Western Religions

An Overview

Both Mesopotamia – roughly the region of modern Iraq – and ancient Egypt produced dazzling urban civilizations. In the former region the pioneer was Sumer, but the glory belonged first to Babylon, and then to its successor Persia. To the west the Canaanites and Phoenicia flourished, and from Phoenicia were planted the North African colonies which became the Carthaginian state. There were other actors on the scene: the Assyrian empire, some Indo-Europeans such as the Hittites to the north, and, folded in between the great powers, the Israelites.

Sumer, Babylon, and Assyria belong to the same sequence, since the latter two empires borrowed their religious forms from Sumer. Basically, too, Canaanite and Phoenician religions were the same. To simplify our story we can imagine little Israel as a center surrounded by Canaanites, Mesopotamian religions, and Egypt. Israel is important to us because its religion proved to be significant for both Judaism and Christianity, and to some degree Islam too. So, whereas the religion of Phoenicia and that of Carthage are buried under the sands of time, and Egyptian culture of the ancient period is to be seen in museums and as great stone monuments in the desert, and much of ancient Mesopotamia has disappeared, there remains a living stream which runs down to us today from the Jordan Valley.

But dead religions deserve respect also: for that reason we will at least sketch briefly some of the features of ancient Near Eastern religions outside that of Israel. We have some literary records and to some degree we can travel into these ancient minds; but this survey will necessarily be highly selective.

Some of the basic dates to keep in mind are these. First, it was around 3000 B.C.E. that urban culture was formed in Sumeria, at the lower part of the Tigris and Euphrates rivers and on the tip of the Pesian Gulf. By 1700 B.C.E. there was a significant dynasty in Babylon, ruling over the provinces of Akkad and Sumer. This First Dynasty of Babylon was overrun by Hittites in 1595. From around 1300 B.C.E., Assyria, with its main capital in Nineveh, was the dominant power in the region and in fact conquered Babylon; it lasted until 612 B.C.E., when Nineveh fell. Shortly thereafter Babylon was taken by the Persians, who dominated the whole region until the coming of Alexander the Great (ruled 336–323 B.C.E.). Meanwhile Egyptian civilization had been established from about 3100 B.C.E. with the start of the First Dynasty. For many years, off and on, Egypt's Asiatic empire, reaching up

Opposite Assur became the predominant God of the Assyrian empire, combining political and spiritual power. The non-human representations of such a god emphasized his remoteness from humans.

into Assyria, was formidable. From shortly before 500 B.C.E. the country's history was checkered, being under Persian domination for a while, then Greek – with Alexander the Great and his successors – and then Roman. In the years that followed 1000 B.C.E., the Phoenicians founded Carthage and Utica in North Africa and other settlements as far as southern Spain.

Mesopotamian Religion

Some Figures from the Pantheon

We do not have full information about ancient Mesopotamian religion, but we do have various hymns and myths which give us an insight into some of the gods in the rich pantheon, headed by the god An, which was the focus of priestly ritual. Though An was nominally the first god, Enlil, the Lord of the Wind, came to play that role; then with the establishment of the First Dynasty in Babylon, Marduk (the local favorite) was promoted to that status.

Enlil is the god of the religious center of the ancient Sumerians, Nippur. As the wind he guides the rains from the high mountains so that they fall upon the plains; without him no grain will grow, and no wealth can be created to provide the splendid urban culture of which his worshipers are so proud. Wind and rain can be destructive, so his good will cannot be assumed. Yet generally the hymns portray him as fatherly. Moreoever, he holds the tablets which decree the fates of human beings. Many gods come to his city to pay respects to him. His consort is Ninlil, the Lady Wind, and different versions of his wooing of her are told. In one he seduces her while posing as ferryman of the river to be crossed to the underworld.

If Enlil is fatherly and benign, Enki (in the Akkadian version he is Ea) is crafty and good fun. He is the god of the underground waters which, welling up, give fertility. In Sumerian cosmology there was the idea that under ground was a great freshwater sea. Their agriculture, of course, depended on irrigation, and this notion accounted both for freshwater springs and the effectiveness of digging wells. In the myths, Enki is ingenious. For instance, the primordial man Adapa has offended the god Anu by breaking the wing of the South Wind; Enki advises him to get the two gods who act as doorkeepers at Anu's palace to intercede on his behalf. But on no account should he eat or drink when he is with Anu. The doorkeepers do their bit, Adapa is forgiven, and he refuses to eat or drink. When asked why, he tells of Enki's advice. There is much amusement for Anu in this. He knows that the food and drink would not have brought death, as Enki had pretended, but immortality, which Enki did not wish.

Another powerful being who had much influence in the Near East and later in the Roman world is Inanna, known in Akkadian as Ishtar and in Assyrian as Astarte. She is a fertility goddess, associated with showers and thunderclouds, and goddess of war. She is also a prostitute and served by prostitutes. She is supposed even to have become queen of heaven, as consort to Anu; although she is usually depicted as wed to her Tammuz, a beautiful

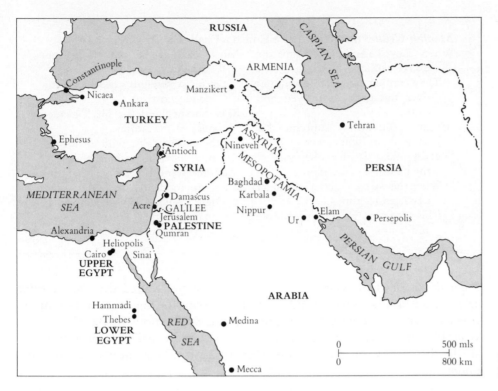

Map 1 The Ancient Near East.

young male. In a famous story she wishes to become queen of the underworld, but the goddess there defeats her and kills her. She is transformed into a slice of rotten meat. When she does not return her maid seeks aid: eventually it is the ingenious Enki who has a solution. He sends two creatures to the nether world, and the queen there grants them a wish. They ask for the meat, and sprinkle it with grass and water – which restores Inanna to her pristine form. In the tale, further complicated adventures follow, which result in Tammuz's banishment to the underworld to take her place there for half of each year.

Finally, let us glance at the great Marduk. He is something like Indra in the Indian pantheon: god of thunderstorms, and like a young bull. The gods were threatened by the dangerous chaos represented by the female deity Tiamat. The chief gods, Ea and Anu, fail to stave off the challenge, and it is suggested that only Marduk will be successful in combat against her. He demands full authority, which they grant him. In a great combat she opens her huge jaws to destroy him, but he drives in the winds and slays her with his arrow. The wind gods capture her in a huge net, and he uses her corpse to create the present universe, cutting her in two like a fish, one part being heaven and the other the earth. Then he organizes the calendar and various other matters and is hailed by the other gods as supreme.

The myth celebrates Babylon, Marduk's city, and its supremacy. But it also reflects the idea that the creation is the bringing of order, the world

---

Marduk Creates the World: The Enuma Elish *Tablets*

When they had granted him the exercise of kingship of the gods,
They confirmed him in dominion over the gods of heaven and earth.
Anshar pronounced supreme his name Asaruluhi:
"Let us make humble obeisance at the mention of his name;
When he speaks, the gods shall pay heed to him.
Let his utterance be supreme above and below!"

Most exalted be the Son, our avenger;
Let his sovereignty be surpassing, having no rival.
May he shepherd the black-headed ones, his creatures.
To the end of days, without forgetting; let them acclaim his ways.
May he establish for his fathers the great food-offerings;
Their support they shall furnish, shall tend their sanctuaries.

---

formed out of chaos, Tiamat. The epic of creation called the *Enuma Elish* celebrates Marduk's victory and is a kind of script for the ritual and dramatic re-enactment of the narrative in great spring celebrations in Babylon every year. It is often cited by scholars of the "myth and ritual" school, influential at the beginning of the twentieth century, to show how we can best understand myth in relation to ritual.

Worship and the Temple

Some of the myths which we have sampled can be seen in connection with the ritual process in the great temples, or ziggurats, erected to celebrate official religion in Mesopotamia. The ziggurats were built on high ground but were also towering structures in themselves, links between earth and heaven. The god lived at the summit. The Biblical story of the Tower of Babel (Genesis 11) reflects knowledge of the Ziggurat of

The mythic dimension: scenes from the *Epic of Gilgamesh* showing Gilgamesh and Ea struggling with a lion, and Arad-Ea crossing the waters of death. Such cylinder seals are similar to examples found in the Indus Valley civilization. This one dates from the late 3rd millennium, B.C.E.

Babylon (for Babel is Babylon). The god living there shows himself to be present to the community and so concerned with its welfare. It is likely that the daily rituals resembled those later prevalent in India, where the god and his goddess were dressed, washed, and so on. At great festivals there was probably the enactment of a glorious drama based upon the myths which have come down to us. The rites would also involve the king, who would become the relevant god for a sacred marriage festival, ensuring fertility in the kingdom.

But some of the myths are free literary creations and are not necessarily linked directly to ritual. Such is the famous *Epic of Gilgamesh*, which tells how Gilgamesh is overcome with great grief at the death of his dear friend Enkidu and sets out to conquer death, traveling to visit the wise Utnapishtim, an ancestor of his. But Utnapishtim has no joy to give: he invites Gilgamesh to try to conquer Sleep, which is the younger brother of Death. But Gilgamesh fails and realizes the fateful truth: Death awaits every person. The epic thus addresses one of the great questions of religion, the fate of human beings in the face of death. (The epic also has an account of the Flood, which partly influenced the Biblical story.)

At this point it is worth turning to the Egyptian experience, which is so much concerned with the nature of death and the quest for immortality.

Ancient Egypt

Our imagination is haunted by the silent great pyramids, from the earliest at Saqqara, south of Cairo, to the great Pyramid of Cheops at Giza, built about 200 years later. They stand with an air of enigma, quite as much as the famed statue of the Sphinx. The enigma is that such huge effort and precise workmanship should have been directed to the building of a tomb – and a tomb of that particular geometrical configuration. When we join this with the fact that the Egyptians became very skilled in the technology of mummification, we recognize a civilization that was very worried by the nature of death and of its hoped-for survival. We note, too, the wonderful sculptured portraits which testify to a desire for remembrance.

The most formative time in ancient Egypt was that of the First Dynasty, which was founded when Menes, about 3000 B.C.E., united Upper and Lower Egypt and built a new capital at Memphis. By the Fourth Dynasty, around 2600 B.C.E., there were resources to build the Giza pyramids (just outside modern Cairo). Between about 1750 and 1580 B.C.E., Egypt was harassed and partly occupied by the Asian invaders known as the Hyksos, and this helped to stimulate Egyptian ambitions in Asia, on the other side of Sinai, to provide a buffer against further incursions. A later Pharaoh, Akhenaten (reigned 1356-1339 B.C.E.), experimented with a new, monotheistic religion and moved his capital to El-Amarna, suppressing the old religion of Amun. But his move was unsuccessful. In 946-712 B.C.E., Egypt was ruled by pharaohs of Libyan descent, and in 664-525 by Ethiopians; and in the two centuries that followed she was twice dominated by Persia. But even after Greek and Roman occupation there was a remarkable continuity in Egyptian culture; and some of the patterns set in the First Dynasty lasted through.

Probably the greatest text of the Egyptians was what has come to be called the *Book of the Dead*, more correctly *The Book of Going Forth by Day*. It is based substantially on much earlier so-called Coffin Texts, so it is partly very ancient; and at the same time it represents the standard Egyptian view of the nature of death and the way to survive it. It was a book to be placed with the dead at their entombment, to help them in their passing through judgment to the afterlife. The mythic scene which underlay the process was the life, death and resurrection of the god Osiris. Next to Re the great Sun God, who often combined with city deities in the form of Amon Re and so on, Osiris was undoubtedly the most important deity in the Egyptian tradition. By the Middle Kingdom period (about 2050-1750 B.C.E.), when *The Book of Going Forth by Day* was assembled, a sacred drama at Abydos, where he was buried, was the focus of much piety, and this devotional concern in which participants identified with Osiris was still popular in the Roman period. The living pharaoh was identified with Osiris' son Horus, as the "living Horus," and a dead pharaoh was identified with Osiris himself.

The influential legend of Osiris, which in some ways prepared the ancient world for the acceptance of the Christian story, was as follows. Seth, brother of Osiris, had a beautifully shaped coffin made. He prepared a banquet and promised the coffin to the guest who would fit it. Only Osiris fitted it precisely, and as soon as he was lying inside Seth had the coffin fixed shut. He sealed the coffin with lead and had it thrown into the Nile. It eventually washed up on the other shore, where it was found by the distraught Isis, Osiris' wife. She had the body returned, but Seth got it and chopped it into pieces and scattered them throughout Egypt. Isis recovered all the bits – save the penis, for which she made a substitute – and reconstituted Osiris. Before embalming him she gave him new life – so much so that Osiris had intercourse with her, and their son Horus was thus conceived. Eventually Horus fought and overcame Seth, but injured his eye in the process. His good eye came to be identified with the Sun and the bad eye with the Moon. The relationship to the Sun meshed in with the cult of the great god Re. Horus was often seen as a falcon, perhaps stretching his wings and invisibly, save to the mind's eye, hooding the whole sky.

Osiris, having overcome death, is the ruling god of death and patron of the process of mummifying the dead. Osiris is there in the afterlife for the judging of the dead, which is described in some detail in *The Book of Going Forth by Day*. The soul of the deceased is weighed against the feather of Truth: this notion of the scales of judgment became a widely

used metaphor. In Chapter 125 of the book there is a formulaic protestation of innocence addressed to the forty-two judges, which gives a good insight into the ethics of ancient Egypt. The person protests that he has not stolen, or been covetous, or killed a human being, or damaged a grain-measure, or told lies, or committed adultery, or had sex with a boy, or been abusive of a king, and so on. The aim of the formula is to make sure that the judges will let the deceased through and he will be able to live in the presence of Osiris and Re. There are other pieces of ritual with which to assist the dead: scarab brooches to stop the heart from speaking against its owner, and figurines of servants, and so on.

Osiris also appears in Egyptian myth as a god of fertility, and his resurrection is associated with the sprouting of grain in the spring and summer, after the "death" of winter. His connection with the Sun, Re, helps to underline this productive capacity, since it is the Sun which triggers off and nourishes the growth of the crops.

The dry climate of Egypt and the technology of well-sealed coffins (one of which was, as we have seen, the undoing of Osiris) and embalming

The ethical dimension: the heart of a person weighed against truth in the realm of Osiris.

meant that the preservation of the dead was an advanced achievement in Egypt. It was an expensive process, but gradually down the centuries the Osiris cult became more accessible.

In Egyptian thought there were, in effect, two souls. One is the *ba*, which is depicted hieroglyphically as a little bird that flutters up to the sky at death; the other is the *akh* or spirit which survives in the afterlife. An individual should be equipped with spells and other precautions so that his *akh* can be perfected. The *akh* is essentially the glorified state of the individual. Such bright ancestors came to be the focus also of a cult of the dead, as in some other societies.

We see in all this the coming together of various factors in the Egyptian experience: a notion of diving kingship, and with it an ideology which favored the preservation of dead pharaohs; the technology of mummification and other processes for the literal preservation of the dead; the resources for huge mortuary tombs and above all the Pyramids (it may be that the cult of the Sun is relevant here, since the pyramidal shape may represent the pouring down of the Sun's rays); the idea of a semispiritual afterlife; the cult of a dying and rising god, Osiris; and the notion that ethical worth should determine immortality, even if flaws in life can be got round by spells and other good advice in the mortuary literature. The confidence of Egypt in dealing with the dead contrasts with the relative pessimism of Utnapishtim in the *Epic of Gilgamesh*.

Canaanite Religion

The Canaanites occupied part of Syria and what is today's Palestine for a long time, overlapping with the Israelites. They also fathered the religion of the coast which was referred to by the Greeks as Phoenician. For these reasons, it is important to understand it in relation to Mediterranean culture as a whole, and as a kind of counterpoint to Israelite religion. On the other hand, it has not left significant traces in the modern world, except in the great Semitic religions.

Much of our best knowledge of Canaanite religion comes from texts found in the excavated city of Ugarit, at Ras Shamra on the Syrian coast. The pantheon, as elsewhere in the ancient Near East, is complex. It is headed by El or God; but the more vital force is the Lord, Baal, who is associated with the weather and rain, and so brings fertility to the people. Among female deities is Athirat the consort of El, jealous on behalf of her divine offspring; and Anat, the rough goddess of love and war, who is Baal's sister and possibly also his mate. Baal has three great adversaries: Yamm, accompanied by great sea monsters; Litan, the Leviathan in the Bible, another great sea monster; and Tunnan, as in Tannin in the Bible.

In the stories there is a sequence about Baal which suggests one great motif in Canaanite religion, which reminds us too of the Osiris myth. Baal fights against the Sea and with a magical club strikes him dead. But this

victory over the Sea, no doubt representing chaos and an uncontrollable element, is not enough. There remains a final enemy, Death, who, like the other gods, is the son of El. Baal sends messengers to Death, but the latter answers that Baal must die like other beings, and Baal submits, taking with him his tools – clouds, lightning bolts, rain and so on. The news of his death rouses Anat to do something about it. She buries him and then fiercely attacks Death, slices him with a sword, riddles him with a sieve, burns him with fire, grinds him with a mill, and sows him in the fields. Baal is restored to power. This whole story is of course filled with the idea of the dying and rising god whose death and resurrection correspond to the facts of the agricultural year. It is a myth, like its Egyptian counterpart, which is about both death and fertility, and about both human life and the supply of plants.

It is obvious from this and other sources that to some degree Canaanite ritual also concerned seasonal fertility. But the texts show there is much more besides. There are rites where the king purifies himself and makes offerings to various gods. Another ritual described offers a bull to Baal for help with fighting off enemies. And there is a third sort of event in which the whole population of Ugarit gather to make public repentance for their wrongdoings, in order to win safety from their enemies. It may be that some of the myths – possibly the myth of Baal and Death – also

Palmyra, an Aramaic speaking city, was the center of the worship of Baal.

Jewelry showing the figure of the great fertility goddess Astarte (Ishtar), 14th–15th century B.C.E., Ugaritic.

had dramatic enactment at sacred ceremonies. Another ceremony concerned the moving of images from one place to another.

I have put some emphasis, in these glimpses of the rich religious heritage of the ancient Near East, on the attitudes to death displayed. This is partly because death is at the meeting-point of public and private life. I have meant to indicate that even the most gloriously collective aspects of ancient religion in the Semitic world had, or developed, significance for individuals – at least those with the wealth to be able to take part in the rituals. It may also be that this theme of the dying and rising god prepared the way for the acceptance of Christianity in the area. Another theme is the idea of the fertility goddess, and in general the cult of fertility. It is something resisted by the prophets of Israel (whom we shall study in Chapter 4), but it was clearly important in the ideology of states which relied on agriculture and sought the extra wealth from rich harvests to pay for their increasingly splendid urban temples and palaces.

The Dimensions of Ancient Near Eastern Religions

We can identify some patterns in the religions of the ancient Near East by looking at their dimensions. At the *narrative and mythic* level there are stories of creation, of heroic encounters with death, of the annual restoration of fertility, and so on. *Doctrinally*, the religions typically recognize a hierarchy of gods, with the existence of the world being dependent on the supreme god. There are many and varied ideas of the underworld. The cosmology typically has three levels. Heaven is the abode of the gods, and earth the sphere of humanity and other living beings. Beneath, the underworld is the milieu of the dead and of the ancestors. The *ethical* is variously well advanced, with codes of kingship and with the notion of a judgment beyond the grave. As to the *organizational* dimension, there is a crucial role for the king or pharaoh as the priest and mediator between heaven and earth – religion is well integrated into the needs of great urban civilizations. As to the *ritual dimension*: the re-enactment of the drama of the dying and rising god at great festivals is important, though more personal rituals developed, relating to a better afterlife. The rituals of the city, state or empire were designed to ensure prosperity. The *material dimension* is seen in the wonderful archeological remains of the various empires, preparing the way through their sculptural traditions for Greek, Roman and, ultimately, art in Western civilization. At the *experiential and emotional* level, there was increased preoccupation with death, and some of these concerns prepared for later mystery religions connected to the dying and rising god. The initiate, in following and identifying with the path of the god or goddess, participated in experiences analogous to those of both the religion of the shaman (see The Americas section, Chapter 8), as well as later Christian patterns of the living identification with Christ.

CHAPTER 2
Zoroastrianism and Manichaeism

Persia's Significance

Persia (modern-day Iran) was a powerful empire from 550 B.C.E., when it became unified, until 687 C.E., when it was conquered by the Arabs. Its religions made an important impact on Judaism, Christianity, and Islam, even though its chief faith, Zoroastrianism, is weak in today's world.

Zoroastrianism existed in six phases. Its early period lasted until the sixth century B.C.E., when it entered its second phase as the official religion of the Achaemenid dynasty. Then there was a period of flux until the third century C.E., when it was reconstructed as the official religion of the Sasanid dynasty. Then there was the persecution under the Muslims, and its migration in part to India. Finally, there is the modern period when it has flourished within a modest population.

Also there was an important current within Zoroastrianism which some count as a separate religion; but it is perhaps better considered as the main stream of reconstructed Sasanid religion. This current is known in the modern West as Zurvanism.

Then again there was a dynamic and marvelously syncretic religion which was founded by Mani (early third century C.E.) and is usually known as Manichaeism (sometimes as Manichaeanism); it remained widespread and influential until the ninth century in China, Central Asia, Persia, and the West. Also with a Persian background was the mystery religion called Mithraism, which was active throughout the Roman Empire, but which we shall discuss in Chapter 3.

Zoroastrianism

The Life of Zarathustra

The name Zoroaster is derived from a Greek mangling of the name Zarathustra. This great prophetic figure lived some time before 600 B.C.E. Late Zoroastrian sources say that he lived 300 years (or less) before Alexander the Great, which might place him around 630 B.C.E. But most scholars think that he was older than that, and there is a rough consensus that he probably was of the tenth century B.C.E. He probably came from the region of what is now Afghanistan, or maybe from just inside the modern Iranian border. It was a region of Eastern Iranian culture.

About his life we have few reasonably hard facts. Later legend was to fill in the spaces and see his career as that of an ideal human being, wise and good. Five songs or *Gāthās* in the scriptures are ascribed to him, and in these he mentions that he belonged to a priestly class. The East Iranian or Indo-Iranian culture had many affinities with the Aryan culture of the Vedic period in India, and so his position was analogous to that of a Brahmin. According to tradition he left home – possibly having already experienced the hard training necessary for becoming a priest – at the age of twenty, and at thirty had a powerful inspiration and vision which led him to begin to preach his new and highly original message.

The main component of this was his monotheism, seeing Ahura Mazdā as the One God: the Wise Lord, as his name says. He fathered twin spirits,

Spenta Mainyu and Angra Mainyu (Beneficent Spirit and Hostile Spirit). They each make a fundamental choice, the one for *asha*, goodness (which corresponds to the *rta* or "order" of the Veda) and the other for *druj*, the lie – in a word between good and evil. That fundamental choice faces each person in her or his life. Zarathustra also seems to have taught the existence of six semi-independent abstractly named entities, the beneficent Immortals: Good Thought, Best Truth, Desirable Power, Great Devotion, Wholeness, and Immortality. Were they a kind of concession to the prevailing polytheism? Perhaps not enough: for opposition from other priests led Zarathustra to leave his native area and become an adviser to the court of King Vishtaspa, a convert to the new religion. There, he was married twice and had a number of children: one of the *Gāthās* celebrates his third daughter's wedding. He died at the age of seventy-seven, assassinated by a priest.

His religion also protested against some features of the prevailing warrior religion of his time, which involved the sacrifice of bulls and the use of the hallucinogenic *haoma*. In various ways, then, he was a threat to established ways. The question which is unclear is how this distant and somewhat hazy tradition came to be adopted as the imperial faith of the Achaemenids. In this the Magi seem to have played an important part.

The Role of the Magi

The Magi are, of course, most famous for having come to Jesus' manger in Bethlehem, wise men from the East. Possibly they were a priestly tribe or caste originating in the west of Persia, among the Medes. They practiced marriage between close relatives, a custom which later spread to Zoroastrians, and they were responsible for dealing with the dead. Their characteristic mode of disposing of them was by exposure of the corpses to animals and birds – a method which has become standard in Zoroastrianism, involving *dakhmas* or Towers of Silence where the vultures can pick the flesh off the bones. As priests who were thought necessary to ritual functions, the Magi played a role analogous to the Brahmin class in India, and with the unification of the empire in 550 B.C.E. they assumed an important role. In any event it seems that they came to adopt Zoroastrian beliefs, though not without embroidering and modifying them, in the service of the imperial state. Their learning enabled the corpus of ancient Zoroastrian texts to be handed down to us, as assembled by them from the fifth century B.C.E. onward. In the Sasanid period they were responsible, it seems, for the reformulation of the religion and its doctrines.

The scriptures divide roughly into three phases: the original poems of Zarathustra, the *Gāthās*, then the rest of the *Avesta*, compiled around the sixth century C.E. but based on collections made about a thousand years earlier; and then the texts in the Pahlavi language, written in the ninth century C.E., during the Islamic period, when the Zoroastrian community was under threat. These last are of an analytical nature, with summaries of knowledge, replies to Christian, Islamic, and other doctrines, and so on.

Angra Mainyu, the spirit of Evil, in his struggle against Ahura Mazda, decides to tempt the ancestors of the human race. This fourteenth-century illustration shows a late Zoroastrian view of the fall of the human race, doubtless influenced by Christian ideas. Angra Mainyu here speaks with the primordial couple, offering them two fruits.

The Drama of the World in Zarathustra's Teaching

In the original teaching of Zarathustra, so far as we can make out, the history of the cosmos is conceived as a drama. If Ahura Mazdā is perfectly good, then evil must come from some source which is both dependent on him (as Ahura Mazdā is the creator of all things) and yet independent of him (for he is absolutely good). The idea that Angra Mainyu, the adversary, is evil because of a wrong choice, is a fine solution to the problem, though the source of the idea of evil still remains mysterious. The evil in the world struggles against the good, and humanity, which is capable of choices, must side with the good. This drama will culminate in a third age when good and evil will be separated and the good will be rewarded with judgment and immortality. This entire picture provided a monotheistic frame, but at the same time conformed to the experience of human beings, which sees the world as a mixed place.

This threefold drama, and especially the concept of the future age when human beings will have pure bodies in a state of resurrection, has been very influential in the history of religions. The idea spread to Judaism, to Christianity, and to Islam. There will at the end of time be a wonderful refreshing of existence, making it glorious again. The Lie will be defeated and humbled: the Hostile Spirit will be driven away and finally annihilated.

And in the process human beings will be made immortal. These ideas were already there in the beginning of Zoroastrian religion, but they became considerably more elaborate as time went on.

High Zoroastrianism

As Zoroastrianism developed into a state cult under the priestly guidance of the Magi, it began to reabsorb features of surrounding religions. Thus, the gods began to reappear within the fabric of the faith, though not the evil *daevas* or demonic gods denounced by Zarathustra. First of all the shadowy and abstract Immortals (Amesha Spentas) became personalized. Perhaps for the prophet they were unseen forces which could possess the good person, but later they were as gods. In the *Yashts*, a section of the *Avesta*, we find various divinities being nominated as being "worthy of worship" or *yazata*. Among these are the Sun and the Moon; a rain god, Tishtrya; Anāhitā and Mithra (to them I will return in a moment); Vayu the wind, the personified Haoma; and various other beings and entities, including the angel-like figures which guard individuals, the *fravashi*. There are also Saosha and Rashnu, who with Mithra judge the souls of the dead. If we define a god as a being whom people worship, then we have here in the *yazatas* the wholesale reintroduction of a kind of polytheism, even if the many gods are subordinated to the One God. It is a little like the situation in the Indian tradition.

In the first state of creation Gavaēvōdāta and Gayamaretan are the prototypes of animals and men; and the latter forms with Zarathustra and Saoshyant a triad of great figures relevant to the times. Eventually three Saoshyants were assumed, one each for the beginning of a new millennium (incidentally this imagery of a thousand-year cycle gained a strong grip on Western imagination, and it reappears, for instance, in Hitler's notion of a Thousand-Year Reich). The last Saoshyant will bring immortality to humans and fight a final battle with the force of evil, who will be destroyed.

This idea of a future summation of history had to be combined with a somewhat different piece of imagery, that of the Chinvat Bridge, which stretches from the great cosmic mountain at the center of the universe to Paradise and becomes as narrow as a razor's edge. When the individual soul reaches the Bridge it is judged by Mithra and the other judges, and is confronted by its image: if good, this image is like a beautiful young girl; if not, like a hag. The bad souls slip off the razor's edge into the fires of everlasting torment, and the righteous proceed onward to Paradise. Eventually this imagery was combined with the other, when Saoshyant looks on the world and restores it to imperishable glory, and the souls of the just are united to glorious bodies, and the sacrifice of a cow drink made of blended *haoma* and fat from the cow will confer immortal life upon them.

But despite the re-insertion of gods and goddesses into the religion, on the whole Zoroastrianism retained its imageless state and did not erect statues or have temples for individual deities. There were some exceptions: King Artaxerxes II (reigned 404–358 B.C.E.) put up temples of Anāhitā in the main

37

cities of the empire. But on the whole the battle against representations of the divines was successful. The Zoroastrians, in effect, combined the ancient Indo-Iranian, nomadic, imageless type of religion with the rejection of "pagan" gods in the name of monotheism: they arrived at the same conclusion as that of the official religion of the ancient Israelites, but from another direction.

Many of these ideas, and their accompanying practices, were further elaborated during the Sasanid period, from the third to the seventh century C.E., which also saw the growth of the Zurvanite myth and theology. To that I now turn.

Divine Time: Zurvān

Already during the Achaemenid and Greek periods there had evolved a series of ideas which later were to be elaborated in the Pahlavi literature, which looks back to the glorious days of Sasanid times. It was an idea which in some ways reversed the thrust of the original dualism of Zarathustra. He had claimed a personal Supreme God and twins below him, one good and one evil. In Zurvanism the dualism was between Ohrmazd (Ahura Mazdā) and Ahriman (Angra Mainyu). These were twin offspring of a higher force, namely Time or Zurvān.

The reason for this way of modifying the original pattern was doubtless that, both in the late Achaemenid period and during Greek rule under the Seleucids, the notion of Time had an attraction. This was partly because of the influence of Babylonian astronomy on Persian culture and the derived astrological means of forecasting good and evil futures, and partly because of Greek notions of Fate. At any rate Zurvanism arrived at a new metaphysical interpretation of the world by sacrificing the supremacy status of the ethical good. Zarathustra had elevated the perfectly good God to the supreme place but sacrificed his power, setting up an evil principle from primeval times who would struggle against him, even if destined ultimately to be defeated. In Zurvanism, a morally neutral Time was elevated to the governing position, with both combatants on an equal footing in the cosmic struggle. Although the good God, Ohrmazd, ultimately wins, metaphysically he is not ultimate.

Sasanid Zoroastrianism in its Dimensions

Zoroastrianism was re-founded in the third century C.E. under various leaders. Some of the *narrative* elements to which we have referred become more elaborate. Thus the Saoshyant or Savior who was to come in the final age was supposed to have been born of a virgin who was impregnated while bathing in a lake where the seed of Zarathustra was preserved – and where it had indeed been guarded by no less than 99,999 *fravashi* over the ages. Time, an increased preoccupation, was divided into segments. The age of the cosmos was supposed to be 12,000 years. This was in four stretches of 3000 years. During the first age, the mental age, Ohrmazd starts his creative

activity and begins the war with Ahriman. They do a deal and agree to mingle for 9000 years. The next stage sees a shift from the mental to the material state. The third sees Ahriman's assault on the creation of Ohrmazd. At the end of that period the good God prepares for the coming of the Prophet, whose revelations begin the fourth age. There are three thousand years left; at the end of each thousand years a savior appears, and the last savior ushers in the revitalized cosmos. All this combined history and myth in an interesting and influential way.

In the *doctrinal* dimension, we have the experiment of Zurvanism as a counterpoint to the monotheism of the more orthodox tradition, which had however made compromises with polytheism. As for *ethics*: this dimension was integral to the fabric of Zoroastrian thinking, which focussed on the struggle between good and evil. On the whole Zoroastrian ethics were highly world-affirming, even if the figure of Ahriman was influential in later world-denying creeds such as forms of Gnosticism and Manichaeism.

Regarding the *ritual* dimension, the main feature was the very complex fire ceremony, with the sacrifice of *haoma*. Fire was thought of as purifying in

For the Sasanids, Zoroastrianism was a powerful State religion, and the emperor combined religious and political functions. Here Shapur I receives the submission of the Roman emperor Valerianus.

essence, and the rites attached to it required considerable time and knowledge. The calendar was also dense with festivals, such as celebrating the *fravashi* on the day of Nō Rūz, or New Year's Day, and at six other great festivals: at the middle of spring, at midsummer, at the corn harvest, in the fall, and at midwinter. Also vital were the feasts of Mithra and of the star god Sirius.

The *institutional* dimension in Islamic times, of course, no longer involved state participation; but over the periods when the religion flowered the priesthood was tied to the imperial system. The Magi, as we have seen, made up a hereditary caste, and they assisted with social affairs, such as the initiation of the young, marriages, and funerals. Whether any among the Magi were religious specialists in a further sense, as prophets or ecstatics, is open to some question. Although Zarathustra himself was a visionary, we do not have much evidence on the *experiential* dimension of the religion.

Finally the main *artifacts* of Zoroastrianism were the fire temples and the *dakhmas* where the dead were exposed. In art the winged disc came to represent Ahura Mazdā; but as an imageless religion Zoroastrianism had less to offer in art and statuary than most other faiths.

But the mental imagery was most powerful. The imagination of other traditions was haunted by the Chinvat Bridge, the resurrection of glorified bodies, the coming of a savior, and the thought of life as a struggle between good and evil.

The Survival of Zoroastrianism

The Zoroastrians dwindled in Persia under Islamic pressure and persecution, though a small minority has persisted till modern times. A number migrated to India during the tenth century onwards, forming the Parsi community. Here we shall briefly examine how a modern strand of Zoroastrianism has managed to persist and, at the same time, make a mark on the mixed culture of the Indian subcontinent.

During the eighteenth century, Bombay began its rise to become the major port of India and one of its greatest cities. The Parsi community, which was largely to be found on the west coast, began to collect in Bombay, to learn English, and to work with the British. Nevertheless, some of the large figures of the Indian Congress and nationalist movement were Parsis, men such as Dadabhai Naoroji (1828–1917).

After 1947 the community was loosened up somewhat, in so far as more non-Parsis were employed in Parsi businesses. It remains well respected, though not without its crises. One has to do with mixed marriages: do the offspring of non-Parsi wives count as Parsi? Indian law confirmed the community's traditional directive, which was in the negative. But though this has led to a weakening of the group (a crisis not unlike that among Orthodox Jews in the United States), new impulses have come from the overseas Parsis. Many migrated, after World War II especially, to London,

Parsis, that is, modern-day Zoroastrians, performing ceremonies in the fire temple, in modern India.

Canada, the United States, Hong Kong, and elsewhere. This overseas group is less traditional in outlook and may eventually have a modernizing effect on Indian Parsis themselves. The traditional Zoroastrian way of dealing with the dead, by exposing the corpses on Towers of Silence or *dakhmas*, is also for practical reasons in decline, and in most areas Parsis are buried. Though Zoroastrianism has survived only in small numbers – maybe 150,000 people today – the religion has had vast influence and is a noble mode of organizing belief in one God. A growing Western scholarly interest in the religion has helped to stimulate, partly among the Parsi diaspora (dispersal), a revival of Parsi studies and the presentation of the religion in a newly sophisticated way.

Manichaeism

The prophet Mani was born near the city of Ctesiphon in Mesopotamia around 217 C.E., just before the establishment of the Sasanid dynasty. He had a visionary experience when he was twelve. A few years later, when he was twenty-four, he received an angelic order to preach the truth in public. He spent his life in energetic missionary work, committing his teachings to writing and to painting. He had a high regard for pictorial art and thought it ought to be part of religious communication; he compiled a book of *Images* to illustrate the doctrines. His missions took him to Baluchistan, and he was granted permission by King Shapur to preach throughout the Persian empire. But after Shapur's death Mani fell from favor: the Magi were intent on reconstructing Zoroastrianism after the Parthian period. He was arrested and died after interrogation and being kept in chains, probably in 277 C.E. when he was sixty.

It seems that Mani thought of his religion as a suitable new state religion for the Sasanid dynasty, and this explains some of the hatred between the Magi and him. He genuinely seems to have seen his doctrines as universal, for he held that in part they made up the essence of the teachings of the three great founders, Zarathustra, the Buddha, and Jesus. He himself was raised as a Christian, in a Baptist denomination influential in his region, and so it became common for Christians to think of Manichaeism as a Christian heresy. But its dominant doctrine, of the separation of good and evil, light and darkness, seems to have owed much more to the Zoroastrian tradition.

Despite the persecution of the new religion for a while in the Persian Empire, it persisted there right into Islamic times. It had great success in going west, spreading through much of the Roman Empire in the century after Mani's death. Its most famous adherent, who then, however, converted to Christianity, was St. Augustine. It was also persecuted by Roman emperors, both before and after the Christianization of the Empire. In 527 C.E. an edict threatened death to followers of Mani, so it must have still had some vigor then.

The basic doctrines of Manichaeism were that the soul has fallen into the material world; that unless something happens it will remain trapped in the round of reincarnation; that God, the Father of Greatness, sends a savior who will rouse those asleep in darkness; and that the way to salvation is by knowledge – direct experience of the Light.

The war which exists between the Father of Greatness and the Prince of Darkness has much to do with sex, for the latter wants to produce as many bodies as possible to house and trap the light. Light lives in the seed, and Mani seems to have woven some Tantric ideas into his religion, about the importance of the retention of sperm. Those who were experts were expected to refrain altogether from sex; the married laity should observe strict monogamy. The Manichaean Church was built along somewhat Buddhist lines, with the clergy living in monasteries and being supported by the lay folk. The clergy were supposed to practice truth-telling, nonviolence, celibacy, abstinence from meat and other impure foods, and poverty.

The myths of origin in the Manichaean scheme are somewhat lurid. As a result of the first clashes between the Father of Light and the Prince of Darkness the world is created, the lower regions being caused by the Prince of Darkness and the sun and stars by the offspring of light. These contests also generate some monsters. Unformed matter causes the demons Ashaglun and Namrael to eat the monsters and then to mate, and they bring Adam and Eve into being. But the Savior is sent from above, who arouses Adam from his ignorant sleep and shows him the light within, which ultimately has heavenly origins.

Manichaeism's ethics were strict and humane, renouncing all kinds of violence for lay and clergy alike. People were expected to give to the Church either a tenth or a seventh part of their earnings. They were to fast on Sundays and during the month before the annual Bema celebration, which was a remembrance of Mani's suffering and death. The Bema itself was an empty throne, and this was a little like the early Buddhist practice of not showing the Buddha. They were to confess their sins weekly and annually at a collective ceremony. They had to pray four times a day.

No doubt the Manichaeans encouraged meditative practices which would bring out the light within. At any rate it is through such a direct knowledge of the Light that the expert could finish the round of rebirth and ascend back to the Light which was the soul's source.

This was a vigorous but pessimistic religion, which may have spread in part because of its claims to universality in bringing together themes from Christian, Buddhist, Zoroastrian, and other sources. In part it may have appealed because of its gentleness. Alongside its pessimism there was also hope, for the faith in a Savior pointed to a way out. With its austerity it may have looked good at a period when state religions were showing their corrupt side and harshness.

We have followed the story of Zoroastrianism and Manichaeism until the close of the Sasanid period. Persia was soon destined to be overcome by the forces of Islam, and entered on a quite different period of its civilization.

CHAPTER 3

Greek, Roman, and Imperial Religions

The Strands of Graeco–Roman Religion

Various cultural currents mingled together in the Mediterranean world to form Graeco–Roman civilization. But the two broadest streams were those of Greece, with its splendid but politically fragmented civilization, and of Rome, with its genius for conquest, law, and synthesis. A stepping stone to the unification of the Mediterranean was the unification of the Greek East and various Levantine cultures through the conquests of Alexander the Great in 336–323 B.C.E. Another was the Roman defeat of the major rival power of Carthage in the three Punic wars of the next two centuries. With the Roman conquest of the East and the final stabilization of the empire under Augustus Caesar after 30 B.C.E., a new Graeco–Roman civilization of great power, beauty, and spiritual vigor came into firm existence.

Certain dead civilizations also contributed obscurely to the later creativity of Rome and Greece, such as the Etruscans in Italy, absorbed by Rome in early days, and the Minoan civilization of Crete and its mainland offshoot, Mycenean culture, which was overtaken by conquest by Greek-speakers. The Roman Empire later synthesized and absorbed many streams of thought and practice from the subjugated peoples. Nowhere was this more obvious than in the case of religion: the cults of Isis from Egypt, Mithras from Persia, Cybele from Asia Minor, and Astarte from Syria; Jewish religion from Palestine; Manichaeism from Persia; and Christianity, also from Palestine, are prime examples, to set alongside such homegrown beliefs as the older paganism of Greece and Rome, the mysteries of Eleusis, Orphism, the intellectual faith of Platonism and its daughter Neoplatonism, Stoicism, and Epicureanism. The empire was a great melting pot of spiritual notions. In this chapter we will sample some of these riches.

First there are the traditional religions of Greece and Rome, up till the flowering within these societies of wider ideas and philosophical movements. So we are dealing with Greece up to the fifth century B.C.E., and Rome virtually till the first century B.C.E. We will then look at the philosophies and new religious movements of Greece and the Hellenistic world till the first century C.E. We will then do the same for Rome before looking at the ebb and flow of religions in the early Roman empire, including Christianity but in the wider context of other movements, philosophies and mystery religions. We will leave later developments to Chapters 4 and 6, which will see the emergence of classical forms of Judaism and Christianity.

Greek Religion

The Pattern of the Gods

The system of classical Greek religion is, in terms of belief and worship, polytheistic. There are many gods, and much later this idea was itself denounced by the monotheistic Christians and Jews. It is true that there was a supreme god, a first among other immortals, a chief. And impressive he was too: the mighty Zeus, ruler of the sky, sometimes joined in a triad with Poseidon, god of the sea, and Hades, god of the underworld. Zeus had destroyed a previous group of deities, the mighty Titans, and their leader Kronos. He was not only god of heavenly light, but also a just and kingly god, who was concerned with justice for human beings, and who supported good rulers. He was father of gods and men, the final ruler. But like a chief, he had his advisers and friends around him, and he could not fully control them. Various of his wives and consorts indicate some of the powers and ideals that he had gathered round his person. His great wife, Hera, helps him to sanctify the institution of marriage. When coupled with the earth goddess he represents the male spirit of procreation in the world. In his mating with Themis, goddess of order, he brings regularity into human and cosmic

---

Graeco–Roman Religion some key terms

Cosmos The universe as an orderly whole.

Holocaust A whole burnt sacrificial offering.

Hubris Overweening pride and the desire to gain equality with the gods, which typically proves disastrous.

Logos Reason within humankind, sometimes treated as the principle governing the cosmos, as in Stoicism and in Philo and Christianity (where Logos is also creator and mediator).

Manes The spirits of the dead: the collective ancestors.

Mysteria Mysteries or mystery religions, such as those of Isis, Eleusis, and Mithras, involving the revelation of truth in dramatic form by initiation.

Mythos A story and, in particular, an authoritative story about the gods.

Numen Spirit, e.g. in a stream, a copse, a mountain or other sacred spot or force.

Philosophia Love of wisdom, or a system of ideas which helps us to understand and cope with life, such as Stoicism or Neoplatonism.

Religio That which binds us to the gods, religion.

Temenos A sanctuary or sacred area often including a temple.

Theos God, or God as supreme being, as in Aristotle's philosophy.

affairs. They produce the Fates which rule over human destiny. And so on. If Zeus's frequent espousals and couplings were sometimes criticized later on as giving a bad example to men, they were from one perspective merely a sign of his various powers. And gods were different from us: they were the immortals, and it was *hubris*, or overconfident presumption, even to compare ourselves to them.

Another deity we can sample among the clouds of spirits in the Greek world came from Cyprus, where she may have been stimulated by the example of the Semitic goddess Astarte. Aphrodite is the spirit of fertility and love, married to the beautiful Adonis. In Homer she turns out to be the daughter of Zeus and Dione. She was to inspire the great sculptor Praxiteles (active *c.* 370–330 B.C.E.) to produce the greatest portrayal of her nude. She was a serious goddess, but she could have her wild side, for in the city of Corinth she was served by sacred prostitutes.

A god of uncertain origin but great influence was Apollo, an ideal young man in appearance and the patron of music, healing, prophecy, and the safekeeping of cattle. He was also, and most importantly, the god of the Panhellenic (all-Greece) shrine of Delphi. He may have been non-Greek in origin, in that he was supposedly the offspring of a Titan, which may reflect some old struggle between the Hellenic gods under Zeus and their predecessors. On the whole Apollo stands for orderly inspiration and creative prediction. He can be contrasted with the much more disorderly Dionysos. The main gods of Greece lived on Mount Olympus, the great mountain of central Greece. But Dionysos was not an Olympian, although it came to be said that he was the offspring of Zeus and Semele. He was the god of wine and the leader of orgiastic feasts and revels. Dionysos was associated with the religious origins of drama, in ritual performances in which sacred narratives were enacted. His cult forms the centerpiece of what is in many ways the most powerful play by the dramatist Euripides (480–406 B.C.E.), *The Bacchae.*

The many gods had a national meaning, but each was also rooted in the individual city-state or *polis*. In the heyday of Greek culture, around 600–400 B.C.E., the *polis* was the typical unit, even if Athens, for example, gathered round it an empire of subordinate cities and their territories. Each little region had its own shrines and gods, so Greek religion was an interplay between the localized cults and the Panhellenic religion, which most of the culture shared. This included the gods of Olympus, central holy places like Delphi, where Apollo's oracle was, the great poets, above all Homer, who became the foundation of Greek education, and the Panhellenic games such as the Olympiad. Both poetry and games were held to have sacred significance.

The Importance of Sacrifice
The central ritual activity of Greek religion was the making of sacrifice to the gods. For the most part it involved the slaughter of animals. It is said that the first sacrifice was brought about by Prometheus. He was a hero

and trickster. He tried to deceive Zeus by making the portion of food he set aside for the gods look good: actually it was the animals' bones covered in fat; the good meat was concealed by revolting entrails and the like. He thought this would be good for the human race; but Zeus, who saw through the deception, cunningly took the bones and failed to reveal to Prometheus that a carnivorous life is one of death. So Prometheus unknowingly chose death for the human race. The institution of sacrifice thus drew the line between the gods, who were the immortals, and the mortal humans.

Animal sacrifices were well integrated into ordinary living, for they were the times when Greeks ate meat. Enjoyment and pious duty were thus harnessed together. Similarly, the priesthood were the magistrates for civic purposes, so again there was no divide between religion and the life of the *polis*.

Sacrifices to the earthly gods, the supernatural deities who belonged to the soil and the underworld, were holocausts, burnt whole. The blood, instead of spurting up toward heaven, as the sacrificer slit the animal's throat, poured downward through a hole in the ground. Instead of a high altar, there was a low altar.

Heroes

Though the Greeks distinguished sharply between gods and humans, there was nevertheless a kind of transitional being or demigod who was important for cities, for families, and sometimes for all Greeks: the hero, who was celebrated after his death with a shrine, and who had attained legendary status. Perhaps he was the father of a colony, or a great ancient hero like Achilles or Heracles. He might be associated with the civic past, or with a profession (as was the legendary doctor, Asclepius). To a limited extent their existence formed an ancestor cult. At any rate the heroes, though not divine, were nearer to the gods than other humans – many were thought to be the offspring of gods, and some attained immortality.

Religions within Religion

In the complexity of the mixture of cults which existed in the Greek world, certain movements had a more personal meaning, and these formed in effect smaller religions within the broad-based Panhellenic religion which loosely unified Greek culture. We can view philosophies such as those of Plato as religions within the greater whole, though different in character from more explicitly religious movements. These include the Dionysian movement, turbulent and orgiastic; Orphism, cleansing and in search of release from rebirth; and the Eleusinian mysteries, sacramental and dramatic.

Let us begin with this last one. It centered on the sacred complex of Eleusis, some distance outside Athens. The annual celebration of the rites or mysteries (from *mustai* meaning initiates, based on a verb meaning to keep silent, for the initiates were sworn to secrecy) involved a public procession from

Some of the most powerful rituals were those of initiation, especially at Eleusis. Here we see a relief of Demeter and her daughter Persephone, whose myth was integral to the Eleusinian rites or "mysteries."

Athens, bathing of the initiates in the sea on the way, and the secret goings-on in the cave and temple of Eleusis. The drama there, the rites, the spoken words, the presentation of sacred images by the light of flaring torches, were said to be profoundly moving. As Aristotle said, you went there not to learn anything but to have an experience (a rhyming jingle in Greek: *ou mathein alla pathein*). The sacred drama concerned the descent of the distraught corn goddess Demeter into the underworld, to which her daughter Kore or Persephone has been abducted to marry the infernal god Hades. Eventually Zeus imposes a solution: Kore is to spend half the year in the world and half below. This agricultural myth was transmuted into a higher meaning, to do with the changing of the life of the initiate. Those who were initiated were then able to feel extra depth to their religious life amid the daily routines of the *polis*.

Orphism was a loosely defined movement named after the mythical singer, whose voice can enchant the beasts and the plants and rocks. Orphism had its own priesthood, who traveled about advocating a pure way of life, involving vegetarianism and other means of self-purification. The Orphics saw the cosmos as having started perfectly, as a Cosmic Egg (according to one version), and then progressively becoming more chaotic. The soul is entombed in the body, the Orphics said, and is doomed to transmigration if salvation is not sought. The whole movement was something of a passive rebellion, in that the ban on meat meant a ban on partaking in sacrifices and therefore in civic life. In a culture in which nothing of importance was ever decided without a sacrifice, the Orphic message must have seemed disturbing and revolutionary.

To some degree there was an overlap between it and Dionysian religion, which encouraged the opposite behavior. The myths were connected, and in Orphism there was the conception that Dionysos had been eaten by the Titans who were burned up by Zeus and whose ashes provided the material for creating the human race – so each person contains within himself the divine spark of Dionysos. Dionysianism encouraged women's orgies in wild places, and frenzied dancing, and the consumption of the raw flesh of animals torn apart – an accepted breach of its own taboo. Or, in its tamer, civic form, it provided for a sort of Mardi Gras as a counterpoint to the solemnity of many other civic religious occasions.

Next, there is the movement, periodically revived, of Pythagoreanism. Here we begin to make the bridge between religious and philosophical visions. Pythagoras (570?–500 B.C.E.) came from Samos in the Aegean, but his main work was conducted in Croton, a Greek colony in southern Italy. There he founded a religious order which also took political control of the city. Pythagoras died in Metapontum, in Asia Minor, exiled from Croton for some reason. His order proliferated and was influential for more than fifty years in the area. This order looked on Pythagoras as a holy man, perhaps divine, who taught various spiritual, practical, and philosophical things. According to his view the ultimate constituents of the world were numbers – an idea which was ultimately to have a profound impact on Western thought. The discovery of the mathematical ratio involved in musical harmony had a large effect on Pythagorean thinking. The world somehow flows from the relationship between the bounded, symbolized by numbers, and the unbounded. The soul was held to be involved in reincarnation; and by a process of purification, by following the precepts of Pythagoras, including food taboos – for instance on the eating of beans – the experts could free an individual from this round of rebirth. So the Pythagorean message was a blend of theoretical, mathematical learning and practical spirituality: and all this was related to political action. As we will see, all these three motifs were important for Plato.

The Love of Wisdom and Religious Goals

Already there were connections between what we would call religion and that activity which was known as the love of wisdom (the literal translation of the term *philosophia*). In modern times, in the West, philosophy has become increasingly technical and theoretical. It is true that sometimes it incorporates a worldview – often that of scientific humanism, in the English-speaking world in particular – but it tends often to define itself in opposition to religion and indeed to the idea of wisdom. But this was not the case in ancient Greece.

Apart from Pythagoras, some thinkers, known as the Presocratics – Thales, Anaximander, and Anaxagoras among them – pioneered speculative thought. Heraclitus (c. 540–c. 480 B.C.E.) said that everything is in flux, and that you cannot step into the same river twice (a doctrine reminiscent of those of his contemporary, Buddha Śākyamuni). Parmenides (b. 515 B.C.E.) saw reality as unchanging Being. Socrates (c. 470–399 B.C.E.) concentrated on seeking the definition or essence of things, asking questions like "What is courage?" and generally stirring his contemporaries to reflect about moral issues – for which he was condemned to death for corrupting the young. The teachings and methods of these men paved the way for Plato, and then for Platonism and later Neoplatonism, which often took a highly religious form.

Plato (429?–347 B.C.E.) was influenced somewhat by Orphic and Pythagorean thought and argued, in his delightful dialogue, the *Phaedo*, for the doctrine of reincarnation. He held that human souls were unable to retain their splendid original state of immortality and so sank down into bodies, to wander through life from existence to existence. But knowledge enables them to rise again to a state of liberation. Knowledge involves knowing essences, which for Plato are defined by the Forms which earthly things imitate and participate in. The World of Forms is where the soul came from, so acquiring knowledge is really remembering. And this, according to Plato, is how Socrates' method of arousing thought managed to work: as Socrates himself said, he was a midwife of knowledge.

The World of Forms is a great hierarchy, with at the top the Form of the Good which informs all other Forms because each is ideal. So the soul, through knowledge, can climb up to the Form of the Good and perceive it in a vision. Plato's intuition was thus both mystical and intellectual, and part of the rigorous training of the disciple had to be in mathematics. In his school in the grove known as Akademos (hence the words "academic" and "academy") he had written over the entrance the words *Mēdeis ageōmetros eisitō* – "Let no one ignorant of geometry enter here."

Plato was not only concerned with theory and vision but also with politics. He made some fruitless visits to Sicily at the behest of the dictator Dion of Syracuse. But most of his life was devoted to education, and it was one of his pupils, Aristotle (384–322 B.C.E.), who took Plato's philosophy in a different direction. He brought the essences down to earth, and developed marvelous analytical treatments of biology, psychology, physics, metaphysics, ethics, politics, and logic, which were to have a profound effect on European thought.

Platonism provided a noble and unified vision which could be set alongside the religion of the mysteries and the new movements, and, up to a point, alongside traditional religion and civic cults. But Plato was very critical of the poetic tradition of Homer and Hesiod and the low morals ascribed to the gods. In Greek religion, around 350 B.C.E., there was a mixture of different levels of public and private religion, with certain high philosophical speculations woven into the fabric of life. In a way Greek religion was like that of the Indian tradition of the same period – not yet synthesized in a cohesive system, but full of potential which was to be realized later.

Alexander and After: Some New Philosophical Movements

Greece was unified, and the city-states tamed, by Philip II, king of Macedon (382–326 B.C.E.) and his genius son Alexander the Great (356–323 B.C.E.) – a pupil, by the way, of Aristotle. In a series of brilliant campaigns, Alexander swept aside the Persian empire, which had long been its polar opposite in politics, thought, and religion. He laid the foundations of Greek-influenced regimes in Egypt, Syria (including Palestine), Persia, and Bactria in Central Asia. In Greece he brought a turbulent but wonderfully creative period to a close and ushered in the age which we know as "Hellenistic." During this time some new philosophies were pioneered which became influential both in the Greek East and the Roman West of the Mediterranean world.

Epicurus (342–271 B.C.E.) taught most of his life in Athens, and made use of the atomic theory of his predecessor Democritus. He argued that everything in the world is composed of atoms in emptiness. The soul too is a composite, and so when a person dies his atoms are dispersed and that is that. The gods are made of refined atoms but exist outside of our world, and they are not concerned at all with what we do or do not do. The best thing is to cultivate moderation in the pursuit of reasonable pleasure and to cultivate the virtue of *ataraxia* or equanimity. Later this worldview was put into poetic form by the Roman poet Lucretius (*c.* 96–*c.* 55 B.C.E.). In his *De rerum natura*, "On the Nature of Things," he sought to dispel fear of the *numina*, gods and spirits.

About 300 B.C.E., Zeno of Citium founded the school which was known, after the cloisters or *stoa* where he taught, as Stoicism. He demythologized the gods, treating them as natural forces. The universe was controlled by mind (itself a material entity, though of a superior, refined nature – and poetically this could be called Zeus). On death we exist no more: but we are superior to animals because we possess reason. The wise person steels himself in the face of ultimate extinction, and bears himself with courage, self-control, and realism in the face of evil and death, which are unavoidable ingredients of the way things are. This austere doctrine had an appeal to Roman nobility, and was taught in Rome by the Greek slave Epictetus in the first century C.E. and in the famous *Meditations* of the emperor Marcus Aurelius (121–180 C.E.), who became emperor in 161.

The latter part of what is called the Hellenistic age saw the conquest of the Greek East by the Romans and the fusion of the Mediterranean world into a single empire. In order to see the religious character of this new age, we need to retrace our steps to look at the nature of early Roman religion.

The numinous figure of the great Greek god Zeus is tempered by the increasing realism and humanity with which the Greeks depicted their gods.

Roman Religion

The Numina and Civic Virtue

Roman religion was focused on deities and spirits who can collectively be called *numina* – mysterious spirits who roused reverential fear. Its gods ranged from the great Jupiter, with his consort Juno, through Mars or War, Venus or Love, and Ceres of the grain harvest, to such specialist deities as Sarrator, the god of weeding, and Januarius, the god of the threshold. The whole of reality and of human activity was punctuated and pervaded by the *numina*.

The aim of public worship in the early Roman system was to ensure that the gods remained or became benevolent. The calendar was a mosaic of feast days for worshiping various gods. March, for instance, started off with a sacrifice to Mars, after whom it was named – and there were days for the blessing of horses, arms, trumpets, and so on. In addition, the various games had religious significance – chariot races, wrestling, boxing, and later on (borrowed from the Etruscans) gladiatorial combats. To administer all these public events there were different classes of priests, headed by the supreme priest, the *pontifex maximus*. There were also the vestal virgins, appointed each for thirty years and enjoying great prestige, who had to maintain the sacred fire in the court of the goddess Vesta. There were also different kinds of diviners, such as the augurs, who predicted the future on the basis of the flights of birds. Curiously, this custom has a descendant in European countries, where people may be superstitious about seeing an odd number, but not an even number, of magpies.

The public rites had their complement in household ceremonies, addressed to the *lares* or household gods, and to the ancestors, honored as *di manes* or divine shades. This system made the Romans a very religiously observant people. As they grew outward, absorbing other cultures, the pantheon expanded. Since, too, the Romans were increasingly exposed to Greek culture, both because of the overrunning of Greek cities in the south of Italy and through the importation of educated Greek slaves as tutors and so on, the tendency was to identify Greek and Roman gods freely – Jupiter and Zeus, Venus and Aphrodite, Juno and Hera. This prepared the way for a blended Graeco–Roman civilization when ultimately the Romans overran Greece and the Hellenic East. This they did effectively from the mid-second century B.C.E., when they annexed Greece, having shortly before razed Carthage; and in 66 B.C.E. Pompey organized the whole of the East, as far as the Persian border, into provinces subsidiary to Rome. Not long after that, Julius Caesar conquered Gaul and started the subjugation of Britain. By the time he died, in 44 B.C.E., the Roman empire was more or less in place. It was taken over, after destructive civil wars, by Caesar's adopted son, Octavian, who assumed the title of emperor (*princeps*) and, in 27 B.C.E., took the solemn, rather religious name of Augustus.

The Spread of Mysteries and Philosophies

Perhaps because of the pluralism of the new empire, and because of the abatement of civic concern in the states which it had absorbed, religion became more individualized and was seen more and more as a matter of choice. The imperial ideology, it is true, required sacrifice to the emperor, as a means of expressing loyalty. But within that limit there was a remarkable flux of beliefs and practices. Among these movements were many mystery religions, like the cult of Eleusis. These gave dramatic shape to the initiation of those who wished to pursue purity or immortality and to take part in the power of the god or goddess.

Already some of the Oriental deities had taken root in Rome, such as Isis of Egypt who had had a temple on the Aventine hill since the second century B.C.E. She brought feminine powers to bear on faith. Isis, of course, restores Osiris to life, and likewise the initiate is given new and restored existence by the goddess. She was regarded as the supreme deity, and the initiate's vision of her is movingly depicted by the writer Apuleius (second century C.E.) in *The Golden Ass*. The hero, who has unfortunately been turned into an ass, is ultimately redeemed from his animalistic existence by the goddess.

A mystery cult that had special appeal to the Roman soldiers was that of Mithras. Mithras was credited with slaying the bull which would renew life, in alliance with the Sun. This myth was celebrated with the sacrifice of a bull

The mythic dimension: popular particularly among Roman soldiers was Mithras. This offshoot of Iranian religion related to the myth of Mithras as the unconquerable Sun.

in the half-underground temple which was characteristic of the cult. The worshipers present at the action partook of a subsequent feast (or, at least, this is a prevailing interpretation of our archaeological evidence). Mithraism became a kind of initiatory club, its rites producing the feeling of renewed life and comradeship.

At a higher level educationally, there came the development of the Neoplatonic movement, especially through the writings and teaching of Plotinus (205?–269 C.E.) and his successors Porphyry (232?–303) and Iamblichus (250?–330). Plotinus was from Upper Egypt and studied with the teacher Ammonius Saccas in Alexandria before setting off on an expedition to eastern Persia in the hope of learning something of Eastern thought. Later he started teaching in Rome, gathering about him some influential disciples. He greatly modified the teachings of Plato.

At the summit of Plotinus' system is the One. It is, in effect, the supreme God and emanates in the form of the Intellect or Nous. This contains within it the intelligible Forms of Plato's system. Beyond that, Intellect has a further emanation, the Soul, in which the Forms are seen in space and time. The Soul is on the brink of becoming the material world, into which the human soul descends. The world has many beauties, though it is a kind of prison that entraps the human soul. The One spreads love or passion (*eros*) for itself to the souls of human beings who begin the ascent back, through intellectual,

Neoplatonism: Iamblichus on the Mysteries

No sacral act can be effective without the supplication of prayer. Steady continuance in prayer nourishes our mind, enlarges the soul for the reception of the gods, opens up to men the realm of the gods, accustoms us to the splendor of the divine light, and gradually perfects in us [our] union with the gods, until at last it leads us back to the supreme heights. Our mode of thinking is drawn gently aloft and implants in us the spirit of the gods; it awakens confidence, fellowship, and undying friendship [with them]; it increases the longing for God; it inflames in us whatever is divine within the soul; it banishes all opposition from the soul, and strips away from the radiant, light-formed spirit everything that leads to generation; it creates good hope and trust in the light. In brief, it gives to those who engage in it intercourse with the gods.

In the catacombs, the Roman piety toward the dead was formalized in niches such as these, where urns containing the ashes of the dead were stored.

ethical, and mystical endeavor, to the One. As he lay dying, Plotinus is supposed to have said: "I am trying to bring back the divine in me to the divine in the All."

Such teachings ultimately had a lot of appeal to Christians who were trying to make a blend between their monotheistic Jewish tradition and the classical culture of their environment in the Roman Empire. Neoplatonism could be detached from paganism and its ideas made use of when formulating a deep Christian theology. Their emphasis on contemplation also gave Neoplatonic writers an edge at a time when monasticism was growing, after the Christian takeover of the Roman Empire in 330 C.E. There was also the pressing need to reaffirm commitment and purity of life in a world gone easy.

So we find in the Hellenistic world and the early centuries of Rome a variety of mostly Eastern mystery religions and philosophies of special appeal to the literate elite. There was also something else brewing, and that was a challenging religion which also had some appeal across the whole empire: Christianity.

Roman Imperial Religion as a Total System

Christians and others were of course somewhat hostile to the imperial religious climate. What others saw as meaningful stories they saw as deceptions. They did not acknowledge that their own narratives might look like sacred myth to others. The various deities represented so many powers and above all forces for the renewal of life. There was a strong air in the empire of the need for propriety, so that the proper imperial and civic rites could be performed. It was essential continually to cement good relations between the Beyond and ourselves. Within the total loosely bound system there were alternative mysteries which pious folk might wish to take part in. Those which did not respect the emperor were subversive and deserving of persecution. The central gods of Rome were meanwhile being integrated with local deities throughout the empire, from Britain to Cyrenaica. This process helped to bring a sense of solemn loyalty to the far-flung parts of the empire. In its own way it was a satisfactory system, for it functioned to a great extent pluralistically.

Yet the imperial religion, which concentrated on the pieties addressed to former and present emperors, contained within itself the seeds of decay. The spread of mystery religions, including Christianity, attested to the concern for dramatic and elevating rituals. They were made all the more powerful because of the focus on a *sole* figure, whether Christ or Isis or Mithras, who commanded intense loyalty. The formalities of the imperial cult were neither intense nor inspiring. It is true that for the educated elite the new Graeco–Roman religious synthesis was hooked up to literature, from Homer to Virgil and beyond, which could be thought inspiring in its way. Indeed, philosophies such as Stoicism and Neoplatonism could command both intellectual esteem and emotional loyalty. But we have seen how the whole system of beliefs and practices was plural, and loyalties became divided. It

was Constantine's perception that an intense religion such as Christianity, strengthened by the persecutions it had undergone, and appealing to all levels of society, would form a very powerful imperial cult. This was especially so as the new faith incorporated ingredients of the older religions and philosophies. It was deeply influenced by Neoplatonism, and it began to take over as churches many of the "pagan" temples.

The End of Graeco–Roman Religion

Naturally the victory of Christianity was not absolute and immediate after the approval of Constantine and the subsequent Council in 325 C.E. Yet it was in many ways very rapid. In 391 the emperor Theodosius ordered the end of pagan sacrifices. The destruction or in some cases conversion of pagan sanctuaries was common. Though the philosophical religions might hang on, they were also taken up into the emerging doctrinal synthesis achieved by the heirs of the Greek and Roman world, men such as St. Augustine (354–430) and the Eastern Fathers.

The result was a blend of two ways of life, for Christianity did weave into its fabric many of the values of the Hellenistic world and the Roman Empire. It was thus able to transmit across a rather chaotic period, from the fourth century onward, a whole complex of Graeco–Roman values which were not entirely buried by Christian orthodoxy. But the Churches did get very preoccupied thereafter with right doctrine, and Christians saw themselves as the true believers.

Although Graeco–Roman religion faded away after the victory of Christianity many of its ideas, especially philosophical ones, remained influential, and reinvigorated Western civilization through the Renaissance.

Among Christians cremation was replaced by burial awaiting the resurrection: the sarcophagus here depicts the death and final glory of Christ, in the center depicted by the Chi Rho symbols, being the first letters of the name Christos in Greek.

57

CHAPTER 4

The Israelites and Early Judaism

The Beginnings of the Israelite Religion

Israelite history provided materials which continued to have religious significance long after the societies which they reflected had ceased to exist. Take, as key examples, the various books of the Bible. It is worth noting, too, that though Judaism, Christianity, and Islam project themselves back in time to Abraham and to the religion of the Israelites – so that it is tempting to think, for instance, of Moses as the founder of Judaism – strictly speaking what we know as Judaism did not yet exist. There is some historic or other connection between Jews and their predecessors the Israelites, of course. But in the period we are talking about, from 1200 B.C.E. or so down to the time of Alexander (say) around 330 B.C.E., what existed was a stream of religious development which swelled into Judaism much later, at about the time that Christianity took its first classical form, two or three centuries after Jesus.

Most of our sources for the story of Israel come from the Bible, supplemented by fairly extensive archaeology. From the perspective of the history of religions we can use the Biblical narrative to establish a fairly clear account of the evolution of beliefs among the Israelites. But we have to use it judiciously as a source, the way we have used other scriptural traditions in this book.

The earliest period of the religion of the Israelites is a kind of prehistory: the period of the Patriarchs, beginning with the narrative of Avraham (Abraham), who came from Ur of the Chaldees in Sumeria. His God is described as El (also the name, as we have seen, of the highest god of the Canaanites). His son Yitshaq (Isaac) was father of Ya'akov (Jacob), who had various adventures: during one he had a dream of a ladder leading up to Heaven, and named the place where he had it Bethel or House of God, which became the cult center, before Jerusalem, in northern Israel. On his return from a visit to Mesopotamia he had a wrestling contest with a mysterious being and his name was changed to Yisra'el. His twelve sons bore the names of the twelve tribes of Israel, and these became a confederacy which struggled successfully to dominate both northern and southern Palestine.

Many of the stories of this shadowy earlier period have become vital in the living faith of those who look back – the story of Avraham's willingness, in obedience to God, to sacrifice his only son; how Lot's wife turned into a

The God of the Israelites was probably an amalgam of several divine concepts. The Canaanite fertility god Baal, here represented in the form of a bronze statuette from 1300 B.C.E., was at first identified with Yahweh but later rejected as an idol.

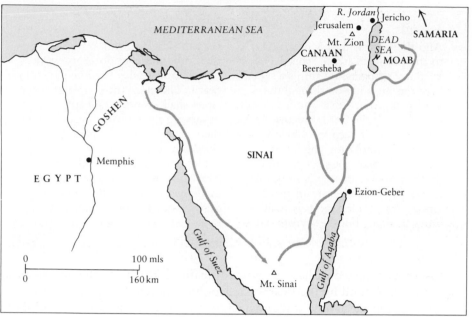

Map 2 The route of the Exodus from Egypt, twelfth century B.C.E.

pillar of salt; the destruction of the evil cities of Sodom and Gomorrah. But we know very little really about the religious shape of the period before the revolution that culminated in the flight from Egypt. This bold rebellion was brought about by Mosheh (Moses), the leader of those Israelites who were working as slaves for the Egyptians before they escaped through the Sinai peninsula. They conquered the land of Canaan in the name of a new religious ideology of commitment to one God, whom they called YHWH or Yahweh (and who, in the West, is often named Jehovah, a partially Latinized rendition of the Hebrew name). Scholars are not certain at all when Mosheh or Moses lived, but it was maybe soon after 1300 B.C.E..

The Mosheh Revolution and the Entry into Canaan

The whole story of Mosheh seems to be a composite one, with different traditions and ideas being woven together in the narrative as we have it. The modern version is derived from four or maybe three sources: the Book of Deuteronomy; the source which scholars call "J" for Jahve (i.e. Yahweh or Jehovah) because it stresses the concept of Yahweh; the closely related "E" (which uses the name Elohim for God rather than Yahweh), and the so-called Priestly source or "P." These were probably composed between about 700 and 400 B.C.E. Much is speculative in these discussions of origins and the composition of texts. But it may well be that Mosheh was indeed the revolutionary leader who did in fact promote the strict adoption of loyalty to Yahweh. This facet became the hallmark of the official religion of the Israelites, and won out as a clear form of monotheistic faith, leaving, in the process, a great mark on the whole historical process.

Exodus

And the Lord said to Moses, "Say to the people of Israel, You shall keep my sabbaths, for this is a sign between me and you throughout your generations, that you may know that I, the Lord, sanctify you. You shall keep the sabbath, because it is holy for you; every one who profanes it shall be put to death; whoever does any work on it, that soul shall be cut off from among his people. Six days shall work be done, but the seventh day is a sabbath of solemn rest, holy to the Lord; whoever does any work on the sabbath day shall be put to death. Therefore the people of Israel shall keep the sabbath, observing the sabbath throughout their generations, as a perpetual covenant. It is a sign for ever between me and the people of Israel that in six days the Lord made heaven and earth, and on the seventh day he rested, and was refreshed."

Mosheh is depicted as having escaped death as a baby by being put in a boat of reeds. Found by the Pharaoh's daughter, he was brought up at court as a prince even though he was an Israelite. But, because he struck and killed an Egyptian for oppressing an Israelite worker, he had to flee into the region beyond Egypt, in the deserts to the east. He lived there with a priest of Midian and worked as a shepherd. During this period he seems to have adopted, in some modified form, the religion of Midian, focusing on the God Yahweh. When later he led the Israelites out of Egypt, in that great event which later Jews would know as the Exodus (Greek for "departure"), he took them to Mount Sinai. During this period in Sinai he experienced the spiritual vision of a bush which was burning and yet was not consumed by the fire. There, he heard the voice of Yahweh, calling him to a leading role in the life of his people and the service of God. It was like several prophetic visions of a much later period.

It was under his chief leadership, though in conjunction with his elder brother Aharon (Aaron), that he led the Israelites out of Egypt in a miraculous fashion. The Biblical narrative lists such events as the plagues on Egypt, the Passover and the parting of the sea, which saved the Israelites and then swamped the Egyptians. These events are commemorated at the great eight-day Jewish family feast, the Passover.

Most important were the events on Mount Sinai, when Mosheh ascended the mountain to converse with the Divine Being and to receive the covenant, including the Ten Commandments which were to become the basis of the Torah, or Law. (I translate Torah as "Law," though some Jews prefer some other appropriate translation such as "Teaching" – they wish to avoid a translation which might reflect what is to their minds an unfortunate Christian disapproval of Law as opposed to Grace, in the New Testament.) Thereafter, it was the loyalty of official Israelite religion to the idea of One God which brought it into conflict with Canaanite religion.

The Temple

The process begun by Mosheh led to the domination of Canaan by the Twelve Tribes, so that a substantial part of the land was under their rule by as early as 1200 B.C.E. Eventually the pattern of leadership changed to kingship. The second king and great hero, David, captured Jerusalem and created the capital there. He had the ambition of building a central temple there, but it was left to his son Shelomoh (Solomon, 965–925 B.C.E.) to do this. His wonderful construction, known as the First Temple, lasted till its destruction in 586 B.C.E.

Its building was a means of centralizing all the cults of Israel in one physical and spiritual place. The advantage was both political and spiritual. It meant that the monarchs had greater control, though on Shelomoh's death political power was split and the Northern and Southern Kingdoms of Israel and Judah emerged. Israel did not survive the destruction of its capital Samaria in 721 B.C.E., the overrunning of the region by Nebuchadnezzar of Babylon, and the subsequent period of Persian rule. The spiritual effect of having the central rites at Jerusalem was that it was easier to wipe out unacceptable forms of practice at the shrines scattered through the land. The Temple came to be a monopoly. It is true that, through the lavish care that Shelomoh bestowed on the Temple and through his desire for a glorious cult, there were elements which went beyond the austere requirements of Yahwistic worship.

Mosheh teaching the people of Israel the Ten Commandments, from an early medieval Bible.

The building consisted of a large high hall, with cedar beams and cedar doors decorated with gold. At the west end was a windowless shrine inside of which was lodged the most holy object of ancient Israel, the Ark. This contained the stone tablets on which the Ten Commandments were inscribed. Above were two gold cherubs. In front of the building was the altar used for sacrifices. Gradually round about it various outbuildings were erected, housing priestly implements and clothes and the like. It was ultimately enclosed in two great courtyards, approached by three sets of gatehouses and three flights of stairs.

After its destruction in 568 B.C.E., fifteen hundred of the elite of Judah, the Southern Kingdom, were taken in exile to Babylon. When some of these exiles returned in 538 B.C.E. they began to rebuild the Temple on the same site. It was dedicated more than twenty years later. Much later still, after many modifications and additions, King Herod the Great in 20 B.C.E. began the reconstruction of the entire complex, creating a beautiful building partially on Roman lines. Such rebuilding in fact continued throughout the period, but ending in the destruction of the Second Temple in 70 C.E.

The altars of sacrifice in front of the Temple must have presented a busy sight, not altogether in harmony with modern feelings. Many animals and birds would be killed, and their blood drained. Many would function as burnt offerings in which the whole of the animal would be engulfed in flames. There would be offerings of grain and other foods too. Since the Temple came to be a place of pilgrimage, the daily killing must have been great, particularly in times of prosperity when many people could afford to pay for sacrifices. In many of the sacrifices, a person gave up something of worth, for instance a goat or a sheep, in a concrete manifestation of his feeling of sin or guilt at something he had done. So the sacrificial aspect of the Israelite religion, like its general worship, was focused on an ethical God.

The Prophetic Tradition

In many religions we can make a contrast between prophetic and priestly types. If the Temple was the heart of priestly religion, something else was the heart of prophetic faith. It was a mixture of vision, vocation, and ethical values. The true sacrifices to God should be, as one prophet remarked, a broken spirit and a humble heart. The inwardness of religion is the vital essence of it. Later Judaism always had something of this split between outer and inner – the very complexity of the Law meant that there were many, many externals in the Jewish religion, but like ancient Chinese *li* they were useless without the sincerity of inwardness.

There were "official" prophets in Israel and Judah, whose job it was to make predictions before military campaigns and the like. There were others attached to cult centers. But the great Prophets, who attained orthodox stature by the incorporation of their teachings into the sacred writings of the tradition, were detached from such organizational ties and were more individualistic in their utterances. Because their proclamations and criticisms were on the side of what became the official religion, their turbulence tended to be vindicated after their deaths. Their critical awareness, based on personal religious experience, provided an indispensable element of renewal in a tradition which had its heavy investment in the expensive rites of the Temple and a detailed understanding of the provisions of the Law.

There are many prophets to choose from, but let us just briefly mention three: Amos, Isaiah, and Jeremiah.

The Book of Amos dates from around 750 B.C.E. and incorporates an account of the prophet's inaugural vision. He saw the Lord at the altar, and so his criticisms of ritual do not stem from a rejection of the sacrificial cult. But he is highly critical of those who think that riches in a period of prosperity are the *result* of the rituals, and are a sign of God's blessing. It is too simple a view in an age of social injustice. God's relationship to Israel is founded on Israel's social and moral duty. The ruling class had better beware. The day of the Lord is not sweetness and light, but darkness. In such ways the prophet attacks the smugness of his time and demands that the externals of worship be tied to inner worthiness of aim and compassion for the poor.

The Book of Isaiah is a composite work, the first part belonging to the eighth century B.C.E., the time of the Assyrian invasions, and the second part to the Persian period. Here we concentrate on Deutero–Isaiah (Second Isaiah). This unknown prophet had a tremendous influence on later religion, through his idea of the Suffering Servant of the Lord (*'eved YHWH*) – a probable metaphor for the people of Israel – who is rejected by his fellowmen, yet bears God's message and has a mission to restore justice. The *'eved YHWH* represents an ideal which places value on faithfulness rather than prosperity. Yet in the end all will be well: Deutero–Isaiah looks forward to the time of the Anointed One, the *Māshīah* (Messiah). He is destined to restore Israel and to usher in a period of cosmic peace, when the wolf will lie down with the lamb, and the leopard with the kid, and the lion with the fatted calf. And then the earth will be full of the knowledge of the Lord.

In the stormy days which led up to the taking of Jerusalem by the Babylonians under Nebuchadnezzar, Yirmeyah (Jeremiah) called on the people to submit rather than resist. He naturally got into trouble as a traitor; but as he saw it neither the Northern Kingdom of Israel nor the Southern Kingdom of Judah had been able to live up to the covenant with God. He did not point his finger at any one class, but at all. Once Israel had entered into the Promised Land, the nation had become unfaithful. Yirmeyah called the people to repentance; but if his call remained unanswered then inevitably the destruction of the land was assured.

As a person Yirmeyah seems to have been depressive. He was unmarried, lonely, a person of strife who stirred things up at the call of God. He wished, indeed, he had never been born. But he felt the prompting of the Lord to speak the gloomy truth to the populace. There was hope, even so; and Yirmeyah predicted that God would make another covenant which would be so written into the hearts of people that they would stay loyal.

In being so convinced that the old Israel would in effect be destroyed, Yirmeyah paved the way for a more individualistic understanding of relationship to God. This was already implicit in the Torah at Sinai, in that its ethical requirements are placed in a personal framework. Much of the religion of the Israelites is based on the idea of a chosen people: but it also relates to individual acts and choices.

In the latter part of the sixth century B.C.E., following a decree of the Persian king, Cyrus the Great, in 538, the restoration of the Temple in Jerusalem was permitted and the exiles returned from Babylon. Under the leadership of Ezra, a large group set out from Babylon, with great financial resources, and arrived in the holy city. Amid the devastation they found that many Jews had married Gentiles and had given up their strict adherence to the lifestyle that had sustained the people before. All mixed marriages were dissolved, and, at the feast of Sukkot, Ezra read out the Torah from a great book at the ceremony in which the notion of a scriptural basis for the religion became an official doctrine. After a period of fasting and the confession of sins, the people undertook at another ceremony several months later to renew the covenant. This meant supporting the Temple and observing the *Shabbat* (Sabbath) and the various laws of the Torah.

Maybe the book which Ezra read out was the Pentateuch or First Five Books of the Bible, which thereafter became the sacred scriptures. Or maybe it was something less. But in due course it was these Five Books that became regarded as the Written Torah. The so-called "Oral Torah," handed down verbally since Mosheh, was considered to be authoritative by later orthodox Jews also. It was an important buttress of Rabbinic Judaism, which we shall come to later.

The Dimensions of Israelite Religion

We have briefly highlighted some key events in the Israelite experience, down to the Second Temple, the influence of the Prophets, and the jelling of Jewish culture. Bearing in mind that this historical period was prior to the coming of the Greeks and Romans and the absorption of the Jewish people into the Graeco–Roman experience, we may now be able to understand some of the main features of the varied dimensions of this religion.

First, regarding *doctrine*. God is seen as supreme and then as alone. It became a monotheistic religion, and therefore different from neighboring faiths and rituals. This development was doubtless due to the revolution in practice associated with the name of Mosheh. Second, as far as the *narrative* dimension goes, ancient Israel had the memory of the Exodus, the homelessness of the desert, and the conquest of Canaan. This narrative held a major place for the idea of the covenant with God. Third, in regard to *ritual*, there was a ban on carved images, which helped to separate Israel from many of the fertility and other cults of the area. This separation seems to have been a constant struggle. The foundation of the kingship, leading to the centralization of worship at the Temple, was an important factor in

In this miniature from the *Golden Haggadah* (Spanish, fourteenth century), the artist portrays the Jews leaving Egypt "with a high hand" – a Hebrew expression meaning "triumphant," but here illustrated literally.

maintaining the separateness and imageless character of Israelite worship. But the experience of exile also meant that an important elite became committed to maintaining the rituals even without the Temple. For this and other reasons, the restoration of the Temple also saw the beginnings of the idea of synagogue worship, in which congregations could take part.

As to the *experiential* dimension, the call of the Prophets became an important counterpart to the conservatism of the priestly tradition, intent on the niceties of sacrifice. The call blended with a sense of ethical destiny, which gave the Prophets their special edge as critics of the kingly and priestly establishment. The visions, too, reinforced the sense of the spiritual presence of God.

The law code, which is already encapsulated in the Ten Commandments, gave Israelites a clear vision of the *ethical* conduct expected of those in a treaty relationship with God. Organizationally, the fact that by the end of this period there was the conception of written scriptures, prepared the way for the rise of a scribal class whose job was to interpret the written texts. These were in parallel with the hereditary priests, whose main tasks related to the Temple liturgy.

The *institution* of kingship was important politically, even if finally not successful. But it came to be even more important in the mythic imagination of the people, who might look forward to an Anointed One who would restore the kingship and usher in a time of great peace and solemn prosperity. This vision came about, in part, because of the political fragility of the Temple.

Finally, as to the *material* dimension, the Temple was the great big artifact on which Israel spiritually depended. Its glory under Shelomoh was great, and its restoration with the return of the exiles from Babylon was a reassurance. But there were other artifacts, such as the scriptures. They could – and eventually did – replace the tablets in the Ark of the Covenant. Perhaps the greatest material thing for the people in the end was the land of Israel. But the land was at the crossroads of great powers – the Assyrians, the Egyptians, the Babylonians, the Persians, the Greeks, the Romans.

Israelite religion was not completely unaffected by the religions of the area. In particular it blended with Canaanite religion as well as separating itself out. The surrounding cultures could easily understand the slaughter of sheep and pigeons on the altars before the Temple, the glories of kingly power expressed by the pillars in front of the Temple, the importance of sacred writings, and the visions of the Prophets. But Israel's blend was very specific, and it had a great capacity for survival. Indeed, many of its customs, and many of its great ideas, were taken up by later peoples.

Judaism in the Graeco–Roman World

From the Israelite religion of the early period through to the emergence of fully fledged Judaism there were several transformations. The older religion was anchored in the land of Israel, but the Judaism of the third century C.E. onward had become a more universal religion, centered on synagogue worship and led by rabbis. Believers upheld the ancient laws but were no longer tied to the Temple, which was destroyed in 70 C.E.

The Changing Fortunes of the Jews

The period from the reconstruction of the Israelite tradition under Ezra to the era of the Roman Empire saw Palestine under Greek rule, that of the Seleucids. It also saw some Persian influences, through the notion of the resurrection, and an increased emphasis on doom-laden prophecies concerning the end of history. At the same time came the elevation of the figure of the *Māshīah*, Anointed One of the House of David, who would come to restore the kingdom of Israel. All this emerges in the Book of Daniel, filled with dazzling imagery. After many attacks on the people of Israel by foreign adversaries, God sends a great leader to guide them in defeating their foes and establishes an everlasting kingdom. The wicked are condemned to perish, and the good live on.

Various parties emerged before the time of Jesus, and it was in this plural and chaotic time that he started his own movement. The Pharisees were looked on as innovators because they introduced ideas like the resurrection of the body which scribal conservatives rejected. The latter belonged to the party of the Sadducees, who preserved the Torah, and had chief control of the Temple rituals. There were Jews who were Hellenizers, won over to the excitements and lifestyle of Greek civilization. There were Zealots, who were involved with plotting armed resistance to the Roman occupation. There were the Essenes and the Qumran community, who withdrew to a secluded life in the desert, in order to preserve the Torah intact and create a counterpoint to the Temple rites. There was the group known as the Therapeutai in Alexandria, who pursued the contemplative life in a spirit of asceticism. There were men like Philo of Alexandria, who took Greek learning seriously and sought to express the higher truths of Jewish belief and practice in Greek terms. These currents of belief flourished in Palestine and more widely in the Roman Empire, for there was an extensive diaspora (dispersal) of Jews even before the fall of the Temple in 70 C.E.

Judaism Defines Itself

Several crises assaulted the Jewish tradition. There was the tragic and tormenting sack of the Temple after an unsuccessful revolt against Rome in 70 C.E. There was the later razing of the city of Jerusalem itself and the building of a Roman city there, Aelia Capitolana, in 130 (leading to the disastrous revolt of Shimon Bar-Kochba, hailed by the famed Rabbi Aqiba as *Māshīah*). There was also the problem posed by the growing Christian movement, getting further and further away (as Jews saw it) from the orthodox scriptural tradition. When Christian ideals triumphed and Judaism found itself having to adjust to the new reality, it had somehow to define itself. We can say that from the fourth century, when classical Christianity took its Roman and Greek forms, we see the formation of Judaism, too, as the religion which is still recognizable today. The long series of experiences leading through Israelite religion, its restoration by Ezra, the confusions of the Greek period, and the need to face up to the destruction of the heart of the ritual cult, now culminated in a fully formed Judaism. Like twins, Christianity and Judaism grew up together. It was not, of course, destined to be a happy relationship. The two religions differed markedly on how they saw the Hebrew Bible, and on most other things.

During the first centuries C.E. the position of rabbis in Jewish life was greatly strengthened. These were men of power and knowledge, charismatic leaders, but above all experts in the Torah. The reason for their prominence had in part to do with the fall of the Temple. There were to be no more sacrifices to God. The glories of the renovated building were gone, and Jerusalem itself was devastated. The religious Jews who wished to perpetuate tradition had to find it in records, in books. Study came to replace sacrifice as the most central Jewish ritual, for it was by intensive study of the Torah

In 70 C.E., the Romans tore down the Jews' Temple and, as a symbol of their victory, carried off its treasures, including the menorah, to Rome.

that the whole of the rest of the ritual life of the Torah-following Jew was defined. Once life had been easier: you could go to Jerusalem. Also, the Jewish religion of the period was already heavily oriented toward the synagogue, and there scripture was preserved.

Christians could take what to Jews was an unkind line: Jesus had foreseen the destruction of the Temple. Jews had been disobedient because they had rejected the Messiah, and indeed had been caught up in the killing of him. A powerful anti-Jewish myth was brewing up in the mind of the Church. Also, Christianity was built on the assumption that the new king had already come. A new age had dawned; there was no great significance left in the Temple. So somehow Jews, by contrast, had to defend their Temple though it was gone. It was preserved in the memory of people. The study of the rules and meaning of sacrifice became a substitute for sacrifice itself in the literal sense.

In certain respects the triumph of the new Judaism, in which the daily life of the Jew was in harmony with the rules, minutely analyzed and interpreted for the changed conditions, was a victory for the Pharisee party. They already had begun to apply laws of purity, essentially devised for priests, to the community as a whole. It was also a victory for the notion of the dual Torah.

There was the written Torah, the first part of the Hebrew Bible, but there was also the oral Torah, which flowed from Sinai (said the rabbis of the new age). This oral Torah became written down, as the Mishnah and its commentary the Tosefta. This collection already existed by about 200 C.E. The two versions of the Talmud – the Jerusalem or Yerushalmi and the Babylonian or Bavli – represent an extensive commentary on these materials. The Babylonian Talmud was, of course, based on long experience in exile, in a foreign land. Exile helped to make the oral Torah more central to Jewish life, when other means of expressing the traditions were impossible.

The development of a great mass of rabbinic interpretations in effect made rabbis the carriers-on of revelation for the community. It gave them a central position, and learning became a central ideal of the Jewish way of life. So what we have emerging is a religion which is based, not just on the Hebrew Bible, but on the two legs of the written and oral Torah. It laid much responsibility on those with learning, and it centered on communities united in synagogue worship. The Jewish family unit was basic. It was there that some of the most vital of ritual activities were performed in the unfolding cycle of Jewish feasts through the year, enlivening and enriching the daily performance of all those duties related to ordinary living which the Law prescribed.

All this was very different from the interpretation of life in the Christian community. Christians had no oral Torah. In many ways, for them the Torah was redundant – the Messiah had already come. The Jewish adherence to ritual observances and rules of purity from a bygone age seemed perverse. For the Christian the right interpretation of the Bible was obvious, and those who did not see it were willful. Thus was born an unfortunate epistemology (or theory of knowledge) which was to fuel later anti-Semitism.

The Deeper Implications of the New Judaism

It is worth dwelling longer on the traumatic changes which had come over Jewish religion. It had to make its way in the world in total exile: even the land of Israel, occupied by an alien power, was foreign to most Jews, who were forbidden to practice the central rites of their tradition. Jews needed to learn to face their nation's scattered or dispersed nature – the diaspora. Attracted by its ethical dimension, many people did convert to Judaism within the bounds of the Roman Empire. They were undeterred by the laws which Jews had to fulfil (becoming increasingly stringent as Rabbinic Judaism took its grip on the community). Despite these conversions, the religion was basically conceived as ethnic. God had entered into a contract with this people, who were mysteriously chosen to witness to his power and goodness on earth. The religious life increasingly became both the mark and the protector of identity. Before, the ethnic group had been loosely identified with Israel, even though many Jews lived in lands far beyond, throughout the Empire and in other centers such as Babylon. But the smashing of the Jews' desperate revolt, culminating in the sack of Jerusalem in 70 C.E., put an end to the pretensions of Jews to rule their own land. Jerusalem and Israel came more and more to be the dreams of those in exile.

Meanwhile, at that time there were, as we have seen, many parties and types of the Jewish commitment: there were the Pharisees, who won out; the Sadducees – too collaborative to be successful; the Essenes and others, who largely perished at the hands of Roman power. There were "heretical" Gnostic groups, who stressed *gnosis* or direct experience of God. (Their pessimistic evaluation of the world led to the erosion of Jewish loyalty to the creator Yahweh.) In addition, there were, of course, the Christians, some of whom continued to fulfill the teachings of the Torah and regarded themselves as both Jews and Christians in the early days of the new movement. All these groups eventually succumbed, because of various forces outside and within the wider community, to the power of Rabbinic persuasion. In the definition of the Jewish faith, Christianity played a notable part. Jews could see an alternative way, and they rejected it (of course, some converted to the new faith, which styled itself the New Israel). Jews were forced to ask themselves not only about the Hebrew Bible, which had been hijacked (from their point of view) by the Christians. They also began to ask themselves the meaning of the laws which they followed in the diaspora and which were, after all, a powerful way of preserving Jewish identity.

At any rate, Jews came to reject different alternatives. They did not accept Christianity which turned aside from the Torah. Jews could not accept Christians' wild claims that the Messiah had unexpectedly arrived. Given the Jewish idea of a messiah, he had failed, and so was not truly the Messiah. The Jewish community perhaps easily rejected the Gnostic beliefs, which themselves were a protest against Jewish loyalty to the Biblical God who was treated by Gnostics as evil. Jews reacted against the Hellenizers and others who wanted a real compromise with Roman and Hellenistic civilization. Judaism thus came to follow a stricter path, but one which offered reality to the Jewish community.

The Jewish Community and the Formulation of a Jewish Worldview

It is reasonable to think of the emerging Judaism as primarily concerned with Jewish practice, rather than theory. It was, after all, observance of the Torah which set Jews apart and so paved the way for their remarkable survival as a national group into modern times. Nevertheless, the *raison d'être* of both the Jews and their religion involved a set of doctrines and myths which were important to them, both in terms of their convictions and their sense of identity. The more philosophical kind of Judaism, in which beliefs were analyzed and defended, had to wait till later. The burden of the Rabbinic Judaism was rational – but rationality was devoted to setting forth and interpreting the demands of practical action. The bodies of literature which massively attested to this were the Talmuds.

Behind the practice, however, lay certain narrative and doctrinal assumptions. These are that God is one; that we are made in his image; that the revelation on Mount Sinai embraced both the sacred scriptures (consisting of the first five books of the Bible) and the oral law, expounded to Mosheh and carrying on as a living tradition to and through the later rabbis; that the destruction of the Temple does not mean the abandonment of the sacrificial system but rather its transformation into the life of study and application; that through the observance of the 613 commandments of the Jewish tradition Jews can manifest their acceptance of the role of Chosen People; that the ultimate importance of the ritual and other regulations was the transmutation of ordinary daily activities into holy processes; and that in the end God will triumph over evil and the People will be vindicated through the actions of a holy leader or Messiah.

Central to these beliefs is the idea that the oral Torah is a continuing revelation in which human beings participate both by study and by daily action. Often Christians and others misunderstand Judaism because they think of Jews as concentrating on scripture. But it is what lies outside scripture, in the narrow sense of the Hebrew Bible, that predominates in the Jewish imagination. The Talmud is a colossal testimony to "continuing revelation." In that continuance the rabbis play a central part, since through their learning and holiness of life they reflect the divine glory and the divine mind.

Consequently, they were able to interpret the order of a disorderly-seeming world. The destruction of the Temple signalled deep disorder, but beyond that disorder lay the order of Jewish life and the orderly classification and interpretation of actions that give meaning to life.

While the rabbis constituted the most important institution of the dispersed people, both in the Mediterranean world and under Sasanid rule in Persia, a more formal system of liaison with imperial governments occurred. In Babylon there had for a long time been such an official, the Exilarch, or leader of the Jews in exile. And in Palestine the Patriarch, who appointed rabbis to the Bet Din, or law court, functioned as an imperial official who counted as a prefect.

Part of the attraction of Rabbinic Judaism, from governments' viewpoints, was that it was passive and co-operative. It is true that Jewish refusal to worship the emperors gave rise to sporadic persecution. But the ultimate victory of Pharisaism ensured that after Bar-Kochba's violent revolt in 132–35 C.E. Judaism could live at peace with the empire.

Jews were widely dispersed, from northern Persia to Portugal and throughout North Africa and parts of Arabia. Judaism's presence in the last-named area helped to prepare the way for a kind of universal monotheism initially based in Arab ethnicity, but seeking a much wider outreach – namely, the religion of Islam. We shall later contemplate the changing fortunes of medieval and modern Islam. For all the tragedies of the Israelite and Jewish experience in Palestine, the final disasters gave new directions to Jewish piety, which helped greatly in the survival of the people and their spread to new areas.

Judaism in the Early Medieval Era

In the Roman Empire, before the conversion of Constantine, conversion to Judaism was not uncommon, but by edict Constantine made it punishable by death. This was a factor in the consolidation of Jewish identity. Nevertheless the Jewish people lived in remarkably diverse circumstances. There were the Jews in Yemen and among Khazars, both countries which for relatively short periods became officially Jewish; there was the great

Map 3 The Jews in medieval Europe.

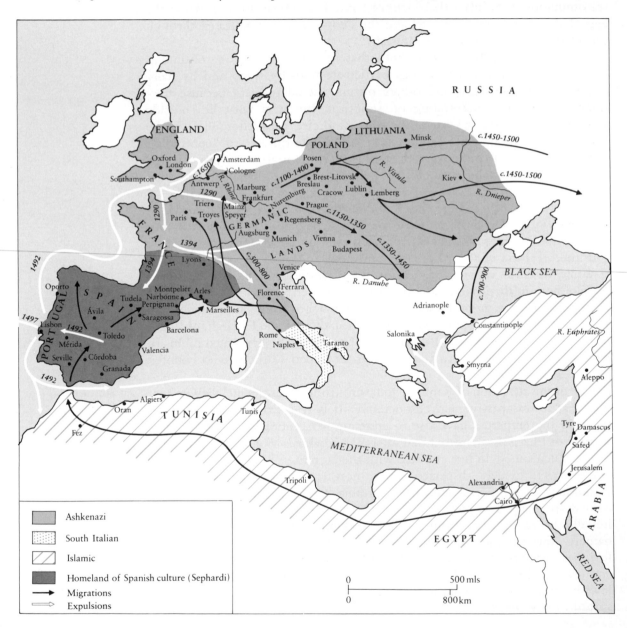

community of Babylon, so influential throughout the Jewish world; the Jews of Palestine, Egypt, North Africa; the Sephardic Jews of the Iberian peninsula, the Jews of Italy, France, Britain; the Ashkenazic Jews of Germany and Central Europe; and later those of Eastern Europe. There was no single circumstance of being Jewish. But there remained, even in these divisions, a reasonable amount of communications, facilitated by the fact that Jews played an important role in trade. Because of the Christian and Muslim bans on usury, money business was largely left to them.

Amid the disadvantages of being Jewish, there were some bonuses. In Islamic countries there was a reasonable place for the Jewish community. Jews were able to benefit from the cultural and philosophical achievements of Arabic civilization, through which they had renewed access to the Greek classics. Especially in Spain there was a great period of Jewish culture, culminating in new forms of poetry, such as the *Crown of Royalty*, by Ibn Gabirol (1021–69), still recited by Sephardic Jews on the eve of Yom Kippur, new commentaries on the Torah, and the like. Yehuda Halevi (1086–1143), as well as writing poems about the love of God and Zion, composed a dialogue and polemic about why the Khazars had chosen Judaism over Christianity and Islam. The greatest philosopher in this creative milieu was undoubtedly Mosheh ibn Maimon, commonly known as Maimonides (1135–1204). He wrote a great commentary, the *Mishneh Torah*, and a famous philosophical treatise, *More Nevukim* or "Guide of the Perplexed." In this he employed the method of the negative way in theology – you can say what God is not, but not what he is. Maimonides thought, with Aristotle, that the notion that God created the world is compatible with the everlasting character of the world (a view greatly disputed by other philosophers). He had great influence also among Christian thinkers, including St. Thomas Aquinas. Maimonides also formulated the famous Thirteen Articles or principles of belief which have remained the most-used summary of the Jewish creed since that time. They fall into three groups. The first concerns God – his existence, unity, incorporeality, and eternity. The second is about Torah – prophecy's validity, the uniqueness of Mosheh's message, the divine origin of the written and oral Torah, the eternity and changelessness of the law. The third group relates to reward and punishment – the omniscience of God, divine compensation for good and evil, the coming of the Messiah, and the resurrection of the dead.

The Jewish Year

It was during this early medieval period that the practice of the Jewish calendar reached its full form. Judaism had always emphasized the sacredness of certain times. Indeed with the taking away of the Temple and, effectively, of the land of Israel, Jews found their sacredness more in time than space.

The weekly rhythm underlined the holiness of the Shabbat (Sabbath) for practicing Jews. At sundown on a Friday – for Jews consider that the day begins with sunset rather than dawn – the woman of the house lights the special candles and says a prayer over them, and there follows a meal which is made holy by being the Shabbat meal. The day lasts till the following sunset, and is the occasion for prayers in the meetinghouse or synagogue. Jewish law forbids work on this day.

As well as the weekly rhythm there is also the yearly rhythm, beginning with the Jewish New Year, Rosh Hashanah, and followed ten days later with Yom Kippur, the Day of Atonement, the most holy day in the year. There is the family festival of Passover, and there are such other originally harvest festivals as Shavu'ot (Weeks) and Sukkot (Booths). In the winter there is Hanukkah, recalling the Maccabees' rededication of the Temple in 164 B.C.E., and there are various other less sacred days. This rhythm of the year helps Jews to re-enact the vital points in their history and their relationship to God.

As well as the ritual year there were the 613 commandments which the pious Jew was supposed to observe, and the net of obligations and customs which the rabbis had woven to cast over life as a perpetual reminder of the Jews' special place in the world which God had made. By following the obligations of both written and oral Torah, the Jew not only followed an ethical path but in effect also a religious path. What counted above all was his or her inner realization of the meaning and dedication implied by the outer acts of conformity.

Jewish Mysticism – the Qabbalah

The inner meaning of Jewish piety was no doubt reinforced by the outer problems of the community. The Crusades, beginning with the first in 1095, were occasions for organized persecution and massacre of the Jews in many parts of Northern Europe. Such anti-Jewish hostility was not far below the surface in most countrysides. Both because they were religious nonconformists in an age when faith was increasingly enforced by a nervous yet powerful Church, and because they were much identified with commerce and lending money, the Jews attracted stereotypes which in turn stimulated oppression. They were expelled from England in 1290 and Spain in 1492, for instance.

It was in Provence, France, and Spain, in the twelfth and thirteenth centuries, that there arose the movement known as the Qabbalah or Tradition, which revived the mystical strand in the Jewish tradition. This had been evident in the so-called Merkavah (Chariot) mysticism of a much earlier time, that of Rabbi Aqiba in the first and second centuries C.E. The "chariot" refers to the chariot of fire in which the prophet Eliyyahu (Elijah) ascended to heaven. This is used as a symbol of the inner ascent of the mystic to the higher realms of experience.

Doctrinally the Qabbalists saw God as the Ein Sof, the endless, ineffable, somewhat like the Neoplatonic One; but from the Ein Sof there emanate ten powers or entities, referred to as the Sefirot. Symbolically they are arranged in a diagram which represents the human form, like a great person. Different lists use different names, but they are as follows: Crown or Thought;

Wisdom; Understanding; Greatness or Mercy; Power or Judgment; Grandeur; Eternity; Splendor; Foundation; Kingdom. These emanations from God are supposed to have played a part in the creation of the world. Most importantly the Qabbalists explored the techniques of meditation and ecstasy, especially Avraham Abulafia (1240–?1291), who may have been influenced by Sufism or Islamic mysticism.

One strand in Qabbalistic thought was that human acts can have divine effects. It means that somehow God needs human beings as they in turn need God. This could give Jews a more profound way of looking at the process of keeping the commandments of the Torah: such acts had their reverberations on high. Maybe such ideas were especially satisfying during a time of increasing oppression in Christian Europe. Eventually the norm in the Middle Ages was for the Jews to be heavily segregated. This was less true in Eastern Europe and Russia where they could begin to open up new agricultural lands. But, especially in Germany and Central Europe, existence in ghettos became typical.

Judaism some key terms

Hasidim (or *Chasidim*) A movement founded in Eastern Europe (Ukraine and southern Poland) in the late 18th century, with an emphasis on mysticism.

Haskalah 19th-century Jewish enlightenment, following on the opening up of Judaism to European thought and culture.

Israel The land which is the focus of Jewish aspiration.

Kashrut Jewish dietary requirements, i.e. what is "kosher" or unpolluted.

Māshīah The "Anointed One" or future king who will establish a new age in Israel.

Mitzvah (plural *Mitzvot*) commandment: there are ten main ones and traditionally 613 in all.

Qabbalah The "received tradition" of Jewish mysticism expressed in such texts as the *Zohar* (13th-century Spain).

Rabbi A teacher of the traditional Torah, and learned teacher and spiritual counselor of a community.

Shabbat The "rest" day, from Friday sundown to sundown on Saturday.

Talmud A major text of the Jewish tradition, in Aramaic, being in two forms, the Babylonian and Palestinian. The former is binding in principle, as to its legal and ethical or halakhic provisions, on all orthodox Jews.

Torah The teaching or law, handed down in both written and oral form to Moses on Sinai: identified in written form with the first five books of the Hebrew Bible.

Yahweh The chief name of God in Hebrew.

The Dimensions of Medieval Judaism

The Ritual Dimension

Ritual life was much more fully elaborated as a result of the victory, from the fourth and fifth centuries in particular, of the religion of the rabbis. The various injunctions of both written and oral Torah controlled the various acts of daily life, serving as a constant reminder of being God's special people. The ritual dimension was in part enacted in the meetinghouse or synagogue but also very substantially in the home.

The Ethical Dimension

Jews were expected to keep to the high standard of the Ten Commandments and other injunctions put forward by rabbis (for instance in the early Middle Ages an edict from a rabbinical court forbade polygamy, being married to more than one woman, even though such a practice was well attested in the Hebrew Bible and was not uncommon among Jews within the Islamic civilization).

The Doctrinal Dimension

The insistence on strict monotheism was vital and remained so: but Jews held a different view of revelation from the surrounding Christian culture. They looked forward to the coming of the *Māshīah*, and indeed their whole myth of history was different from that of Christians, for whom the Anointed One had already come. The sufferings of the Jewish people were still a necessary continuation of the special dedication of this community to God. The surrounding Christian culture did not take kindly to this myth of history: they thought that Jews were frustratingly willful in their refusal to see the true meaning of the Old Testament (which of course they did not even see as an *Old* Testament). The vast interpretations of the Talmud and the whole idea of the oral Torah were ill understood by Christians.

The Experiential Dimension

The Jews appreciated the experiences of light and fellowship in the round of the calendar year and the rhythms of the Shabbat. They also explored the whole experience of the mystical union with the Divine, through Qabbalistic techniques.

The Organizational Dimension

Jews were able to retain some cohesion between parts of the Semitic world through travel in pursuit of trade. Rabbinical courts were not uniform in judgment, but the vast accumulation of interpretation of the Law gave a structural resemblance between diverse parts of Judaism. In the Islamic world there were wider openings in the lovely civilization about them, which gave them some room for maneuver. Christendom glittered less and was more

During the Middle Ages, ornate cases were crafted to contain the scroll of the Torah. This one, of copper inlaid with silver, was made in Damascus in 1565.

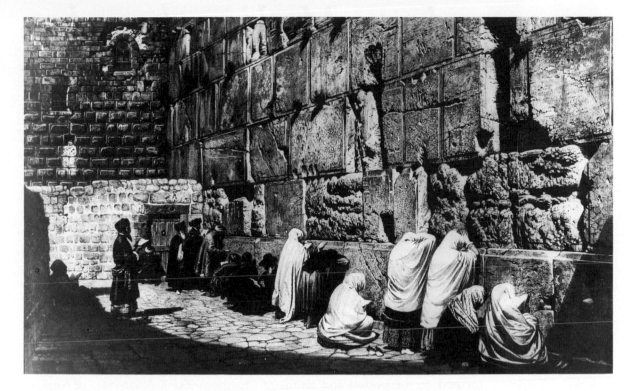

oppressive, so that Ashkenazim (German and North European Jews) were more driven in on themselves and so more conservative and withdrawn than the Sephardim (Jews of Spain and Portugal) and other "southern" Jews.

The Material Dimension

The chief places for ornamentation and the use of artistic forces for religious purposes lay in the decoration of synagogues and religious manuscripts. Early synagogues contained various mosaics, depicting the Ark of the Covenant; the *menorah* or seven-branched candlestick; branches of palm trees and lemons; even signs of the zodiac. The Ark containing the scrolls of the Torah was the chief liturgical focus in the Synagogue, and the containing material came to be increasingly decorated. In early synagogue buildings there seems to have been no special place for the women, but later they came to be segregated in galleries.

As Judaism entered the Middle Ages it had to live with what appeared to be a more and more monolithic Christianity in the West. It existed among Eastern Christians also; but much of its life was passed within the Islamic world. Yet any security that they had there was threatened by reconquest. The position of the Jews in Spain became problematic as the Catholics gradually drove the Muslims from the peninsula during the centuries up to 1492, when they were finally eliminated. And that was the signal for the expulsion of the Jews.

The ritual and narrative dimensions: the Western or "Wailing" Wall of the Temple destroyed in 70 C.E. is the most sacred spot for Jews: praying there unites them with their ancient sufferings and dedication to God. The above scene was in 1867.

CHAPTER 5

Late Medieval and Modern Judaism

Jewish Emancipation and the New Europe

From the late Middle Ages onward, persecution and other factors shifted the center of Jewish life eastwards in Europe. It is true that in Britain, France, and Germany a Jewish elite managed in the eighteenth century to obtain status, in the German principalities especially, through good posts in court circles as fiscal administrators, physicians, and so on. But the large population density was in Poland and Russia. In the late eighteenth century over 800,000 Jews were absorbed into Russia, and were allowed to settle within the so-called Pale, comprising present-day Lithuania, Belorussia, the Ukraine, and the shores of the Black Sea. Poland was also an area of settlement, though not actually within the Pale. It was in Eastern Europe that the great awakening known as Hasidism occurred.

In some ways the path had been prepared by the Sabbatean movement, focused on the person and claims of Shabbetai Tsevi (1626–76), of Smyrna in Turkey, who had been proclaimed by a follower (Rabbi Natan of Gaza) as *Māshīah* or Messiah. It seemed a suitable time, for the sufferings of the Jews were extreme at this time. Not only had they been expelled from Spain and Portugal: they were subjected to a great wave of killings during the Cossack uprising of 1648–58. Shabbetai Tsevi was a charismatic, if somewhat eccentric, figure, and Messianic expectations were aroused throughout Jewry. When in 1666 he was confronted with the choice of death by torture or conversion to Islam, he chose the latter. There were those who followed him still, and the movement was to go underground and re-emerge in Poland under the leadership of Ya'akov Frank (1726–91), who eventually converted to Catholicism. But the fact that many Jews throughout Europe and the East had been fooled by Shabbetai Tsevi left its mark. A more patient and at any rate different solution to the problems of the Jews had to be found.

One movement which did have a long-term effect was Hasidism, associated with the Ba'al Shem Tov (or Besht for short), the "Master of the Good Name," which was the title given to Yisra'el ben Eli'ezer (1700–60). The Besht, in his area of the southern Ukraine and the Carpathian Mountains, revived the ideals of the Jewish Qabbalah, but in a popular way. He was a charismatic healer, a mystic, and an inspiring teacher who emphasized the need to practice *devequt*, the constant communion with an ever-present God. It was a pious movement, and orthodox, except perhaps in organization. It stressed warmth of feeling as well as training oneself in

Jews in Samarkand: in the Russian Empire Jews were subject to pogroms, notably at Easter 1881.

communion – but this was all within the structure of strict obedience to the law. In the fifty years after the Besht, the Hasidim tended to form their own communities. In the process, they came up against the Gaon of Vilna, who was the supreme Jewish legal figure in Eastern Europe, and who came to oppose the Hasidim with some alarm and bitterness. But in many ways it was a revitalizing force, giving inner meaning to the outer performance of the Torah – and it had a special role to play as one of the main strands of Jewish Orthodoxy in the United States.

In contrast to the inward-looking strain of Hasidism, the central Jewish experience of the eighteenth and nineteenth centuries was the wider spread of emancipation, and with it the fuller entry of Jews on to the scene of the dazzling culture of the times. For many, this was a giant step into the world of Beethoven, Kant, Goethe, and Gainsborough. The year (1791) when Jews

79

were defined as full citizens of France – the first European country to do this – Boswell's *Life of Johnson* was published, and Mozart's *Magic Flute* was performed. For Jews, who in much of Europe had been confined to the ghetto, or segregated area of a city, the transition to a wider life was in many ways exhilarating. (The ghetto system had been used earlier in Muslim countries also.)

To some degree the two greatest Jewish philosophers had prepared paths that liberated Jews could take. Barukh Spinoza (1632–77) had left Judaism behind but not betrayed it by embracing some alternative faith. He was an urbane humanist; later, many Jews were to retain their Jewishness but without the religion. Spinoza, by the way, pioneered Biblical criticism from a historical point of view. The other philosopher was Moses Mendelssohn (1729–86), who espoused deism, or the Enlightenment belief in the God of Reason, a God somewhat abstractly represented. He defended Judaism as a system of revealed legislation in which the ceremonial side of life was laid down as a constant reminder of the truth. In effect he proclaimed the feasibility of being German in culture and Jewish in personal practice. He foreshadowed later forms of both Orthodox and Reform Judaism.

Varieties of Judaism and Jewishness

As more and more countries achieved freedom and religious toleration in the nineteenth and twentieth centuries, Jews were faced with various new choices. These choices were to become clearer in the United States, where emigration from pogrom- and poverty-laden Eastern and Central Europe rendered it the prime center of Jewish life. But basically they were as follows: there was complete assimilation into the new nationalities, usually not possible because of consciousness among the population that you were Jewish; there was cultural assimilation, while remaining Jewish in faith, particularly through the new kind of Judaism that emancipation helped to create, Reform Judaism; there was Orthodox Judaism, now somewhat modernized by carrying on the precepts of the religion as far as possible within the new national environment; and later, at the end of the nineteenth century, there were the prospects opened up by the ideology of Zionism which sought a national homeland for Jews themselves. Zionism, like other nationalisms, went with a modernizing program. Because of this, and its attempt to force the *Māshīah*'s hand, so to speak, it came to be largely opposed by the Orthodox.

The transformation of Jewish religion into a private rather than a community matter was heralded by the response which prominent Jewish figures gave to Napoleon when he convened them into what came to be called the Sanhedrin (after the Jewish Council in Jerusalem). The point at issue was whether they were truly French citizens, or were they a nation within the nation? They answered that Israel is no longer a nation, and that those aspects of the Torah which applied to those days were irrelevant. Nor were the arrangements for partial autonomy made in some parts of Europe any more relevant. So in effect they were fully French in citizenship and Jewish in religion.

This response was a foretaste of a general view current for the rest of the nineteenth century in Europe: Judaism was a universal faith, an ethical monotheism, and did not need the clothing of ethnicity. Nor did it need the symbols which once were relevant – the return to Zion, the rebuilding of the Temple, and the restoration of Israel. These pictures of the future were played down by the Reform Jews, and they were not quite realistic to the Orthodox. Ironically, their concrete content was affirmed by the Zionists, many of whom were not religious Jews.

Napoleon's enlightened views, such as they were, did not spare France from anti-Semitism, which broke out in 1894 in the affair of Alfred Dreyfus (1859–1935). Here was a Jewish officer charged wrongly with selling secrets to the Germans and only cleared in 1906, after he had spent years on Devil's Island, a French penal settlement in the Caribbean. It was in part because of continued anti-Semitism, especially in Austria–Hungary and Russia, that the idea of Jewish nationalism flourished. The official stamp came with the first Zionist Congress held in 1897 under the architect of modern secular Zionism, Theodor Herzl (1860–1904). Anti-Semitism also contributed, in the second half of the nineteenth century, to the first wave of migration to the United States.

North America: The First Migration

The destiny of Judaism and of the Jewish people was bright in America. But it was not without pain that the solutions to living in the modern world were worked out there. The price of toleration was that religion had to become substantially a private matter. Although Jews could assemble in living areas in the big cities, they did not have the relative legal independence that they had sometimes achieved in Europe and the Middle East.

The first main wave of migrants to America, often German in origin, were ready for modernization. By the end of the Civil War a reasonable affluence had been achieved in the community, and the formal organization of American Reform Judaism was appropriate. In 1869 a group of rabbis formulated a statement of belief which rejected the notion of a personal *Māshīah* and of the restoration of Zion, in any literal sense. Briefly, Jewish expectations were demythologized. A few years later Rabbi Isaac Wise (1819–1900) formed the Union of American Hebrew Congregations and through that organization started Hebrew Union College in Cincinnati, which remains the premier instructional center for Reform Judaism. Reform Judaism was supreme in America. It sought to present Judaism as a universal religion, working for the establishment of God's kingdom. Human beings would there be united and sanctified, and not within the structure of a divisive community. Worship was remodeled, anglicized and (from the Reform perspective) purified. It corresponded much more to Protestant norms, and the buildings tended to be called temples rather than synagogues.

It was liberal and modernist in theology and combined up-to-date literary and historical scholarship with traditional Jewish learning.

At the time when Reform Judaism was taking shape there were new waves of migrants from Eastern Europe – many of them Hasidim, and most of them concerned not with German-style Reform but with Polish- or Ukrainian-style Orthodoxy. The Orthodox became self-conscious in this Orthodoxy as a reaction to the shape of Reform. The first attempts to deal with this theological problem of new immigrants (half a million up to 1900, and more than a million more between 1900 and 1914) were not successful. But the Jewish Theological Synagogue – reshaped in 1901 – proved more effective, and Solomon Schechter (1847?–1915) was brought over to head it up. But the direction in which it developed was toward a third force in Judaism, namely Conservative Judaism, which combined a high degree of liberal scholarship with a conservative view of the practice of Judaism.

Orthodox Judaism created the Yeshiva University for the training of rabbis and others. Since this included secular studies it was fairly adaptive. Indeed, American Orthodoxy has tended to live successfully within the economic and social institutions of the United States, while keeping to the practice of the Torah. The beliefs of the Orthodox tend to be conservative, considering the Torah as Pentateuch to have been revealed by God at Sinai, and conforming closely to traditional laws or *halakhah*. For the Orthodox the Conservatives have moved too far and the Reform Jews have abandoned the substance of the faith. But after World War I times there were further developments, with the increased influence of Hasidism and the variation on Conservatism known as Reconstructionism.

Opposite This Alfred Stieglitz photograph shows Jews in steerage (the lowest class on a transatlantic steamship), bound for the New World shortly before World War I.

This 1892 cartoon shows antisemitism at work: the notion is that refugees from Russian persecution are filling up New York and forcing its inhabitants to move West.

83

Meanwhile in all this was the complication of Zionism. Generally speaking, the Orthodox and many Conservatives were anti-Zionist. The secular aspirations of the Zionists were unacceptable. Even so, there were some religious Zionists, who later were to become more important in the state of Israel itself.

There was also a fifth movement in regard to Judaism – away from it: Jews who left the Jewish religion and sought their destiny in the wider delights and challenges of American society.

The Impact of the Holocaust

The Holocaust posed tragic questions about the relation of the Jews to a Christian-dominated civilization. Neither Protestantism nor Catholicism had an altogether honorable encounter with Hitler, but there were martyrs to the faith, notably Dietrich Bonhoeffer (1906–45). Yet how could Western society have created the Holocaust or *Sho'ah* – the killing of about six million Jews in Europe in the concentration camps and gas ovens of the Nazis? Other groups were also terribly treated, such as Gypsies, Russian prisoners, and many others. But anti-Semitism was a vital ingredient in Hitler's thinking, and a central part of the Nazi ideology, which was drenched in thoughts of pure Aryan blood and so forth. Christianity had a role in the creation of anti-Semitism – first because of old accusations, from the New Testament time onward, that the Jews "killed God." Secondly, a naïve belief-system held that the Jews culpably failed to recognize that the Old Testament foretold Christ. Thirdly, the Crusading spirit had fostered a general distrust of foreigners, which focused on Jews. And there were several other reasons. Christianity is only now coming to terms with this past.

But the Holocaust has, of course, been even more of a trauma for Jews. Many a German Jew was proud to be German until Hitler, and so in a number of other countries. So there was the initial shock of rejection. But when the full awfulness of the Holocaust unfolded, there was a deep question shockingly posed to believing Jews: How could a good God have produced such a calamity? Some have turned away from the faith. Others have seen it as just an extreme case of the free will with which the Creator has endowed people. Others have seen it as opening up a new period of Jewish history, when faith in God and adherence to the Covenant become absolutely voluntary. This is tenable because the monstrous event of the Holocaust releases Jews from their obligations (this position is found in the writings of Irving Greenberg). Some Orthodox Jews have seen it as a punishment for sins, maybe for Zionism. But such an interpretation scarcely rings true – for so devastating a punishment the sin would have to be disproportionately monstrous. Meanwhile hope continues, for it was partly out of the ashes of Europe's madness that the state of Israel was built, achieving independence in 1948 and surviving miraculously through several wars.

Causes of the Holocaust

It is important in reflecting about modern Jewish history to diagnose the causes of the Holocaust. Probably the principal one is the rise of modern nationalism. The Jew here was in an ambiguous position. While in old multiethnic empires, notably the Austro–Hungarian, Jews were among a whole variety of groups supposedly loyal to the Empire, the new nations presented a different picture. For instance, they began to fashion a language and a history which emphasized the particular ethos and history of the nation. As we have seen, nationalism in its extreme form was manifested in the Nazi ideology. But anti-Jewish feeling was apparent in seemingly milder patriotisms, for instance in France and England. To complicate the situation, most nations in Europe had their special religions, welded into the fabric of the emerging states and expressed through the rituals of the monarchy and so on. While Jews might integrate very fully with the language and culture of the nation where they lived, they were typically adherents of an alien religion, which, by its very persistence, was a challenge to orthodox Christianity. So the new nationalisms were fed by a remembrance of the Christian past, even when they were secular in tone.

More than this: the period from the early nineteenth century to the early twentieth involved the rapid development of industrial capitalism. This brought about tremendous social change and suffering. Many people left the countryside for the growing – and often horrendous – cities. Nationalism itself provided some sense of identity for those caught up in this flux of human social change. But the Industrial Revolution also fueled fears about the new capitalist order, with its international ramifications and liberal ideology. For indeed liberalism was itself a worldview which promoted both new bourgeois-dominated politics and free trade. It is not surprising, then, that new countervailing values were to arise – for instance, socialism, as a protest against the new regimes and against the new nationalism, too. Typically, it proclaimed itself internationalist. But it could also contribute to a fear of dark, universal forces: a sense of international conspiracy. The Jews were a convenient target for a new anti-liberal paranoia, as a people who had deep cross-national links and a history of engagement with finance. And so it was not difficult to stir national feeling against the Jewish "conspiracy," Jewish high finance and so forth. It was not difficult for nationalism and socialism to combine, both in the Nazi phenomenon and in Communist Russia, thereby reinforcing old stereotypes, and intensifying older European anti-Semitism.

But the Holocaust did also have its particular causes, which resided in psycho-history and some peculiar conditions in Central Europe. Hitler himself was a kind of religious figure. He came to prominence rapidly after World War I, rising from the ashes of a Germany defeated and then humiliated by the Allies, later to be afflicted with the terrible plague of the Depression. Hitler supplied a vision which had, as we have already more than hinted at, a religious flavor and power. As an Austrian drifter in Vienna, he

A Jew surrounded by German soldiers in Berlin, 1933, the beginning of the Nazi period.

easily picked up and transformed, with a strange passion, the anti-Semitism of that great city. This, combined with his apparently heroic wartime record, his extreme nationalism, and his charisma, made him a lens through which German resentments could burn. He was also assisted by the extraordinary docility of the German system and of the officer class. Another factor was new technology. During World War II Hitler could impose his Final Solution in a new way, more horribly efficient than older massacres. So a manic vision could not merely be executed, but done so with discipline and method, rather than simple hatred and anarchy.

The effect on the Jewish people of the Holocaust and the founding of Israel was to concentrate them densely in North America and in Israel – for many Jews from Arab and Muslim countries also migrated there. There are, of course, other centers of Jewish life, such as South Africa and Britain, but the center of gravity has shifted to the United States. Modern Israel, meanwhile, has come to occupy a more vital place in the thinking of most Jews than did even the old Zion.

The Postwar Period

Reconstruction in America after the Holocaust

Judaism experienced a revival after the war, especially in the 1950s and 1960s. Since the latter decade in the States, the Hasidim have attracted a large number of previously unaffiliated young Jews into their ranks. Their uncompromising Orthodoxy is attractive for the formation of Jewish identity in a period of religious flux (especially as many young Jews entered new religious movements and took up Buddhism, etc., in the 1970s). Other Hasidim in the United States include the Satmar variety, out of Hungary and Romania. A leading figure among them, Yo'el Teitelbaum (1888–1982), argued that the terrors of the Holocaust were divine retributions for Jewish unfaithfulness – for becoming secular and for joining Zionism. This is an extreme instance of Orthodox resistance to the Zionists.

In the 1970s there was a new movement for the formation of study and worship groups, called *havurot*, for highly committed Jews. There were more Jews who were converted back into the faith, somewhat similar in spirit to "born again" Christians. Division among the Conservatives over the ordination of women was a negative factor. But, on the whole, Judaism

Map 4 Hitler's Final Solution and the genocide of the Jews.

became highly vigorous by the 1980s, despite a decline in the overall number of practicing, especially Orthodox, Jews. This decline is in part because of legal requirements for marriage. Throughout the modern period intermarriage between Jews and Gentiles has been widespread, and it has favored Christian groups rather than the Jewish community.

The State of Israel

The other way in which Judaism developed powerfully in the time since World War II was in its links with Israel, founded in 1948. As we have seen, some religious Jews were against such a state. But otherwise loyalty to Israel could attract secular Jews, Reform and Conservative, together with some Orthodox to the cause. It gave Jews a much greater sense of solidarity, following as it did on the Holocaust which itself did not discriminate among Jews.

Israel itself is the realization of the Zionist program formulated in the first Zionist Congress in 1897. But it contains religious ambiguities. Zionism was a secular nationalism. Many of its better-educated supporters were and are socialists, and Israel was for them the heralding of a new age. In the communes or *kibbutzim* which were planted in Palestine the ideal of collective living was realized, often with a strong aura of socialist idealism. Because of the strong connection with nationalism, Zionism sometimes took on a right-wing political hue, as in the thought of Vladimar Jabotinsky (1880–1940). As for religious Jews, they were often opposed to the Zionist movement, or indifferent to it; the plans to hold the first Zionist Congress in Munich were called off owing to the objections of German rabbis.

However, there were religious supporters of Zionism, most notably Avrahim Yitshaq Kook (1865–1935). A mystic and scholar who became chief rabbi in Jaffa from 1904, he saw in the Holy Land the promise of a renewal of the faith. In this he was opposed by most of his Orthodox co-religionists. He also argued for goodness in all the major religious traditions and for an openness toward all faiths.

His son Tsevi Yehuda Kook (b. 1912) went beyond earlier religious Zionists, who had believed that the task of the Orthodox was to keep the status quo in Israel against the encroachments of the secular way of life. He was involved in the forming of a militant and activist form of Orthodoxy, concerned especially with expansion and the planting of settlements on the occupied West Bank of the Jordan (occupied after the Six-Day War of 1967). This movement is known as the Bloc of the Faithful, or the Gush Emunim.

The ambiguities of religion in Israel are perhaps most poignantly symbolized by the group known as the Neturei Karta (Guardians of the City). Nearly all hyper-Orthodox Hasidic Jews, they often stone cars on the Shabbat and demonstrate strongly against violations of Jewish law in Jerusalem. They are a close community, live in one area of the city, are permitted to govern themselves, pay no taxes, do not go to war, wear traditionalist clothes, and study the Torah. They are anti-Zionists in the new Zion.

Orthodox Jews praying in gratitude for the foundation of the state of Israel, won May 14, 1948. Twenty minutes after the proclamation of the state, it was recognized by President Harry Truman.

The problems, however, lie more deeply in the logic of the state of Israel. Since it was formed on a national basis, it is a state essentially for Jews. But the identity of Jews has been preserved largely by religion. This leads to necessary tensions when state hopes to separate itself from religion, as befits a democracy. To complicate matters further, the new Israel took over what was essentially a hangover from the Ottoman Turks. They had given the Jews of Palestine and elsewhere in the empire, under the *millet* system, a measure of control over their own affairs and the administration of their own law through a chief rabbinate. By a law of 1953, the rabbinate has jurisdiction over family and personal law (so there is no civil marriage in Israel). Since the rabbinate is Orthodox, it means that Reform and Conservative Jews have

An aged Ethiopian Jewish woman arriving in Israel during the last days of the Ethiopian civil war, in 1991, when a massive airlift brought out many of these people, known as Falashas.

no status in these matters in Israel. For Jews, citizenship is by the norms of the *halakhah*, the law: but the state professes to be secular. That is one problem. The other relates to the status of non-Jewish citizens. It is obvious that Muslim and Christian Arabs will not be allowed to use voting rights to overthrow the Jewish state, so in this way the status of these groups is likely to stay somewhat inferior. And yet the institutions of Israel are pluralistic and democratic, for the most part. This tension will no doubt remain unresolved. Meanwhile the Palestinians will see themselves cruelly deprived of their homeland.

On a wider front, the effect of the setting up of the state of Israel has been to drain many other countries of Jewish populations. Many of the Jews of India, who date from early times in the west of that country, notably Cochin in Kerala State, no longer have viable communities. Many of the Jews of the Islamic world – from countries such as Morocco, the Yemen, Iran, and so forth – have gone to Israel, driven by the modern hatred toward Zionism among contemporary Islamic countries. The last main area for Jewish migration to Israel is the ex-Soviet Union, which under the old regime coralled and oppressed Jewish culture. Particularly since 1990, and the spectacular collapse of the Soviet system, many Jews have gone to Israel, though social and other pressures in that country have not always greeted them with a cheerful experience. Others have taken off for North America.

In all this turmoil of Jewish experience, two obvious landmarks stand out. One is the Holocaust during World War II, ending in 1945, and the other is the foundation of the state of Israel in 1948. These have basically altered the dynamics of Jewish life, and have led to opposite reflections – on the place of suffering in human (and Jewish) life, and on the nature of power. These two forces can tug at the heart of every Jew, whether he or she is secular or religious.

Changes in the Dimensions of Jewish Religion

As usual in many religions there is a polarization and mediation in the way they are thought and practiced. So it is that in modern Jewish life we can perceive different ways in which the dimensions are expressed.

The Ritual Dimension

The ritual aspect of Judaism is at its most complex among the Orthodox. This is especially so among the Hasidim, who are strong particularly in Brooklyn, where many Lubavitcher and Satmar followers settled during and after the Holocaust. They reinforced Orthodoxy in America. Conservative Judaism also exhibits practical conservatism, but with the addition of integrating worship into modern life by more modern means. Reform Judaism has a ritual presence not unlike that of Protestantism. The detailed application of Jewish law or Torah in the other branches gives every transaction of daily life a secondary layer of meaning, reminding observing Jews of the presence of God and the need to obey his commandments. The high holidays define time, so that temporal aspects of life are accentuated in the unfolding of the sacred year. By contrast, of course, there are Jews whose affiliation to the traditions is vague. And there are secular Zionists, who have embraced the rituals of socialism and nationalisms.

The Ethical or Legal Dimension

All the above variations reflect differing views of the ethical and legal requirements of Judaism. For Reform Judaism the ethical monotheism of the faith lies at the heart of Jewish obedience – but for Conservative and Orthodox Jews the array of commandments remains an ethical obligation as well as a religious inspiration.

The Organizational Dimension

Generally, it is the Torah-based learning which gives a special place to the rabbi (or for the more guru-like figure of the Hasidic *rebe*). Among the Reform Jews the organization of Jewish life has become so much more flexible that it has embraced women rabbis – one of the signs of modern feminism in religious culture. Again, this is partly because the rabbi is seen in a broader context, and has a more explicit role in the Reform as a social activist and pastor. Organizationally Judaism has adapted efficiently to American life. Orthodoxy, by comparison, has a state-instituted role in forming the religious and family law of the state of Israel – despite Hasidic and other backlashes against the secular Israeli state.

The Material Dimension

The most significant icon of modern Judaism is the land of Israel – *eretz Israel* – which serves as a magnet of Jewish loyalty and whose capital, Jerusalem, contains the holiest sites of Jewish history.

The Narrative Dimension

It is here that the deepest rifts in Jewish thought exist. This is first because the Orthodox reject modern scholarship about the Bible. They adhere to the belief that the Pentateuch was written by Moses, that the story of Creation is to be taken literally, that the Oral Torah was instituted at Sinai, that Jewish history has unfolded according to the texts of the Hebrew Bible and Talmud, and so on. In short, they reject that whole compromise with modernity which, in different ways, the Conservative and Reform wings of Judaism have made. Often, in rejecting the state of Israel they tell the story of the future in a traditional way, and deplore the apparent attempt to force the hand of God by creating the new Israel. On the other hand, conservative movements which favor the new state interpret history to their advantage, in seeing the right of Jews to settle in the occupied territories.

But, still in relation to the narrative dimension, there has naturally been profound anguish and division of opinion about the meaning of the Holocaust in history. In the last thirty years especially, there has been a torrent of theological reflection, history writing and practical memorializing of the events of the Nazi period. The fact that Jews in Central Europe had often responded so enthusiastically to the Enlightenment and post-Enlightenment glories of Western culture, made their succumbing to the dark side of these very forces doubly ironic and tragic.

The Doctrinal Dimension

Modern Judaism has had the dilemma – similar to parallel Christian and Muslim dilemmas – of how to integrate intellectual discoveries and traditional values. While all Jews may agree on the existence of God (though pragmatists have arisen who have seen the framework of religious life as being more important than formal belief in God), the modes of belief on some fundamental matters have fallen apart. Also, as we have seen, the question of traditional belief in Biblical narratives affects other more doctrinal issues.

The Experiential Dimension

Sometimes the answers to these problems have been sought in the experiential dimension. For instance, the Jewish philosopher Martin Buber (1878–1965) emphasized the idea of the I–Thou relationship, in contrast to the I–It relationship. The one highlights profound interpersonal contact; the other represents our intercourse with objects. We manipulate them, and indeed we may often use personal beings in the same way. The I–Thou relation with God is for Buber the most significant and vibrating experience. In this he combines Jewish mystical and prophetic traditions. His existential-ist emphasis had a strong influence during the post-World War II period, and there was some revival of Jewish mysticism. But regarding experience in general, there were two paradoxes that Judaism had to deal with. One was that the experientially based Hasidim (that is, they grew out of Jewish mysticism in Eastern Europe) were the most law-celebrating form of the religion. Second, many of those who were more free-floating in their pursuit of religious experience defected to other traditions. That is, many young Jews were going into Zen centers and the like, and deserting their ancestral religion. The outflow of Jews, especially to experience-affirming religions, has been notable.

The Future Developments of Judaism

The Jewish diaspora is diminishing, and by two forces. One, sadly, is through the massacre of World War II, and the other is the suction effect of Israel. It is reasonable to suppose that the future polarity of Judaism will be between North America and Israel. Judaism as a religion will perhaps be under greater pressure to explain itself – to give a more glowing account of its destiny and meaning in an increasingly globalized world. Both Christianity and Islam have had a patchy history in understanding and accommodating the Jewish alternative. New forces, such as world Buddhism and the Hindu tradition, have had difficulty coping with the major Western religions and have almost no grasp of the meaning of Judaism. There is also the challenge to Judaism in the West constituted by the drift of many Jews to a secular life, not to mention recent manifestations of Eastern religions and the like. There remains, too, the abiding search for peace in the Middle East, likely to preoccupy most Jews and to divert them from the less urgent task of making their faith understood to a wider world.

These challenges remain, but at least Judaism has survived the worst period in its history. Most Jews have been determined that Hitler should not have his final victory – the disintegration and fading of Jewish culture. There is little doubt that Jews and Judaism have continued to make a glittering and vital contribution not only to American culture but to that of the wider world in Europe, South Africa, Latin America, Australia, and elsewhere.

CHAPTER 6

Early and Medieval Christianity

Christians and Jews in the Hellenistic World

Jesus' Movement as a Jewish Sect

Yehoshu'a, or Jesus, (of Nazareth) lived at a stormy time, when political tensions were running high. The Jews had already shown themselves stubborn in the early years of the new Roman emperor cult, and this was to be a continued source of friction. Their exclusive monotheism may have been noble, but it also appeared, to the imperial administrators, to be strange. Jews were divided religiously, as we have seen, but these divisions also signified political ones. There was a stormy edge of revolt in Jewish society, and it was eventually such a revolt that led to the destruction of the Temple.

Yehoshu'a's movement ended up by being strikingly successful. He came from an obscure part even of the Jewish world, namely Galilee. He had a very brief and fairly turbulent public career of two or three years, after his baptism by his cousin Yohanan (John). Another strong preacher, he, like Yehoshu'a, considered that the time was at hand when the kingdom of God would be ushered in. Yohanan was a wild man but a prophet, deliberately wooing the empty places and the landscape beyond urban civilization. Yehoshu'a, on the contrary, mixed with men and women of all walks of life, pure and impure, high and low, and worked in cities. He preached a message resting on the conviction that a new age had arrived with his coming, and that he had a specially intimate relation with God, whom he called Abba, Father. He often referred to himself by the mysterious title "Son of Man," found in Daniel and elsewhere. But he also saw himself firmly embedded within the Jewish world. He would expound the Torah (or First Five Books of the Bible), the then scripture, which was to be expanded into the so-called Tanakh, or "Law, Prophets, and Writings." Combined, these make up the full Hebrew Bible, and became, with slight variations, the Old Testament of the Christian community as it grew away from the Jewish mainstream. Yehoshu'a also frequented that important institution, the synagogue. Synagogue worship, congregational in style, was an important facet of orthodox Jewish life already, in cities such as Capernaum where Yehoshu'a himself taught.

He gathered around himself a group of men disciples and women followers, and began healing and teaching in a striking way. His parables and stories sometimes seemed esoteric but they were vivid. It was chiefly through such stories, and through colorful and lively sayings, that he taught, judging from the style of what has come down to us. He may well have claimed to be *Māshīah* or Anointed One, and his family had some claim to be linked to the House of David. If he did use the idea, he used it in a novel way: not meaning a warrior king, come to restore Jewish rule, but as a Suffering Servant, a new sort of king with a crown of thorns. Many of his teachings used old concepts in new ways, and this maybe was a source of misunderstanding. At any rate he came into sharp collision with the ruling council, or Sanhedrin, and was handed over to Pontius Pilate, the Roman administrator. He was condemned to execution by crucifixion, with a notice on the cross to the effect that he was "King of the Jews." The transformation which overcame his group a few days later, when they came to believe in his resurrection from the dead, was the source of the vigor with which they carried on the movement.

So, apart from all the other currents in Jewish religion of the time, we have the continuation of Yohanan's group and, more significantly in the Graeco–Roman world, the Yehoshu'a movement. This came to be transmitted by Paul, teaching especially in Greek and traveling to the various Jewish centers – that is, the main cities – of Greece and Asia Minor and then to Rome itself. And not only was there Paul but other vigorous disciples also. By not requiring circumcision of Gentile converts, Paul provided easy access into some of the nobler features of the Jewish tradition. The monotheism of the new movement had an appeal to reflective Gentiles, and the ethics were inspiring in many ways to people in the empire. This new offshoot of Jewish religion, full of verve and some apparent secrecy, had the appearance of a new mystery religion.

Also around this period there grew up other religions with Jewish connections, which are collectively known as Gnosticism. Precisely what form they took on the ground is obscure – but in content, though not in organization, they resembled Manichaeism. It was a Gnostic teacher, Marcion, whose doctrine was that the God of the Old Testament was evil, who edited and in effect censored Paul's letters. In addition, he forced the growing Christian community, in the second century C.E., to set about the job of deciding which writings they used were canonical, or approved by the community as containing God's truth. The formation of the Christian Bible in the second and third centuries C.E. was one of the signs that the religion was crystallizing into that fully fledged form which we know as Christianity.

The Success of Christianity

In all this rich interplay of religious movements, rituals, belief systems, and customs, and amid shifting allegiances within the overall stable framework of the empire, why did the Christians win out?

The new mystery religion had some inherent advantages. First, because of its Jewish monotheism it was universal in scope. Second, in looking to a God–human in Jesus it presented a theme very familiar to the Graeco–Roman

The emperor Constantine, who symbolizes the triumph of Christianity over ancient paganism, is here portrayed as a Christian, bearing the cross in his hand.

world. Third, it was able, from the third century onward in particular, to pick up themes from the Platonic tradition which would make the faith appealing to the educated person. Fourth, the nature of its "mystery," a sacred meal, was coupled to a scheme of initiation which meant much more in the way of commitment to beliefs than the other mystery cults. Fifth, periodic persecution, which Jews also experienced, reinforced the solidarity of the group. Sixth, the empty formalism of the emperor cult and the marked pluralism of belief among the imperial elite pointed to the lack of a coherent state ideology. It was the Christians' good fortune that Constantine I (d. 337) saw in Christian teachings such an ideology, and reorganized the Empire with it as official teaching. It was at his command that the first great Council of the Church was called. This and other Councils constituted a meeting of bishops, chiefly, who claimed to represent the whole Church and so could make authoritative pronouncements on doctrine and discipline. Seventh, the new religion had consistent organization, with its system of overseers or bishops – it was only matched in this by the Manichaeans. Eighth, it was able to fight off its pessimistic Gnostic rivals and the Manichaeans with its relatively positive attitudes to the world.

The Dimensions of Early Christian Religion

By the second century, Christianity was beginning to settle down. In *doctrine* it affirmed that there was but one God, who had created the world without any hindrance, so that it was basically good. Its *mythic* dimension affirmed, however, that the first humans had disobeyed God and had been driven from Paradise. Yet God wished to save the human race, and the people of Israel had been chosen as the instruments of this. By keeping faith in one God going, till the time when the Savior came to earth, they were crucial to the whole salvation-history. Christ on earth had died for human sins and had made available God's grace to the faithful. Those faithful were basically the churchly community. The grace came, in particular, through the ritual participation in Christ through the thanksgiving service, held typically in wealthier members' houses.

In *ritual* there were the sacraments, like baptism, by which after a course of instruction a believer was admitted to the group. There was the eucharist, typically followed by a communal meal, in which the followers of Christ showed their mutual love and solidarity – love was the root of the *ethical* dimension. Christians got a good reputation for raising the status of women in marriage, for faithfulness, and for that general goodness summed up in the Ten Commandments. The *institutional* dimension, with areas looked after by bishops and with a priest, as far as possible, for every community, was flexible in times of strife. Certain big bishops, those of Rome, Antioch, and Alexandria, had special prestige; and so, later, had the bishop of the new imperial capital, Constantinople. They were also beginning experiments with monasticism, and this was later to be a vital stream of organized meditation and illumination in the Church. In religious *experience*, there was stress on the vision of Christ, in line with Gnostic practice; but also, and perhaps above

The breaking of the bread, from the Catacomb of Priscilla, Rome, second century C.E.

> ### Christ the Creator: John's Gospel
>
> In the beginning was the Word, and the Word was with God, and the Word was God. The same was in the beginning with God. All things were made by him, and without him was not any thing made that was made. In him was life, and the life was the light of men. And the light shineth in darkness; and the darkness comprehended it not.
>
> There was a man sent from God whose name was John. The same came for a witness, to bear witness of the light, that all men through him might believe. He was not that light, but was sent to bear witness of that light. That was the true light, which lighteth every man that cometh into the world. He was in the world and the world was made by him, and the world knew him not. He came unto his own, and his own received him not. But as many as received him, to them gave he power to become the sons of God, even to them that believe on his name, which were born not of blood, nor of the will of the flesh, nor of the will of man, but of God. And the Word was made flesh, and dwelt among us (and we beheld his glory, the glory as of the only begotten of the Father), full of grace and truth.

all, the feeling of the Love of God which was manifested in the gatherings of Christians, inspired by the Spirit. It was early in the life of the community for there to be much *art*, especially in the context of Jewish imagelessness. But as a material object they did have the Greek text of the Hebrew Bible and of the new scriptures of the rising community.

The Christians had a human parallel to the Gospels and the other writings: they had the source of truth seen in the lives of the martyrs and the saints. It was the Christian holy men and women above all who showed the power of God and the grace of the new community – as they saw it – in the proliferating congregations of the empire.

The Trinity Doctrine

The Council of Nicaea was summoned by the emperor Constantine in 325 C.E., as we have seen. It was the culmination of a process in which the Christians had been defining themselves increasingly in terms of what they believed. Doctrinal orthodoxy was important to establish from an imperial point of view, given that the faith was destined to become the ideology of the imperial state. But why was it so important too for the Christian leadership? In part at least the reason was that Christianity was not like Judaism, a mainly ethnic religion in the sense that you became a Jew by being born into the traditon. Yet it defined itself as a New Israel. How was that Israel to be defined in practice? To a greater and greater extent the definition had to be by belief.

Already in the years leading up to its dramatic success, in the hard days of martyrdom and underground conversion, the Christian community had had to fight off reinterpretations of its message which were considered to be dangerously wrong. It had fought off, in particular, various Gnostic groups who had often, in their pessimism about the world and the flesh, seen Yahweh the Creator God of the Old Testament as being evil. Christians had insisted on the underlying goodness of the world despite the Fall of Adam and Eve. The Christians had also had to react to the synthesis offered by the Manichaeans, who saw the teachings of Jesus, the Buddha, and Zarathustra as converging in the worldview of Mani.

Also Christians had – while respecting Greek philosophy – resisted the seductions of Graeco–Roman paganism. They drew a line between Jewish or Christian stories and pagan ones. The latter were just stories, while Christian narratives, based on real facts, were indeed historical. It was from this negative appraisal of myth that the modern colloquial sense of myth being a false story has come.

Christians had already debated some of the issues concerning the relation between their faith and the glittering culture in which they found themselves, and through which they were making their way. The Latin-writing "Father"

The doctrinal dimension: at councils, such as the Council of Nicaea in 324, the more abstract doctrinal formulae of Christian orthodoxy were formulated and affirmed. Here, under the supervision of Constantine and Pope Sylvester, the heretical books of Arius, Victorinus and others are consigned to the flames. The clothing and other details are anachronistic and belong to the sixteenth century C.E.

(a title Christians gave later to the most vital theological figures of the period), Tertullian (160?–?225) belonged to the literary circles of Carthage in North Africa, and used his literary and rhetorical training through many influential writings. But he was very rigorous in drawing the line between pagan ideas and practices and Christian ones. He is credited with the famous question, "What has Athens to do with Jerusalem?" Yet ultimately it was the synthesizers who won out. It became, if not necessary, at least helpful, to define some of the central doctrines of the community through Greek philosophical terminology. This essentially is what happened at Nicaea in regard to that most characteristic and yet also baffling teaching of Christianity, the Trinity doctrine.

Constantine, in particular, was worried by a serious rift in the Christian Church over the status of Christ. There was a group under the leadership of a priest called Arius (250?–336), of Alexandria in Egypt, which made Christ noneternal, being himself created by God; but on him the Father bestowed divinity. The slogan of the movement was "There was [a time] when he was not." Part of its motivation lay in the desire to preserve monotheism more clearly.

The Christian faith had found itself in a strange position in regard to Jesus. From both the practical and the theoretical point of view it wanted to affirm the divinity of Christ; but it was, after all, a movement which had come out of the Jewish tradition. It had suffered persecution because of its unwillingness to compromise with pagan polytheism. It was firmly committed to belief in one God.

From the practical angle, it was involved in a central ritual, the Eucharist, which involved the worship of Christ. It was blasphemous to worship anyone except God: so Christ must be God. This was the practical part of their affirmation of Jesus' divinity. But theoretically too they needed the idea. Christ died for our sins, in a state of solidarity with humanity, with human beings. He made amends for our sins. So he must be one of us. But as Savior he must be divine, because it was blasphemous to hold that anyone but God could put away sins. So from the perspective of the doctrine of salvation, too, Christ had to be divine, though human at the same time. All this generated the search for formulae which would deal with these problems. This formula would make it plain that the Christian was not committed to worshiping two or more gods, but only one God. It would make sense of the two natures (divine and human) of the selfsame person. The threefoldness, by the way, of God was arrived at since the Spirit of God which guided the Church from within was also regarded as divine; so any formula that applied to Christ should also apply to the Holy Spirit.

These issues came to be debated at various Ecumenical (or all-Church) Councils, of which seven are recognized usually as canonical Councils, stretching from Nicaea in 325 to Constantinople in the ninth century C.E. The resulting formulations did not always work, for they brought about splits in the Church often enough, and led sometimes to mutual charges of

Christianity some key terms

Atonement At-one-ment, that is, the bringing together of humankind and God through the death and resurrection of Christ.

Baptism The sacrament of immersion in water, or being sprinkled with water, whereby a person is initiated into the Christian Church.

Bible The collection of books which are treated by Christians as the record of God's revelation.

Christ The anointed one or Messiah who is the agent of salvation.

Church The community of Christians on earth and in heaven.

Communion Known also as the Eucharist in Anglicanism, the Mass in Roman Catholicism, and the Liturgy in Eastern Orthodoxy: the primary sacrament of sharing bread and wine as Christ's body and blood.

Grace The power of God entering into humans to empower them to good deeds and salvation.

Ikon A picture used in Orthodoxy as a window on heaven, and an object of devotion to the faithful.

Love Greek *agapē*, the reverential affection for other human beings which is the primary Christian virtue.

Sacrament Any of the rites instituted by Jesus, which are believed to be means to grace. The key sacraments are baptism, confirmation, the Eucharist, penance, holy orders, matrimony, and anointing of the sick.

Sin The estrangement of humans from God, thought to be due to the actions of Adam and Eve in the first instance.

Theosis Process of becoming divinized or like God: the goal of Eastern Orthodox spiritual effort.

Trinity God as Three in One, as Father, Son and Holy Spirit: being three persons or centers of consciousness in one being.

heresy. The history of doctrinal definition has not been a very happy one; and yet the Christians felt themselves impelled toward it as a means of saying what the New Israel was.

The eventual outcome of Nicaea was a highly important pronouncement on the nature of the Trinity. In Greek terms it was declared to consist in three *hupostaseis* in one *ousia* or three entities in one being. In the Latin somewhat different language was used, with a rather different effect. God was said to be *tres personae in una substantia* or three persons in one substance. These became classical ways of defining the Trinity, and constituted the achievement of St. Athanasius (296?–373). But Arianism, though banished from orthodoxy, continued and made great inroads in the conversion of Northern Europe in subsequent centuries.

Map 5 Europe in the early medieval period.

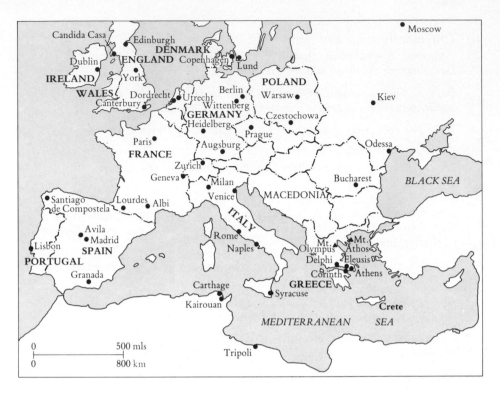

Roman versus Greek Forms of the Faith

In the early part of the fourth century C.E., the decision was taken to divide the Empire in the sense of having two capitals, one located in Byzantium or Constantinople and the other in Rome. This naturally reinforced the cultural divisions within Christianity. The ritual of the Eastern Church became more complex as it took over some of the features of Byzantine court ritual. There was especially in the East the veneration of paintings of Christ and the saints – the holy ikons. The style of churches which was gradually evolved took on a domed appearance, with the interior of the dome representing heaven. The mysteries of the Liturgy or Eucharist took on a heavenly aspect.

Affecting both East and West was the evolution of monastic life. It was especially attractive to Christians to have an alternative way of life in celibacy and austerity, when the Church, because of its political success, was encountering the corruptions which were attendant on that. The Church took the line that a priest's ability to conduct a Eucharistic service is not impaired by his personal unworthiness. But there was also recognition that there needed to be new outlets for the heroic ideals which had carried the Church forward. These were to some degree fulfilled in the monastic movement. The great symbolic figure in the Christian imagination was the legendary St. Antony of Egypt, close associate of St. Athanasius. He wrestled with temptations in the desert and helped found a group of hermits whose way of life later formed the basis of monasticism in both the East and West. Thereafter until the Reformation nuns and monks were an integral and vital part of the organization of all Christianity and nurtured within their establishments both the practice of meditation (and the pursuit of mysticism), and the main elements of study and scholarship.

Northern Europe and the East–West Split

The drifting apart of the two main wings of the Church was assisted by the different political fates of the two parts of the empire. The East was stabilized round the Byzantine monarchy. This empire might make concessions to the Huns along the Danube and the like, but basically it was not till the coming of the Muslims in the seventh century that it really lost great tracts of territory, and even there it retained its heartlands. On the other hand the West was badly overrun by barbarian peoples from the latter part of the fourth century onwards. The Goths had been mainly converted to Christianity before they broke into the imperial domains, but it was an Arian form of Christianity that had been preached by the great missionary Ulfilas. The destiny of Northern Christianity was in part determined by the baptism in 496 of Clovis, king of the Franks, who helped tame the Goths on behalf of orthodox Roman Christianity. It was to deal with the Arian heresy that the Western Church, at a Council at Toledo in Spain, inserted the clause *Filioque* into the Creed, that is, into the agreed formula for expressing the faith of the Church. We shall return to the implications of this. Meanwhile the alliance between the Franks and the Church led to the ultimate foundation of the so-called Holy Roman Empire with the coronation of Charlemagne as emperor in 800 C.E. The bases of medieval Christianity, with its North–South axis in the West, were being laid.

The question of the small clause, *Filioque*, meaning "And from the Son," was more serious than at first sight might appear, and for two reasons. The meaning of the insertion was that the Holy Spirit proceeded from the Father and *from the Son*. According to Orthodox theologians in the East this upsets the balance of the Trinity, which according to them consists in a perfect unity of Persons in which the Father eternally generates the Son and from whom the Holy Spirit eternally proceeds. The Father, so to speak, enhances a balanced unity. But secondly, and worse from the point of view of the Greeks, the formula was added by the West without consultation with the East and was indeed the usurpation of authority by the Bishop of Rome, that is to say, the Pope. He was claiming for himself a role in the formation of new doctrines. Only a Council recognized by the whole Church could do this. These questions, first of doctrine and secondly of the authority of the Pope, have plagued relations between the two great wings of the Church ever since. They helped to confirm the mode in which these parts of Christendom were drifting apart.

As both parts were projected forward into the medieval world, the one as spiritual heir of an empire that effectively had broken up, and the other as the official religion of an empire which was also subjected to increasing external pressures, they differed somewhat in doctrine, organization and practice, and we can see something of these divergences by looking at the dimensions of the religions.

The Dimensions of Christianity East and West

The Organizational Dimension

In the West we have a gradually more centralized organization under the Bishop of Rome, the Pope. But it was a monarchy of a spiritual or religious nature, and the increasingly fragmented nature of Western Christendom maybe made it the more imperative that Rome should be seen as an authoritative center. In the East, so long as the empire lasted, there was a form of what came to be called "Caesaropapism," or *symphonia* in Greek, where the emperor considered himself one with the apostles and played an active role in the determination of Christian doctrine and discipline. In fact, however, the Patriarch of Constantinople and the other leading bishops of the Eastern Church often stood out against the emperor. It was therefore a dual system of rule by the secular and religious heads. But obviously the power of the emperor was great, and some emperors played a vital role in controversies, such as the debate about ikons. But from the seventh century great regions of Eastern Christianity came under Muslim rule. In such conditions the Christians were considered a separate community. They were administered through the leading bishop or patriarch of each area, which gave the Church a limited secular function.

In the West the priesthood came to be secular; but in the East an ingenious relationship between monasticism and parish clergy was worked out. If, after training, a priest did not marry, he became a monk. It was from the ranks of the monks that bishops were elected.

The Material Dimension

The early Church had used decorations, for instance in the catacombs. With the coming of official recognition worship moved out of houses and villas which were used or donated for worship. Pagan shrines were suppressed, and their sites or buildings taken over. The basilica form became dominant in the West. This was originally a long building with high windows and aisles which was used for secular purposes. Now it was used religiously, with the end portion being screened off and used for the altar and the seating of the clergy, the central part for the faithful, and the forecourt for postulants (those who wanted to become Christians). Those who were undergoing instruction had to withdraw from the nave to the forecourt or the aisles during the Mass or liturgy proper. The Eastern tradition favored the domelike structure whether on the base of a Greek cross or on a longitudinal base in the manner of the basilica, as in the famous Hagia Sophia in Constantinople built under Justinian in the sixth century. Its great domes and vaults were covered with gold mosaic; its columns gleamed with polished marble and porphyry. It exuded golden light from within, seemingly weightless, a glorious example of the Byzantine style.

The tombs of rich Roman Christians had long displayed sculptures, but the East retained a ban on three-dimensional representations, as offending against the commandment forbidding graven images. But the ikon or picture of Christ or Mary or a saint became increasingly popular. It came to be customary to screen the wall between the nave and sanctuary with such holy pictures. But from 723 to 842 the Eastern Church was torn apart with a swaying struggle over ikons. The iconoclastic (ikon-smashing) party was dominant over much of this period. In the Western Church this notion that there was something heathen and heretical about the use of holy pictures and sculptures did not appear until the sixteenth-century Reformation. The excommunication by the Pope of the Easterners on this score deepened the rift which grew worse with the crowning of the Frankish King, Charlemagne, as Holy Roman Emperor in Rome in 800, he taking the significant title of Augustus. The ideologies of the Western empire and of Christianity were here fused. In the East the pro-ikon party won in due course, and since that time the reverence of ikons has been a central element in Eastern piety – much more important in fact than the use of pictures in the West.

The Doctrinal Dimension

As for doctrine, there were differences in emphasis, though not very great. The dominant theologian of the Western Church, until the medieval period, was undoubtedly St. Augustine of Hippo in North Africa. Converted from Manichaeanism under dramatic circumstances, he was a pioneer of different literary forms – of autobiography in his *Confessions* and of historical interpretation in his *The City of God*. In this latter book he contrasts the City of God with the City of Earth, of which Rome is the prototype. He does not, strictly speaking, identify the City of God with the Church, but he did come to accept that the earthly power might be used to ensure conformity of doctrine – a license for the state, under the Church's guidance, to persecute heretics. But more importantly, he laid great stress on original sin, the sin of Adam and Eve, which was transmitted down the generations. It was God's incarnation, and his gift of grace, that overcame sin and brought salvation.

Augustine attacked the Celtic monk Pelagius (died 418) for affirming human free will. He laid the groundwork for the doctrine of predestination – that the individual from the beginning is chosen by God and predestined to salvation (or alternatively *not* chosen and predetermined to damnation). This somewhat negative emphasis was carried on in the Western Church, which tended to underline Christ's death as an atoning sacrifice for sin, thus putting us right with God. By contrast St. Athanasius emphasized how God became human in Christ so that humans might become divine – and the Eastern Church tended to stress this idea of *theosis* or divinization. These are only diversities of emphasis.

The experiential dimension: a sixteenth-century ikon of Christ seeks to combine the majesty of the numinous feeling of the worshiper and the senses of serenity arising in the contemplative life.

105

Doctrinally, also, the two sides split, as we have seen, over the *Filioque* clause. Eastern theologians have always stressed the important spiritual message of a correct view of the Trinity, more intensely than their Western colleagues.

The Narrative Dimension

As to the narrative of the New Testament and beyond, the Western Church put a great emphasis on the role of St. Peter, first Bishop of Rome. The commission to Peter by the risen Christ, "Feed my sheep," and other texts, were used to back up the Pope's primacy. Also Rome was seen as center of the world, after Jerusalem. The death of both Peter and Paul in Rome was an important ingredient in the whole story of the faith. But whereas in the West the secular Rome was decadent, in the East it had fused very easily with the Church, and the golden glories of Byzantine art added a new dimension to the Graeco–Roman experience.

The Ritual Dimension

Regarding the ritual dimension, a vital divergence was in language, since Latin was the Western vehicle of worship (so that later in the Middle Ages, as vernacular languages forked off from the Church's language, a certain alienation was bound to occur). In the East the liturgy was in Greek, and in a number of other languages that, like Greek itself, remained in secular use. More importantly, the style of the Eucharist in the two traditions began to pull apart, especially with the Eastern use of ikons. There was also the fact that the main ritual action was more concealed, since the altar area was thoroughly screened off by the wall holding the ikons, the *ikonostasis*. The light is there behind the screen, and the priests make forays into the congregation: the Little Entrance brings the Gospel to be read, and the Great Entrance bears the bread and wine. The church is a representation of heaven, and the movement is from God to humans. The Roman churches, which were longer buildings, were more a movement up toward God.

The Western Church came to list seven sacraments as being recognized – the Eucharist, Baptism, Marriage, Confirmation, Absolution, Ordination to the Priesthood, and Extreme Unction (for the dying). But the Orthodox had a wider view, including other rites such as blessing the house, burial, blessing water at Epiphany, and so on. Both Churches celebrated Good Friday, when Christ died, and Easter, when he rose from the dead. But the Eastern celebrations of Easter are more dramatic, replete with the spreading light of candles in the early hours of Easter Day and the proclamation "Christ is risen."

The Experiential Dimension

Both East and West were committed to the monastic ideal, and within that the practice of contemplation and the notion of an inner, mystical union with the divine grew. Later, as we shall see, the Eastern Orthodox experimented with breathing techniques and the like, and the use of the Jesus Prayer, "Lord Jesus Christ have mercy on me a sinner," said in connection with breathing in and out. The importance of spiritual visions of God and the Virgin remained in both wings of Christendom, and these were expressed in diverse ways in the art of East and West.

The Ethical Dimension

The ethical injunctions of the two Churches were very similar. If anything the Western Church – in part because of St. Augustine – had the gloomier view of sexuality, which was the cause of the transmission of original sin. The increased spread of the ideal of priestly celibacy also had its effects on preaching. Celibacy and virginity were both held up as high ideals. These replaced, in part, the other great way of bearing testimony to faith, martyrdom, which faded somewhat in the more relaxed days after Christianity became the official religion.

Movements away from the Centers

Other Eastern Churches and Eastern Missions

We have so far been concentrating on the Greek Church of the Eastern part of the Roman Empire. But the Church from early days could be said to have an even more Eastern presence. There were the Aramaic-speaking Christians of Jerusalem, dispersed after the destruction of the Temple in 70 C.E. and the subsequent forcible expulsion of the Jews. Their successors were the Syriac Nestorian Church, based initially in Antioch, and spreading outward. It was led by Nestorius (381?–?451), who was identified with the heresy known as Nestorianism. This affirmed that Christ has two natures, one human and one divine, rather loosely united. Nestorians came to control the diocese of Seleucia–Ctesiphon in Mesopotamia, and through that had an immense missionary activity to China, Central Asia, and India. Syriac Churches were an important part of the Eastern Christian world, even if formally in schism with the Orthodox.

In Armenia, Christianity became the official religion of the court even before it did in the Roman Empire, in 314 C.E. under Tiridates III. The country had previously been largely Zoroastrian. The Armenian Church, using an Eastern-type liturgy, accepted the first three Councils of the Church, namely those of Nicaea in 325, Constantinople in 381, and Ephesus in 431.

In Egypt and Ethiopia, Coptic Churches became established, so called from the language which they used – an ancient Egyptian tongue written in a variation of the Greek alphabet. Ethiopia became especially important in later Africa because it represented an ancient black kind of Christian faith. This was an important symbol to remember in the colonial era when the dominant structures of Western religion were in the hands of whites.

Meanwhile, Byzantine Christianity was reaching north toward the peoples of Eastern Europe and Russia. From early days it had made some inroads

The ritual dimension: an Egyptian Coptic priest in his vestments, twelfth century C.E. Victoria and Albert Museum, London.

107

into what is now Romania; but it was not until the early Middle Ages that the great mission work of St. Cyril and St. Methodius was to be effective. But it is best for us first to see some of the work of the Latin missions which had a bearing on the area of Eastern Europe also.

Outreaches of the Western Church

Probably the most important Church on the fringes of the West was that of the Celts in Britain and in Ireland. The British-born St. Patrick (390?–?460) was kidnapped and enslaved by the Irish in his youth, learned their language, and later returned to Ireland where he had a substantial role in the evangelization of the island. The Romano–British Church also played a part in the Christianization of southwest Scotland through St. Ninian, who set up a center of study and monasticism in the Wigton peninsula. Later St. Columba from Ireland set up a monastery further north in the island of Iona.

The Celtic Church had a characteristic form of monasticism with monks and nuns together, and held to some customs not shared by the Roman Church, toward which it had some antipathy. But in 664 the Synod of Whitby led to a truce between the Celtic Church and the Roman, dominated in Britain by the Anglo-Saxons who had been converted as a result of the mission of another St. Augustine to Canterbury in 597.

The British Church made its contribution later on to the task of converting the Germans and others in Northern Europe who had mostly lain outside the old Roman Empire. It was crucial for Christianity to move north, for in the seventh century it was hit by an obliterating storm from the south. The followers of Islam conquered the southern part of the Mediterranean and the Near East, thus slicing off a large part of both the Western and Byzantine Empires. They came into Spain and overran most of it and Portugal. Northern Europe was brought in to redress the balance.

The dynamism of Christianity in Britain and the strength of the Franks combined in the converting of Germany. The most notable missionary was St. Boniface (a native of Devon in the west of England), who worked in central Germany, in Hesse and Thuringia. In 716 he cut down the sacred oak at Geismar, a signal that paganism was being replaced by the Christian faith. In the tenth century two Norwegian kings brought the faith to Norway: Olaf Haraldsson, who became a martyr by dying in battle, and Olaf Tryggvesson who also pressured Iceland to vote for Christianity as its public religion in the significant year of 1000 C.E. Poland, Hungary, and Bohemia were also converted from the West, as was Croatia.

And so by the eleventh century Europe from Sicily to northern Norway was effectively Christian – only in Spain was there a substantial Muslim presence. In the eastern part of Europe the Orthodox mission was also fairly successful. There were parts of the Baltic still to convert, but the main work was done.

It was sometimes done from the grassroots, by lonely missionaries, and, more importantly, by the planting of monasteries. These could train local vernacular clergy, provide learning, help with agricultural development, and supply a good example of Christian living. Sometimes, however, the acceptance of Christianity came from the top. Kings, emerging stronger in a period of chaos, could use Christianity as an instrument of rule. The new religion supplied learning, which could be used in administration, and possessed a body of law. It was, moreover, universal in its values and could be harnessed to a military worldview, despite the peaceful monks. It could promise greater consistency than the old pagan cults, which it was not afraid to attack, even physically.

Eastern Mission – the Conversion of Russia

The achievements of missionaries out of Byzantium were equally important, and especially those of the brothers St. Cyril (826?–869) and St. Methodius (815?–884). Both were in good positions, one as professor at the imperial university and the other as a provincial governor. But they withdrew from these occupations and began mission work together, first among the Khazars, who lived northeast of the Black Sea, then in the Balkans. Their most lasting achievements were the devising of an alphabet (the so-called Cyrillic script) for the Slavic languages, and the encouragement of worship in the vernacular languages. Christianity infiltrated into Russia from various directions, and in 988 Vladimir, Prince of Kiev, was baptized. He was married to a sister of the Byzantine emperor, and it was Eastern Christianity that took root in Russia. Again, the Christian religion, losing ground in the south and east of the Byzantine empire, made substantial advances in the North.

So far we have extended the story of Christianity beyond its chief formative period, which was in the fourth and fifth centuries C.E. We have seen it evolve into its main classical forms. We shall next look at it in its greatest premodern period, that is to say, the so-called Middle Ages – both in East and West. This was a time of glory and achievement for a Christian-dominated civilization, faced, however, with a perhaps more glittering culture, that of Islam.

Medieval Christianity

Eastern Christianity: Outer Retreat, Inner Advance

The Seljuq Turks took Jerusalem in 1071, and this heralded disturbing times for the Byzantine empire. Their advance into Asia Minor was marked by the capture of the emperor in the same year, and soon they were at the walls of Constantinople. Their victory at Manzikert, when the emperor was taken, was a decisive affair in European history. Thereafter, Asia Minor or Anatolia would become the heartland of the Turks, and the boundary between Islamic East and Christian West would lie culturally between that region and the Greek islands. Constantinople held out.

The Turks also triggered the new movements known as the Crusades. The holy places of Palestine were now closed to Christian pilgrims, so the Papacy instigated the Crusades in 1095. The First was quite successful: Jerusalem was taken and remained in Christian hands for nearly a hundred years. But the Fourth Crusade was diverted, and Constantinople was sacked. A Latin kingdom was set up there – this trauma undoubtedly weakened a restored Byzantium. A new empire, that of the Ottomans, out of Anatolia, threatened the empire and made its way deep into the Balkans. So in many ways the Greek East was on the defensive during the medieval period. The ultimate fall of Constantinople in 1453 signaled a new great captivity for the Greeks. The center of Eastern Orthodox power shifted to Moscow, perceived now as a Third Rome, the other two (Rome itself and Constantinople) having failed in their destinies.

But during this troubled period some remarkable developments took place in Eastern piety. Monasticism was renewed, especially on Mount Athos in

The material dimension: monks gather at what is supposed to be the oldest church in the monastic republic of Mount Athos in Greece. It is a replica of the original built by Constantine.

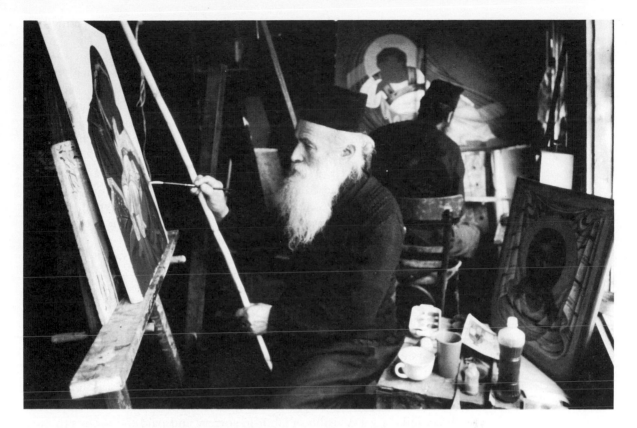

northern Greece, which became in 1052 a kind of self-governing monastic republic. The male celibate life of contemplation and the performance of the liturgy became the key focus. One of its inhabitants for a time was St. Gregory of Sinai, a famous mystic, who had so strong a desire for the solitary life that he had judged the liturgy irrelevant, and had had to leave Sinai for a wandering life. He settled in Bulgaria, where he became the prototype of the later Russian *starets* or wandering holy man. More orthodox in his mysticism, and perhaps the greatest Eastern Orthodox theologian, was St. Gregory Palamas (1296–1359). Highly educated at the court in Constantinople, he became an ascetic at the age of twenty, residing on Mount Athos for a while, practicing the methods known as Hesychasm (literally quietism). Here the expert used physical means, including control of the breathing, in order to gain higher states of consciousness, culminating in a vision of the divine light. One fierce critic castigated the Hesychasts as being *omphalopsychoi* – people with their souls in their navels. Gregory argued that though God in himself is inaccessible and indescribable, he possesses uncreated energies. The human being can participate in the light which was displayed on Mount Tabor at the transfiguration of Christ. This uncreated light appears within the human being. It can be perceived if the human being can concentrate his intellect or *nous*, which is usually distracted, since the Fall,

Monks painting ikons. The ikons serve as "windows on heaven," of which the most glorious was Christ himself.

111

by the things of this world. The training in Hesychasm is, in effect, a method for ascending to the light within.

In attaining to God's uncreated light the human in effect becomes a god. He undergoes *theosis* (a great theme in the Orthodox tradition which we saw being expressed in the fourth century by St. Athanasius). St. Gregory Palamas, in setting forth this scheme of salvation, repeated and summed up some of the central motifs of the Orthodox tradition. Moreover, his defence of Hesychasm ensured the important place of the contemplative quest in the life of the Church.

Although the Church had to experience the rule of the Ottomans throughout Greece and the Balkans, from the fall of Constantinople in 1453, its renewed vigor in the preceding period made possible its survival. Also the religion was making headway in Russia, and the ideal of the Third Rome helped to give Russian Orthodoxy a messianic flavor.

Western Medieval Culture – A New Civilization

In the West the Middle Ages saw the creation of a relatively unified civilization, with its center of gravity in Northern Europe. There, great monastic foundations had helped with the spread of agriculture and the creation of new wealth. Monastic reform, indeed, was one of the main bases of the medieval culture. Thus the Abbey of Cluny, founded in Burgundy, France, in 910, provided a leading powerhouse of influence and reform. Under Abbot Hugh in the eleventh century, it underwent great expansion, and established many daughter houses. Many of these were well endowed, as rich lay folk saw a division of labor in society and paid the monks to pray intensely on their behalf.

The new orders in particular were to have profound influence. First, there were the Dominicans who were brought into being by St. Dominic (1170–1221), who wanted to get together a band of preachers who would live the good life of poverty. Initially he had in mind the conversion of the so-called Albigensian heretics in the South of France. But his order had a wider role in education, and then in the exercise of the Inquisition. Second, the Franciscans, created by St. Francis of Assisi (1181/2–1226), whose strict ideal of poverty later caused some rebellion among his own followers, were an influence on ordinary people. Their preaching and hearing confessions in the context of a modest way of life was very different from that of the princes of the Church.

The Middle Ages also saw a new mobilization of the ideals of knighthood on behalf of the Church. The Crusades created a new channel for the energy of often violent and turbulent princes and warriors. The Orders of militant monks, above all the Templars and the Teutonic Knights, who pushed the bounds of Christendom northeastward along the Baltic coast, captured some of the austere values of Christianity on behalf of military action. This was very much on the assumption that battling on behalf of Christendom was a way of fulfilling the Gospel.

It was also an age of revived learning. Through the Arabic translations and then the Latin translations of Arabic, scholars had some access to Aristotle and other Greek writers. They proved to be a stimulus to new reflections, and above all to the synthesis achieved by the Dominican St. Thomas Aquinas (1224–74). His many and magisterial writings, especially his *Summa Theologica* and *Summa contra Gentiles*, left a lasting stamp on Catholic thought.

Aquinas' whole system was based on a distinction between what can be known naturally by reason and what has to be derived by revelation from God. The former domain is extensive, for by Five Ways (five main arguments), you could establish the existence of God. God also, by these proofs, was good, intelligent, incorporeal, and so on. So a pretty large edifice of philosophy was built by Aquinas on this essentially intellectual foundation. Supplemented by revelation, it provided a great system of ideas which defined the mental basis of the Christian life. Much of his work looked to Aristotle, but Aquinas made use of many other sources, such as St. Augustine and the writings attributed to Dionysius the Areopagite, the convert of St. Paul.

Therefore, the distinction established between reason and faith gave a definite role to the philosopher, as governed hopefully by reason, in the illumination of the Christian faith. At first Aquinas' dependence on Aristotle, then not popular, made the authorities suspicious of his doctrines, but their rigor and clarity gave them great power in later thinking.

Popular piety was far removed from such speculations. It was warmly practical, and concentrated on such activities as venerating relics, on hearing the Mass, and on pilgrimage. Holy journeys to Canterbury, Rome, Compostela, and Jerusalem created much merit for the faithful and wiped away many sins. The whole system of Crusades also was a kind of pilgrimage. Great enthusiasm was generated in a newly selfconscious Christendom ready to flex its muscles against the infidel. Alas, that included the infidel at home – Jews and heretics were often persecuted. Thus, in the thirteenth century a full-scale Crusade was undertaken in southern France against the Albigensian heresy – so called after the city of Albi, a main center. Its followers professed a kind of Manichaean doctrine, affirming the world evil and the Church corrupt. In 1233 the Dominicans were charged with the job of rooting out the heresy. Much cruelty was involved in putting down the movement, which had a threatening effect on the Church. This was partly because the ethical standards of the *perfecti*, or those committed to the higher life of Albigensian religion, were notably higher than those of many of the contemporary clergy.

Also important in medieval Christianity was a flowering of mysticism. In some ways the most powerful figure was the Dominican friar Johannes Eckhart (1260?–?1327), whose philosophical account of the inner experience of God was daring and exciting. For him the creature gets his very being from God – God indeed is the only being, truly speaking. The mystical life

The ritual dimension: Canterbury was a major pilgrimage center in the Middle Ages. This scene depicts a group from London arriving at Canterbury Cathedral.

consists then in striving to be conscious of the divine being within oneself. This is in accordance with what Bernard of Clairvaux had said – that to reduce yourself to nothing is a divine experience. But Eckhart's theology met opposition, and some of the propositions he affirmed were condemned.

There were tensions in this civilization, however, heralding the split which followed from the Reformation. There was the gap between the growing vernacular languages and the official Latin of the Church – hence the suspicion with which translations of the Bible were viewed by Church officials. There was the persistent question of the supposed poverty of the clergy and its contrast with the magnificence of the Papacy and many of the princes of the Church. There was the cost of many of the huge and wonderful edifices that the Church was building across Europe. There were the political tensions between the kings and princes north of the Alps and the Papacy in Rome. There were the discomforts of ecclesiastical power in many spheres.

But the culture of Western Europe was nevertheless vigorous, as was seen by the way in which it was expanded northeast and southwest. The Muslims were being driven back out of Spain. New wealth was being created in Italy. The infidels were at bay in the Mediterranean. New techniques were being pioneered for exploration, and by the fifteenth century Portuguese ships were edging their way round Africa. In 1453 the fall of Constantinople brought classical learning flooding into Europe as scholars escaped the Turks.

How should we sum up Western Christendom at this time, during its medieval dominance? It was proud, conformist, increasingly confident against the infidel, complex in doctrine and philosophy, and catering to the masses in the richness of its kinds of piety. Masses, pilgrimages, the condemnation of heretics, beautiful frescoes on church walls, stained glass windows, statues of the saints, illuminated books, vast cathedrals, soaring spires, the pomp of prelates and the vestments of priests, candles, holy water, the veneration of relics, the hope of glory and horror of hell, the chances of reducing one's time in purgatory, the feast days and fasts, the processions, the preachings of Crusades and other ventures, the lives of saints, the austerities of hermits, the composure of nuns, the great abbeys of monks, the grace of the Virgin, the prayers in Latin, the solemn chants – all these contributed to a mosaic of religious practices which channeled piety toward the sacred Trinity. For the intellectual, credible; for the pious, rich in devotion; for the mystic, deep in theology; for the woman, ideal in the Virgin; for the man, a vigorous and militant faith: the Church was involved in a memorable synthesis.

It was a synthesis which would split – partly because of the Renaissance, partly because of the great voyages and the new colonial ventures, and most of all because of the religious revolution known now as the Reformation.

Worlds that Disappeared

The Celts

The medieval Christian world submerged the paganisms of the north and west and east. The Celtic, Germanic, and Slavic religions would become a romantic memory. Yet their spirit somehow lingered on. Let us end our account of medieval Europe by sampling these religions – so far, that is, as we can get at them from our fragmentary sources.

Caesar remarked that the god the Celts worshiped more than anyone was Mercury: he was probably identifying that god with Lugh, who occurs across the Celtic world. He was the young one who vanquished the demons. Like David, he killed the giant Balar with his slingshot. He was the deity of the harvest who associated with deep fertility goddesses. Above all he was a symbol of sacred kingship, and presided over the other world. Later he was to merge with one or two Christian saints. In all this we have echoes of other Indo–European ideas.

Likewise with the Druids, supposedly rooted out from Britain by the Roman general Paulinus in 62 C.E. Roman accounts of the Druids are melodramatic, yet there can be little doubt that such a priestly class existed – it was part of the deep structure of Indo–European societies. Their chief function was to preside over the sacrificial life of the people. A record of the twelfth century C.E. from Ulster tells of horse sacrifice still being performed. The king had to mate with a white mare, and then bathe in the soup made of it, eat some of its meat, and lap up some of the broth. There are echoes of the Indian horse sacrifice here, from the other end of the Indo–European world. The priests had access to sacred knowledge and could exclude a person from the sacrificial cult, thus banishing him from society.

As for fertility cults, these no doubt lie behind the legend that St. Patrick drove the snakes from Ireland, serpents being above all symbols of fertility. And eventually no doubt the Irish, like other Celts, could find some solace and substitutions in the new Christian order. Christ, like Lugh, as a young man defeated the hosts of Satan. And Celtic saints could easily reincarnate the goddesses. The Irish goddess of learning, a figure like the Roman Minerva, who delighted in knowledge of nature and the fruits of the earth, and commanded poetry, in effect became St. Brigid of Kildare, whose monastery of Cell Dara was on the site of a holy oak. She and her nuns, according to a later account, guarded a perpetual fire (like Vestal Virgins, no less) surrounded by a hedge, to which no male had access.

Celtic religion was close to the other world, so that there were many points of access: caves, streams, and sacred trees of varying kinds. The Christian world took over many of these sacred spots to build churches, and saints were associated with healing springs and the like. The magic of the Celtic world was transformed for the sober purposes of Christian living, and to win the hearts of those whose poetry was always bubbling to the surface.

The Vikings

The Scandinavian seafarers were remarkably effective, and sometimes destructive, in their foraging into foreign lands to settle. They dominated the east coast of Ireland and the Isle of Man, southern and western Scotland, England, Normandy, the Baltic coasts, the rivers of Russia, Iceland, and parts of Greenland. Their impact on monasteries in the Christian West was often severe. But eventually they also succumbed to Christian ideology. In this they were helped by some of the figures of the Scandinavian pantheon.

In the great religious center at Uppsala there were images of the three great deities Odin, Thor, and Frey. Odin is the father of all, master magician, knower of great runes (or *mantras* as we might say, looking to India), dealer in law, ruler of the underworld. Thor is lord of the air and thunder, and is a great warrior deity, given to taking great drafts of intoxicating drinks, and so somewhat like Indra. If Odin is master of the priestly power, Thor incarnates the warrior power; while Frey deals in fertility. His mount is a swift boar, which was in this ancient world a fine edible creature. His sister Freya is the most powerful of the female divinities, very promiscuous, who has sex with all the gods, thus giving them vital power.

This quartet is far removed in spirit from the Trinity and the Virgin. But the hero Balder, son of Odin, is of a different cast: young and beautiful, he has nightmares. His mother Frigg makes all things swear never to harm her son, but forgets the mistletoe. One of the gods, blind Loki, throws a branch of it at him – it pierces him, and he dies. He is buried in a ship with his grieving and dying wife. The goddess of the nether world will not release him unless all things weep for him – and they all do, except for one giantess. He will not return till after history finishes in the great storm of Ragnarök. This end-of-the-world motif is very vivid, and came to be reinforced in Christian times. It is the twilight of the gods, *Götterdämmerung*.

Some scholars think that the myth of Balder owes something to Christian influence, which may be so. But in the form I have just set forth it is of course thoroughly "paganized," and the new Christian message coming from missionaries would still sound fresh and call forth echoes. But in the dark and stormy world of Germanic myth the atmosphere is very different from the medieval Christian myth. The latter is wrapped in a clothing of reason which lay far beyond what counted for knowledge on old runic shores.

Slavic Themes

Again in the Slavic lands we find the dominating force of the Indo–European gods. And yet below them we can also see the outlines of an ancient pre-Indo–European goddess, who deals in death and fertility. She is both a hag and a virgin, a sign of matrilineal society, a moist Earth Mother, pregnant before the spring. The white god Belobog is ruler of the day and year, and contends against darkness and death. In the Slavic world the bipolar oppositions are powerful: light and dark, day and night, life and death. There is almost a Zoroastrian feel to pre-Christian Slav religion. Among the gods Perun, a god of thunder and associated with the oak, was powerful in dispensing justice and in fighting against enemies. And as elsewhere the ancestors were strong to protect folk. When a rich person died he was dressed up in his finery and seated in a boat, to take him to the other shore. His weapons were placed around him. His wife was stabbed and seated beside him, to share in his life beyond life. The boat and all the finery and goods were burnt in a great blaze, and feasting would continue for days. Thereafter, people would maintain the cult of the dead for years to come.

The round Slav temples on hilltops, with images of the gods within (images which have virtually all perished), might give kings and chiefs power here and there. But with the building up of Kiev as a city, new knowledge and new values had to be taken up. Islam had its advantages as an ideology, and Judaism had been taken up by the Khazars. But as it happened it was the Orthodoxy of the Byzantine empire which had the greatest appeal, and so Christ had to be identified with the god of light, and Satan with death and darkness. The light had to be found within, in the mysticism of the Church.

It was these and other forms of culture across the North European plain which were absorbed and submerged in the new Christianity. It turned out that the poetry of the Celts, the story-telling of the Scandinavians, and the religious intuitions of the Slavic peoples, took new forms in Christian civilization. The Cross was pictured like a world-tree, Yggdrasil, with the judgment seat of the new God beneath it, and with Christ not Odin hanging from it. Thus the fusion of North and Christian South sets the seal on European medieval civilization.

CHAPTER 7

Christianity in the Modern Era

The Unleashing of New Forces from Europe

World history changed around 1500. Europe had been a rather peripheral civilization before then, often struggling not to be overrun by Muslims and Mongols. After 1500 it unified the oceans by great sea voyages, it radically altered the shape of its primary religion, Christianity, and it began processes culminating in the development of modern science, capitalism, nationalism, liberalism, and industrialization. These were powerful and sometimes fascinating, often devastating forces. They bred among other things colonialism, and with it great alterations to other continents and ways of life. North America came to be dominated by white men. Hispanic culture permeated the rest of the Americas. The African slave trade shifted large numbers of blacks to Brazil, the Caribbean, and North America. Later on, Australia and New Zealand were overrun by whites, and white settlements at the Cape bred a new area of conflict. Colonial empires were established in India and later most of Southeast Asia, in Indonesia, in the Caribbean, in Africa, and in North and Central Asia. Only with difficulty could China and Japan fight off European empires. Oceania was dominated by the West, too. By the end of the nineteenth century there was scarcely a part of the world which did not feel the impact of colonialism. It was as if in 1500 Europe was just a branch of world history, and thereafter the world was part of European history. So this was a new turn in the story of the human race.

The new European civilization, very different in many ways from that of the Middle Ages, was glittering, dynamic, rich with ideals, and often cruel. The Renaissance marked a new explosion of literary and artistic creativity. The Reformation marked a new reshaping of Christianity in the West. Science and capitalism released new forces of material creativity. The Enlightenment generated new hopes of political freedom and liberal thought. The eighteenth century saw inventions like the steam engine; new economic theories, as in the seminal work of Adam Smith (1723–90); lovely architecture and music; new philosophies and methods of agriculture; and two basic revolutions, one in America and the other in France.

Opposite The experiential dimension: the divine love pierces St. Teresa in this sculpture by Bernini, in Rome.

Christianity and the New Dynamic

Christianity's position in all this was ambiguous. There developed the idea of a rational universe created by a God with a mind analogous to the human mind. This, in turn, prepared the way for the confident exploration of the

physical world which marked the work of such key figures as Galileo Galilei (1564–1642) and Isaac Newton (1642–1727). The events which came to be known as the Reformation undoubtedly helped to spread new thinking and a speculative cast of mind. But there were reactions *against* freedom of ideas on the part of the Churches too. Christianity felt challenged by the new forces released in Europe and America. It had to make accommodations to them in a way similar to those later made by other religious traditions that were threatened by these forces from outside, through the impact of Western trade and colonialism. Christianity had to cope with the effects of the new science on its traditional picture of the universe. The trial of Galileo for heresy and the intellectual debates over Evolution in the nineteenth century were two main instances of this. It had to cope with the industrial revolution, which created new classes of urban people, alienated often from the traditional rural values of much Christianity. It had to cope with the state in the era of nationalism and new systems of education. It had to cope with liberal ideas which often eroded traditional modes of authority. In all this it was also divided, because of the fragmentation brought on by the rise of Protestant-ism. But it had new sources of dynamism – revival in the New World, powerful missionary activity in the colonial era, and the exploration of new forms of belief and practice.

The nineteenth century also saw other ideologies than those of the prevailing liberalism. Most notable was the creation of Marxism, which was to have an enormous impact on the twentieth century. There were ideas of the corporate national state, too, which were to be one of the sources of Nazism and Fascism. All these in their different ways provided a challenge, and indeed alternatives, to traditional religion.

In the following sections we will first look at the religious meaning of the Renaissance, then at the beginnings of the Reformation – Lutheran, Calvinist, and radical; then at the Counter–Reformation, the reshaping of Catholicism in Europe; then at the Enlightenment and the rise of nationalism; then at Eastern Orthodoxy and the Russian move eastwards; then we break with the chronological approach of the chapter to examine the spread of Christianity and colonialism since 1500; then we look at Christian responses to the new knowledge and liberalism of the nineteenth century; then at new ideologies like Marxism; and finally at Christianity in Europe during the twentieth century. In the next chapter we will see some of the same themes, but in the very different context of North America.

The Renaissance and Its Religious Meaning

That broad movement of culture, especially in the visual arts and in philosophy, which we know as the Renaissance, had its high point in Italy in the years around 1500, when Leonardo da Vinci and Michelangelo were at the height of their powers, and the Papacy was a brilliant patron of the new arts. It was a period when, under the stimulus of a rediscovered classical civilization, the artists and sculptors transcended their Roman and Greek heroes. It was a time of a brilliant and colorful depiction of reality in painting, which glorified this world even more than the next. It was also a period of freer thought and humanistic scholarship. Desiderius Erasmus (1469?–1536) used the new Greek and Latin scholarship to rediscover Christian origins. He was critical of dogmatic theologians who, by their disputes, overlaid the morality of Christ and his human face with the crust of stale speculation. Examples of the freer thought were a succession of Italian Neoplatonists: Marsilio Ficino (1433–99), Pico della Mirandola (1463–94), and Giordano Bruno (1548–1600). Ficino propounded a version of Neoplatonism, with a Christian clothing put upon it. But he believed in a kind of unchanging philosophy which had been taught by various teachers in various traditions. Pico showed that the Aristotelian and Platonic philosophies can be blended and are compatible. He was also influenced by Ibn Rushd and the Qabbalah. He was on the edge of heresy. Bruno had a vision of an infinite universe, both in time and space, whose atoms are universally interrelated. He saw God and the universe as like two sides of the same piece of paper. But his doctrines were denounced as heretical and he was burned at the stake.

All these figures had a fresh vision derived from the Hellenistic world, which had been opened up by contemporary scholarship. Ancient civilization

Erasmus of Rotterdam was a noted classical scholar whose humanistic learning was one of the roots of the new attitudes leading to the Reformation.

was perceived as oriented toward humanity and therefore replete with humanistic values. Moreover, the new learning and the new art were substantially patronized by the Papacy, and the values of the Florentine Renaissance were carried over into the Vatican. As a triumphant expression of these values, St. Peter's in Rome was being rebuilt at huge expense.

The Reformation: Theology and Political Power

Luther's Influence

The sale of so-called indulgences (permits, so to speak, to escape so many years of Purgatory, a sort of halfway house to heaven where the soul is purged of sins not deadly enough to consign it to Hell) was a factor stirring unease in Germany and helping to fuel the fire started by Martin Luther (1483–1546). Some of the proceeds from the indulgences sold in Germany were destined for St. Peter's. Some were being set aside to pay for the election expenses of the Archbishop of Mainz. This was unbeknown to Luther, who sent the Archbishop a copy of the 95 Theses, or propositions for debate, which he presented on October 31, 1517. The Archbishop's move to investigate Luther's orthodoxy helped to give publicity to the whole affair.

Luther was the son of a copper miner and was born in Eisleben in Thuringia, Germany. He went to university at Erfurt and after his first degree went on to study law. But in the fall of 1505 a vow which he made to St. Anne during a shattering thunderstorm caused him to abandon law and become an Augustinian friar. Eventually he received a doctorate and taught at the new university of Wittenberg from 1513 onward. Before that he had had a trip to Rome, which he thought would be a fine spiritual experience – but he found the holy city reprehensibly worldly. This was one of the seeds of doubt which were sown in his mind over the years. It was in 1517 that his momentous Theses came out. Some time before then, he had had a profound evangelical experience which altered his attitudes and led him into the main claims of his theology. Basically, the claims he made were two. First, in theology we should rely on scripture alone; and second, our salvation depends not at all on works but on faith alone – or to put it another way, it depends solely on the grace of God.

This rejection of the idea that good works or other human means can make a difference led him to denounce a whole slew of Catholic practices: indulgences, which rested on the absurdity of buying God's favor; celibacy in the priesthood and among monks and nuns; pilgrimages; Masses for the dead; and so on. A great deal of Catholic popular piety was swept away. Also the pretensions – as he saw it – of the Church to exclusive knowledge and understanding were pushed aside. Luther himself translated the Bible and wrote and composed many hymns, thus helping to forge the German language. The struggle for reform was also the struggle for vernacular languages against the dead hand of Latin. There was already restlessness in

Germany over the power of the Papacy. As it turned out, Luther's at first purely theological dispute with the Church made a good pretext for princes to seek some degree of extra independence. Luther received protection, very important for his cause, from Frederick, Elector of Saxony. Furthermore, as the revolt against Rome spread, various princes adopted forms of Lutheran practice, which gave them a large ecclesiastical as well as political control over their lands.

The Reformation movement was greatly assisted by the printing press. The Reformers used the pamphlet as a powerful genre of writing, and they brought theological controversy into the market place. The preacher also helped to give wide dissemination to the new ideas. So the movement spread, partly for political reasons. But its inner basis was piety, love of God, the sense that salvation can come only from God, and a disrespect for the bureaucratic apparatus of the Church at large.

There was military and political conflict. At the Peace of Augsburg in 1555, the principle was admitted (a concession to realities) that *cuius regio eius religio* "Of whom the rule, of him the religion." In other words, the prince or king determined the religion of his subjects. Germany and other parts of Northern Europe came to be divided between Catholics and Protestants, and, fatefully, Lutheranism instilled obedience to the state.

The abolition of monasteries with their rich lands was also a temptation for rulers. It provided means for consolidating their influence, by granting lands to those who helped them. It resolved here and there some pressing financial problems.

Luther was a formidable writer. Pamphlets, theological treatises, translations, hymns poured forth from his pen. Much owing to his activity, the services of the Lutheran Church took on their rolling and spiritual form, and their tender sense of the loving mercy of the Divine Being. The sonorous sounds of Luther's German could give the congregations a new sense of the validity of their faith.

Calvinism

With Luther the cork was out of the bottle. It is fine no doubt to be able to use the Bible as one's authority, but it is a book, or rather set of books, of many meanings. Interpretations could vary very easily. So there followed other Reformers who took a rather different line from Luther's. The most notable of these on the more orthodox or "magisterial" end of Protestantism was John Calvin (1509–63). By "magisterial" here is meant those Reformation movements which sought alliance one way or another with the state. The "radical" Reformers detached religion from politics in this sense – though such a move was itself perceived as intensely political.

Calvin was a French lawyer, who had written what was originally a slim book, *The Institutes of the Christian Religion*, later greatly expanded, and who took part in the Reform in the city of Geneva. Though he left for a while,

The revolutionized authority: all the paraphernalia of Roman Catholicism, such as the monastic life, the papal tiara, and the keys of the kingdom supposedly entrusted by Christ to his Church are outweighed by the Bible in this Calvinist picture. The person organizing the weighing is Calvin himself.

he was invited back and put into practice his notion of a political society which was committed to true religion and morals. His form of Church government, known as presbyterianism, became a characteristic of Reform churches of his tradition elsewhere, as in Holland and Scotland. But his most characteristic teaching was his doctrine of predestination. If salvation is by God alone, then he has already chosen who is to be saved and who is not. What you do does not affect this divine destiny. So good works are merely symptoms of salvation and cannot affect the outcome. Such predestinationism took a strong hold on the intellectual imagination of one wing of the Reformation. It was a rather philosophical variant on the theme of "by faith alone," of the Lutherans.

Also, for the Calvinists the most vital thing was the preaching of the Word. Thus, Calvin altered the plan of the cathedral in Geneva. The altar was taken away, and half-way along the church is the pulpit, with pews gathered so that they face the pulpit, not the altar. The very rearrangement of the furniture of the church signaled a large change in ideas. The Bible as preached became the norm. Good conduct was something that happened in this world, not something that had to be specially cultivated in nunneries and monasteries. Virtue was democratized, and a somewhat puritan acceptance of the work ethic was a consequence. Some, notably Max Weber (1864–1920), have seen in this worldly austerity a clue to the creation of capitalism. Much creation of wealth by hard work and little spending through puritanical abstention add up to savings which can supply the capital for building up enterprises.

The Radical Reformers: Anabaptists and Others

But the most radical of the Reformers were those who began to see religion as a matter of individual faith. In going back to the Bible and trying to re-create the ethos of the early Church, some Reformers rejected infant baptism. Only adults could gauge their faith and have the experience of conversion. They were dubbed Anabaptists or "Rebaptizers," and later, more simply, Baptists. They were radicals because their emphasis on personal and individual faith meant a break with the idea that some collective body such as the state could decide what its citizens' religion ought to be. This simple but revolutionary idea caused great unease among Catholics and Reformers alike. The Anabaptists were often persecuted by both sides. One favorite way of disposing of them was by drowning in a river – an ironic and cruel comment on the rite of baptism.

Among early rebels of the Anabaptist tradition was Thomas Müntzer (1488?–1525), who believed in a new socioeconomic order and the imminent coming of a new age. A well-educated person, he became a Lutheran pastor, but wound up being chaplain to a large-scale peasants' revolt. This was suppressed with cruelty at the battle of Frankenhausen, and Müntzer was taken, tortured, and killed (1525). Another violent uprising was the setting-up of a revolutionary kingdom of the Saints at Münster in 1534, also suppressed. The major leader turned out to be Menno Simons (1496–1561), originally a Catholic priest, who was much harried by authority. He was finally able to settle with his followers on the German coast. Later this expanding group was able to get land in Eastern Europe and Russia, many being skilled at drainage and the opening up of new farm lands. Their successors, known as Mennonites, became an important strand in North American piety.

From these Anabaptist beginnings came various nonconforming groups – Baptists, Congregationalists, or Independents, later the Quakers, and others who argued for the separation of true religion and the state. They were also significant as some of the spiritual ancestors of North American religion (see Chapter 8).

But initially the Reformers who favored alliance with the state prevailed amid a wide struggle for power with Catholicism. In England, Henry VIII (reigned 1509–47) broke away from Rome for political and other reasons and closed the monasteries. Elizabeth I (reigned 1558–1603) reversed the effects of the short reign of the Catholic Mary I (reigned 1553–58) and established the Anglican Church in its present form. The Queen became governor of the Church and was able to decree rites and ceremonies, religion being controlled by submission to the credal statement known as the 39 Articles. The later English Civil War led to various compromises between the more Catholic and Lutheran parts of the Church and the more puritanical and Calvinist. So the Church of England became another variant on the Reformation. Scotland, however, became Calvinist, and Ireland persisted in largely Catholic practice.

The Shape of Europe after the Reformation

As a result of various armed and propaganda struggles Europe divided on the principle of *cuius regio eius religio* (p. 123). Much of northern Germany, which was still of course divided into many states, was mainly Protestant; the South and Austria were Catholic. Poland and Hungary, and Italy, Croatia, Spain, Portugal, and most of France were Catholic. Lutheranism predominated in Scandinavia. In Eastern Europe Orthodoxy was powerful, as in Russia and elsewhere. But the Islam of the Ottoman Turks was encroaching on the Balkans, eventually threatening Vienna. In Spain, not long before the Reformation, the last Muslim power had fallen to the militant Catholic Crown, and it was this form of the faith that went with the Conquistadores to the New World.

At this point it is useful to pause and consider the great transformations that had been effected in Christianity as a result of the Reformation. It was in effect a new founding of the faith, and one which the Catholics themselves had to recognize and act upon, for they themselves underwent that reshaping of their own institutions in the movement known as the Counter-Reformation.

The Dimensions of Reformed Christianity

The Ritual Dimension

In the ritual dimension, the Reformers effected both major and minor changes. They all, however, involved the use of vernacular languages. Latin was got rid of – although it remained the language of theology. Lutherans and Anglicans kept to a ritually simplified version of the Eucharist as their most frequent service. But Presbyterians and the radicals tended toward treating the Eucharist as a solemn occasion to be conducted on special occasions or monthly. Their staple diet was the worship service, with the preaching of the sermon as the centerpiece. The new churches which were to be built reflected this, as we shall see (p. 131). The authority of scripture was a cornerstone of the Reformation, and the importance placed on the Word of God led to a more educated clergy.

Many aspects of ritual piety were swept away, even among Lutherans and Anglicans, such as pilgrimages, the use of the relics of saints, and statues of the Virgin Mary. Indeed the latter was considered by most Reformers as having attained inappropriate status in Catholicism. Devotion to her became, until the Anglo–Catholic revival in the nineteenth century, strictly a badge of Roman faith. In general a great simplification of rituals took place. There was a change in the doctrine, too. The central Catholic notion that the bread and wine are converted into the body and blood of Christ at the Eucharist was greatly modified. Bans were introduced on practices such as the actual veneration of the consecrated bread (or Host, as it was called), which itself became a notable feature of Catholic piety in the period after the Counter-Reformation.

Opposite Quakers in their meeting house. A woman preaches – and this indicates the freedom from social preconceptions which was found in the Society of Friends. Even at their meetings the Quakers do not doff their caps (a sign of servility).

Map 6 Europe after
the Reformation.

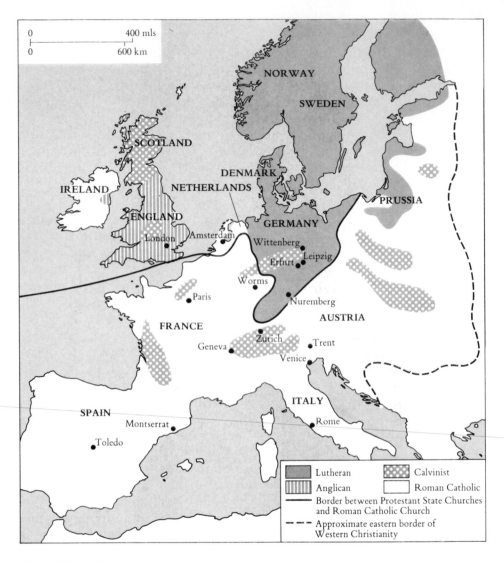

The Ethical Dimension

In ethics, there was a revival of the ideals of austere life, but in quite a different
context. Temperance and self-discipline were for everyone. No distinction
should be made between lay people and monks and nuns, or between persons
from the Church's history given the title of saints and the ordinary members
of a Christian community. Nor was there a radical difference between pastors
on the one hand and their congregations. The pastor might be specially
trained for his office, but the priesthood belongs to all believers. And so there
was a renewal of ethics in the Reformation and a more serious and
challenging call (so the Reformers would think) to the life of justice and
righteousness. Christianity should permeate every part of life. This was also
Catholic doctrine, but the Reformers argued that the practice was otherwise.

Catholicism had made too many concessions to human weakness.

The Doctrinal Dimension

It was above all the thought of God's grace which held the center. Partly this was going back to St. Augustine – more, it was going back to the reading of St. Paul's Epistles. Salvation was in the gift of God. The Protestants often re-emphasized the spiritual holiness and terrifying wrath of God, the more to underline his sweetness and mercy in bending over to lift up humankind. And though the mood of the Reformation was often highly intellectual, especially among the Calvinists – and though, indeed, the movement helped to give an impetus to the reordering of European universities and the unleashing of great energies of philosophy – nevertheless the main trend was against the use of reasoning to find out about God. That is, the Reformers stressed above all the central importance of revelation, and by that they meant the Bible. So Aquinas' great edifice of an alliance between faith and reason, between revealed and natural theology, was dismantled.

The Narrative Dimension

The Bible, no longer screened by a learned language, now spoke directly to people's feelings – it became the great fount of narrative. Printing brought it into many households. You could judge about matters of truth by referring to it, without relying on learned commentary or priestly exposition. It became a series of dramas against which men and women could measure their lives. They could relive the wanderings of the Israelites in the desert, the bad times of Jeremiah, the visionary life of Daniel, the ministry of Christ, the heroisms of the Apostles. The Old Testament, which on the whole had been kept away from the laity by the Catholic hierarchy, was a rich source of ideas and stories. Something of Jewish life could be relived in a new key, especially the keeping of the Sabbath, according to new puritanical rules.

Sometimes the Protestants took the narrative imagery with deadly seriousness in interpreting their own times (for example, the messianic expectations of Thomas Müntzer, which we have glanced at). The Roman Church came in for most negative treatment: the Pope was the Antichrist, and his Church was not the bride of Christ but a harlot. Bitterness became commonplace in the strife which succeeded the Reformation.

The Experiential Dimension

The emphasis which existed in the Roman Catholic Church on mysticism diminished. So did the training of the self in the contemplative life, which was very much the ideal of the monasteries and convents. There were one or two notable Protestant mystics, such as Jakob Boehme (1575–1624), who had a great influence on the formation of the Quakers, and, on later German philosophical thought, above all G. W. F. Hegel (1770–1831). But the disappearance of the cloister in favor of the hearth led to a greater emphasis on personal devotion and family prayer. It led to a warm pietism, rather than the exploration of the depths of the soul. The re-emphasis on the Old

Testament also led to a perception of the wrathful and numinous character of Deity, a feeling of utter dependence on the Holy One, and a sense that we are all unworthy. Only from the Holy can holiness flow, and only by grace are we saved from sin.

The Institutional Dimension

The Calvinists ruled by a democratic method, having local committees, general assemblies, and elected leaders. Each congregation called a minister to serve it. The Lutherans and Anglicans were much less radical in reshaping their systems. They kept to the use of bishops, priests, and deacons – the three-fold order of the early Church as they saw it. The monarch had a regulative say in the affairs of the Church, and the Church-state alliance was solid. Therefore, it was necessary to regulate those who did not conform.

The institutional dimension: in Lutheran countries the king or prince controlled the Church, and likewise among Anglicans. Elizabeth I, here seen praying, was Head of the English Church.

The Reformers used methods of persecution, as did Catholics. In their countries, nonconformists and Catholics did not have civil rights, or had only restricted ones. It was not until the nineteenth century that all of these disabilities were removed. In England, Catholicism was for a time the virtual equivalent of treason, because the war between Spain and England, culminating in the defeat of the Spanish Armada in 1588, was also an ideological or religious war. Loyalty to Queen Elizabeth meant loyalty to the religion which she headed. The Virgin Queen replaced the Virgin Mary.

It was religious regulation which led some of the more radical puritans and reformers to emigrate, either to the ill-defined lands of Eastern Europe and the Baltic or to the New World. But ideals of toleration made headway in Europe after the Thirty Years' War (1618–48) sickened and exhausted those who had engaged in religious struggle. John Locke (1632–1704) was one of the notable theoreticians of toleration.

The deepest crisis for Reformers lay in the removal of papal authority, in the sense that they rapidly found how interpretations of the Bible could vary and form the basis of conflicting systems. The Bible was a paper Pope, but who was to ensure conformity of belief and practice? This was one argument for the alliance of Church and state: the state could enforce unanimity of doctrine. So it was that Anglicanism had the 39 Articles by Act of Parliament – and Protestants were expelled from Austria in 1597 and eventually from France in 1685. Other groups sought a different mode of inner conformity by having rather democratic procedures and agreement on teachings. But the crisis of authority has remained with Protestantism, which is why it is divided into so many denominations and sects.

The Material Dimension

Catholic churches which were taken over had their more outstandingly un-Protestant features removed, and the interior was sometimes reshaped, as at Geneva. New buildings were much plainer, especially in Calvinist countries – plain white walls, no stained glass, no ornamentation, but a great pulpit, plus a communion table. In Calvinism singing of hymns was discouraged – only the singing of the Psalms, for they were truly Biblical. Even in the Church of England, under Puritan influence, it was illegal to sing hymns until 1820, though the practice had come in earlier with the influence of Methodism. Often a form of iconoclasm occurred, as when Oliver Cromwell's troops smashed up a number of English and Scottish churches and cathedrals.

The effects on painting were to secularize it. No longer was there a demand for altarpieces and holy pictures in Protestant parts of Europe. The Dutch took to interiors, portraits, seascapes, landscapes, and the English to landscapes and portraits. A tradition arose which helped to stimulate the great eighteenth-century Scottish portrait artists. All this was part of a new and more objective vision of people and nature which had vast effects in the formation of modern scientific thinking.

This Dutch interior shows the simplification of the ritual dimension brought about by the Reformation.

These, then, were some of the revolutionary effects of the Protestant Reformation. It led to a new creation of Christianity: sober, rhetorical, bookbound, devotional, dogmatic, national, plain, but endowed with energies which stimulated trade, exploration, science, nationalism, democracy, and conflict.

The Counter-Reformation and the Formation of Modern Catholicism

The dreadful crumbling of the Roman edifice in the first stormy years of the Reformation called for some remedy. It was only, however, in 1545 that the Papacy succeeded in calling a general Council, at Trent, which lasted intermittently until 1563. This had profound effects in clearing up abuses within the system and in providing for a revitalized Church with greater centralization. Its chief effect was to reject reconciliation with the Protestants. But the appointment of bishops and priests was reformed; training for the clergy was reorganized and made more intellectual; the Vulgate or Latin Bible was revised; the administration of the Church was reshaped; doctrines of the seven Sacraments and of justification by faith were reformulated; and loose ways of dealing with indulgences, the cult of saints, and so forth were tightened up. The strength of the central government of the Church was enhanced. All those things of which the Protestants were most critical – including the devotion to the Virgin Mary, the cult of saints, pilgrimages, the adoration of the Host, the central place of the priesthood, and the ecclesiastical hierarchy – were reaffirmed in practice.

At about the same time there was forged a most powerful weapon for mission activity and the reassertion of Catholic values: the Society of Jesus, founded by St. Ignatius Loyola (1491?–1556). He had been raised mainly at the court of Spain and had embarked on a knightly and military career. The bad wounds he received at the battle of Pamplona led to a long convalescence when his reading stimulated conversion to the religious life. He went to the Holy Land and on his return to Spain founded a small order of priests – not monks – which was to become the Society of Jesus, its members being known as Jesuits. He gave a military flavor to the rigorous training he devised, and his *Spiritual Exercises* was a powerful manual for those who would serve Christ in the world. He put his new order at the disposal of the Papacy. With its iron discipline and highly intellectual training it became a significant factor in the reconquest of parts of Europe for the Catholic Church, working in France, southern Germany, Austria, Poland, and elsewhere. It was also very effective in the mission field in India, China, Japan, and Latin America.

The Council of Trent, a little ominously for the future of the Church, also created the Index of Forbidden Books. For four centuries and more it was involved in censoring the reading done by Catholics. It was all part of the discipline necessary to hedge around papal authority. But within the limits of doctrinal orthodoxy the Church took on renewed vigor. In 1622 it set up a missionary department, the Congregation for the Propagation of the Faith (*de propaganda fidei* – from this word came the modern "propaganda"). In the welter of new voyages, discoveries, and colonies, there were vast gains for Roman Catholicism to offset the European losses. The Baroque style of the seventeenth century gave new magnificence to churches – with lush post-Renaissance holy pictures, highly decorated ceilings, marble altars, and twisting candleholders, golden monstrances wherein the Host was held up for devotion, elaborate side chapels, statues of the Virgin in blue with stars about her head, and the new forms of liturgical music. This was to culminate in the Masses written by Joseph Haydn (1732–1809) and W. A. Mozart (1756–91). New orders also grew, and there was a revival in mysticism, with St. Teresa of Avila (1515–82) and St. John of the Cross (1542–91), among others, forming a famous school of Spanish mystics.

As a result of these and other factors the Roman Catholic Church was revitalized in its religious life. It managed to fuse a new intellectual discipline with the piety of ordinary people and so to cater for traditional populations. But it bought some of its advantages at a great cost, which was to become apparent with the period of the Enlightenment and the rise of European nationalism.

Enlightenment, Capitalism, and Nationalism

The breakdown in authority which the Reformation and its aftermath displayed had its philosophical effects. The Reformation had elevated faith above reason, and for some thinkers, reason rather than faith should reign. The terrible struggles of religion stimulated the desire for toleration, and with it rationality. There arose a rationalist current in European life and thought which cultural historians call the Enlightenment. Part of the new movement enthroning reason had its origins in France, with such writers as the fiercely anticlerical Voltaire (1694–1778), and Montesquieu (1689–1755), social theorist and urbane moralist. Its French climax was in the work of Denis Diderot (1713–84), who edited the massive *Encyclopédie*.

In Germany among the most vital figures was Gotthold Lessing (1729–81), dramatist and theologian, whose *Nathan the Wise* was a drama devoted to pleading for toleration, with its central figure of the fine Jew. And there was Immanuel Kant (1724–1804), who combined two great themes of the Enlightenment, the importance of reason and the essential need to be critical. He had been awakened, as he said, from his dogmatic slumber by reading the skeptical writings of the Scotsman, David Hume (1711–76), who was both a philosopher and a noted historian. Already the advance of a more scientific approach to history was beginning to cause rumblings over the truth of scripture, or at least over its claim to absolute truth. This was to bring acute troubles to the maintaining of Biblical authority. If the Pope of Rome had been rebuffed, and the paper Pope was weakened, then where would authority be found? That was to be one of the great themes of religious debate in the nineteenth and twentieth centuries.

It was another product of the Scottish Enlightenment, Adam Smith (1723–90), who laid the foundations for capitalist economics, which was one strand in the great changes that were overtaking the world. Consider the inventions of the era: in 1775 came the manufacture of steam engines; in 1793 Eli Whitney revolutionized the cotton industry with his new cotton gin; in 1814 the first practical steam locomotive was built; in 1831 Faraday demonstrated the principle of the electric dynamo; in 1846 ether was used as an anesthetic in an operation ... and so on. It was a marvelously inventive age, in which the sciences really began to show their practical utility. In agriculture there were also great changes, with the use of rotation of crops, and later the varied reaping and other machines which made the opening-up of the North American prairies so advantageous. In short, we come rapidly on the period of Industrial Revolution and the high age of early capitalism. It was a period when the middle classes asserted themselves. This was one of the meanings of the French Revolution in 1789. Another meaning was nationalism.

Already, of course, the national idea had shown its muscle during the Reformation. But the Industrial Revolution and the Enlightenment together gave it new impetus, for in the nineteenth and twentieth centuries nationalism and modernization were associated. Larger units of operation were needed, and the nation-state could provide these. Liberalism was thought to be the politically dynamic mode of conducting the new creation of wealth. A new literature sowed the idea of national cultures.

From the time of the French Revolution onward the fight for national identity became irresistable. National aggrandisement became natural. Empires were a corollary. The very nations which fought for unification and freedom were also involved in the acquisition of colonial empires – Holland, France, Germany, Italy, Great Britain, Denmark, and others. So we see, entering the stage of world history, this explosive force of nationalism, which by its very tendency to expand stimulates further nationalism in others, and which has become the general principle by which we are all governed. We have a United Nations, not United Persons.

All this paved the way for the making of new ideologies which had something of a religious flavor, even when strongly antireligious in belief, such as Marxism. Because the idea of the nation-state is a bit weak on doctrine, it has tended to blend with wider ideologies and religions. Italian nationalism blended with liberalism, as in its own way did French. British imperialism dedicated itself to what it saw as Christian civilization. Irish nationalism had its doctrinal guarantor in Catholicism.

In other ways, too, nationalism functioned like a religion. Its myth was the national story, to be taught in schools, once modernization had produced universal education. Its rituals were the flag, the national anthem, the military marchpast – all pioneered in France with the tricolor, the *Marseillaise* and the citizen army. Its ethics were those of the good citizen, law-abiding, taxpaying, ready to fight – or, if a woman, ready to help produce the babies of the nation. Its priesthood was the teachers, and its saints were the heroes and poets of the past. Its organization was that of the state itself. Its emotions were those of patriotism and nostalgia for the homeland. It was, in short, a powerful religious force with which all traditional religions had to make some sort of accommodation.

In the new Europe of the nineteenth century the relations between religion and nationalism were varied. There was the pervasive idea of the national religion in such countries as England and Sweden. But now citizens who were not of the majority faith had to be accommodated, too. There was overt hostility between the Church, eager to retain its territorial foothold in the Papal States of Central Italy, which were thought of as a guarantee of its independence, and the largely liberal nationalist *Risorgimento* (resurgence). There were new compromises when Germany became united, with divisions of the educational system, but the general thought was that Christianity is for personal life and the state is for public duty. Folk now died for their country, for the most part, not for religion as such. Where religion or ideology and nationalism combined, then you got a very powerful force. Incidentally, the multinational empires were destined for trouble by the very fact of nationalism, and all of them in Europe crumbled.

Russia and the New Learning

The Muslims, in the shape of the Ottoman empire, had more or less occupied the territories of the old Byzantine empire. As a result, the whole realm of Eastern Orthodoxy was cramped for living and breathing space. It continued to survive under the Ottomans but its possibilities as part of the so-called *millet* system (which allowed for subcommunities such as Christians and Jews to follow their own laws and to be administered through their own leaders) were limited. But Russia, already vast and destined to acquire an even vaster empire to the east, was there to represent the Faith. Moscow was to be the Third Rome, destined in hope to lead the forces of the faith in the restoration of a purified and true Christianity, now that the second Rome was conquered and the first Rome was corrupted and weakened by Protestantism. Although Christianity was established first at Kiev, this center of power was shattered by the Mongols. Moreover, despite the fact that there were important other Orthodox Christian centers at Novgorod and Pskov these were fighting a hard battle for self-preservation against the Teutonic Knights pushing forward from Prussia. It was Moscow, therefore, which succeeded in becoming the new capital. In the late sixteenth century its archbishop was dignified with the title of Patriarch and became the major Orthodox religious leader outside the Islamic captivity.

After the defeat of the Mongols of the Khanate of Kazan in eastern Russia in 1552, the way was open for the annexation of lands to the east. By 1689 virtually all of Siberia was taken over, mainly because of the lucrative fur trade. Under Peter the Great (reigned 1682–1725) and Catherine the Great (reigned 1762–96), Russia conquered areas of the northwest and of the Black Sea coastal region which enabled it to open up new seaports at St Petersburg and Odessa, greatly enhancing trade. But Peter's modernization also involved controlling the Church. The Patriarchate was abolished, not to be restored till 1918, and the Church was ruled by a synod. Already there had been schism. In the seventeenth century Patriarch Nikon (1605–81) had tried to bring in reforms of the ritual, and this was seen as questioning the special calling of Moscow to be the Third Rome. What Nikon was trying to do was to bring Russian practice in line with that of Byzantium. A large breakaway group known as Old Ritualists or Old Believers continued in the old ways, despite persecution. The majority of Ukrainians, for separate – largely nationalist – reasons, constituted themselves the Uniate Ukrainian Church, in communion with Rome but using Eastern rituals and customs.

The new lands to the east, which extended into Alaska in North America, were subject to considerable missionary activity in the eighteenth and nineteenth centuries. This was also a time of revived spiritual life. The practice of Hesychasm was brought in from Mount Athos, and texts of Greek spirituality were translated. The figure of the holy elder (the *starets*) became a regular feature of Church life. He was a person who by his charismatic personality and saintliness was considered to have treasures to teach –

somewhat like the Hindu guru, but in the very different religious and cultural milieu of Russia. The most famous of all such holy men was St. Serafim of Sarov (1759–1833), who entered the monastery of Sarov as a young man on the advice of a *starets*. From 1793 till 1815 he lived as a hermit near the monastery. In the years 1815–25, retiring to a cell, he was inspired by divine revelation to counsel people and speak with them. For him the heart of the Christian life was experiencing the grace of the Holy Spirit, and the light of the Spirit reportedly shone from his countenance for those who approached him for healing, advice, and prophecy.

Such figures had profound influence on some of the great writers of Russia, including Fyodor Dostoyevsky (1821–81) and Leo Tolstoy (1828–1910). They in turn formulated profound religious ideas in their writings. Dostoyevsky, in his famous novel *The Brothers Karamazov*, portrayed a *starets*, Father Zosima, who presented anew the ancient Christian faith. But his vision was purified in a way by the scarifying critique of God produced by Ivan in the novel, and his story of the Grand Inquisitor of Spain who gives short shrift to a returning Jesus. Tolstoy in his later years preached a simple love and pacifism which were to earn him excommunication from Orthodoxy but the gratitude of M. K. Gandhi, whose mind he helped to form.

But despite the Orthodox Church's strength, clouds around it were forming. The Russia of the late nineteenth century was divided between modernizing Westerners – often armed with strange new revolutionary theories, from liberalism to anarchism – and Russophiles who put their faith in the old Russia, the wisdom of the peasant, the holy mission of Russia in a suffering world, and so forth. In 1861 the serfs were liberated, and Russia embarked on a new wave of modernization. But its effects were impaired by poor leadership. In 1905 Russia was humiliated by the Japanese at the land battle of Mukden and the sea battle of Tsushima. Unrest gave a foretaste of revolution, as workers demonstrated in the streets and troops shot them down. The doom of the monarchy and of the old order was sealed by defeat in World War I. With that collapse there came revolution.

Meanwhile, it should be noted that Tsarist expansion had continued as the frontier of the Empire was driven south through Central Asia, so that now it contained a substantial Muslim population on the borders of Afghanistan and Iran.

Imperialism and the Spread of Christianity

The development of modern Christianity naturally had marked effects on the missionary enterprise. Spanish and Portuguese Catholicism, itself deeply affected by the effervescence of the Counter-Reformation, went on to influence Latin America in profound ways – at first, as a predatory invader. Protestant ideas penetrated North America, and later, in the nineteenth and twentieth centuries, helped to shape African and Pacific Christianity, as well as some areas of Asia, notably Korea. The Orthodox Church, meanwhile,

The social dimension: liberation theology has brought out the meaning of changing social conditions for the poor. Here is a base community in Panama, part of the movement to reform both the Church and society from the bottom up.

made deep inroads into North Asia, as the Russian Empire spread to the Far East. Sadly, over the last 500 years, much mission work carried out in the name of God has accompanied horrifying cruelty toward, and economic exploitation of, native peoples. Occasionally, however, certain trends of Christian expansion have helped the indigenous inhabitants to fight for human rights and national liberation.

Catholic Missions in Latin America

It was not until about 1520, nearly thirty years after Columbus' first landing, that the Spaniards were fully convinced that what they had found was really a New World. At that point, the discovery of these vast lands and their exploitation were taken up with a kind of crusading zest. The expulsion of the Muslims from Spain had been a tough business, but it fired the Spaniards, and to a lesser degree the Portuguese, with a Catholic zeal. And to complicate matters, there was the Reformation, causing Europe to disintegrate religiously but reinforcing the value of commitment to the Catholic cause. The fact that the Spaniards acted in the New World with great cruelty and greed should not blind us to the fact that they thought themselves to be doing God's will. The Church followed on the heels of the Conquistadores, and there was held up before the eyes of the faithful the prospect of a great extension of Christ's work.

The general attitude to indigenous religions, such as the Aztec and the Inca systems, was one of horror and disdain. The Aztec practice of human sacrifice was not easy to take. But the true horrors lay in the general idolatry of the New World's inhabitants. The gods were often seen by Catholics as creatures of the Devil. So much, therefore, of the native culture had to be rooted out. Disentangling culture from religion was itself a problem, and a good proportion of the region's literatures and creations was simply destroyed.

The spirit of the conquest was one of dedication to a sacred cause at the same time as the opportunity for hugely exploiting the conquered population. And because of the advent of the Counter-Reformation the Church had the motivation and the apparatus to carry orthodox Catholic faith to the New World. The conquest was then in its own way a crusade.

The astonishing ease of some of the conquests was uncanny. It lay in the fact that the two great empires the Spaniards encountered were so centralized. The Spaniards struck at the brain of these empires and paralyzed their bodies. Their superiority lay in their horses and muskets, and their ships and cannons. The rapidity and glory of the conquests boosted the self-confidence of the victors and their belief that their civilization and religion were immensely superior to those of the peoples they had come to dominate.

By 1700 the Spanish domains in the New World were immense, running from California and Texas to Patagonia and from Ecuador to the Caribbean. The Portuguese ruled over the huge area of Brazil, after some fighting with the rival Dutch (who kept a base in Surinam). But certain areas were highly important and others thinly populated and marginal. The rich and densely populated places were Peru and Mexico (known as New Spain), together with part of the Caribbean. It was during the period leading to the consolidation of power over so great an area that the way of life of the New World was worked out and in this the Church played a leading part. The fact that the nations of Central and South America are steeped in Catholicism today is due to these sixteenth-century Spanish conquests.

The Catholic Legacy: Liberation Theology

This set of ideas, which came to prominence in the 1960s, was heavily influenced by Marxism. It blended a Marxist analysis of the social situation with the Catholic and Christian values evident in the New Testament. The Pope's Council of 1962–65, "Vatican II," had given a great impetus to Biblical scholarship, and the new thinkers saw in the New Testament especially a revolutionary concern for the poor on the part of Christ. They argued that the Church's prime duty was to raise the life of the poor. They were often critical of older attitudes which glossed over the present miseries because the faithful could be sure of the joys of heavenly bliss in the life after this one. The movement, therefore, was very critical socially, revolutionary in spirit, concerned with altering the structures of existence, and anticapitalist. It led some priests into actively participating in revolutionary struggle, as in the case of the Sandinista revolution in Nicaragua.

The Liberation Theology movement also emphasized some other things, apart from the analysis of the present condition of the poor of the Third World. They were very keen on a practical approach (they used the Marxist word "praxis" here as a slogan for their commitment to realizing ideas in

Archbishop Romero
assassinated in San
Salvador, March 24,
1980.

practice). They were keen too on starting at the grass roots, like a number of earlier reforms in the Catholic tradition. They wanted to raise the consciousness of the poor (and this often meant the Indians), who too often were filled with a kind of fatalism which traditional Catholicism did very little to puncture. So it was with "base communities" that the movement realized its ideas – the creation of small communities of lay and clerical people organizing social betterment, Bible-reading, and the raising of local consciousness. Over 200,000 such communities have been set up in Brazil and elsewhere in the continent.

Liberation Theology has come to have a wide influence beyond the Latin American scene, being of some special attraction in the Third World and also among those involved in the Church struggle in South Africa. Among the prominent exponents are Gustavo Gutiérrez of Peru, Juan Luis Segundo of Uruguay, Leonardo and Clodovis Boff of Brazil, Hugo Assmann of Costa Rica, and (among Protestants) José Miguel Bonino of Argentina.

Protestantism in Latin America

Protestantism has had a spectacular increase during the twentieth century. Its three roots are, first, migrant Churches in such countries as the Argentine, Chile, and Brazil, with a large number of German and other European immigrants. Second, and more important, there are (mostly American) Protestant missions who have worked among both Catholics and Indian tribes, where Biblical evangelical preaching has made large inroads. Third, spontaneously arising Protestant groups from within Latin America, especially Pentecostals, have come to the fore. Pentecostalism has also had some prominence within Catholicism, as elsewhere in the world after Vatican II. There may be as many as eighteen million Protestants in the Latin American region, compared with a few hundred thousand a century ago. But the statistics are hard to find.

The success of Protestant preaching was worrying enough at one time to be put on the agenda for Catholic Bishops' conferences, together with the impact of Freemasonry and other matters. Until fairly recently relations between Catholics and Protestants have often been bitter, with Catholics trying to hold on to old monopolies and Protestants often taking a severe evangelical line against Catholic superstitions (as they saw them). The reasons for Protestant success, in Latin America as elsewhere in the Catholic world, are varied. One is that the individualism of Protestant religion makes sense in a capitalist, urban environment. Second, Protestant emphasis on religious experience and conversion is direct, appealing, and promising for togetherness – such feelings become the glue of new communities. Third, it is natural that people should awake to the essential pluralism of the religions and within the religions of the world. Catholicism can no longer claim to be the sole possibility.

All this is part of an increasing ferment in the Latin American scene. Among Catholics the meeeting of bishops at Medellin in 1968 is commonly regarded as a turning point, when the voices which awakened the social conscience of the Church were significant and loud, and when the Church seemed to acknowledge the need for new structures both in Christian life and in society. This call, with the attendant Liberation Theology, has made the Latin American Christian scene central to the religious history of the world.

The Penetration of Christianity into Black Africa

The massive spread of Christianity is undoubtedly the greatest change to come over the African continent. It is now the majority religion of black Africa. One might at some preceding stage have expected that Islam would become the dominant faith. It has indeed made some progress, but rather small compared with that of Christianity.

In the eighteenth century, apart from the rather few Christians around the coasts where Europeans had settled or established trading posts, there was little Christianity at all, except in the ancient kingdom of Ethiopia. But toward the end of the century Christian opponents of the slave trade arranged for a group of emancipated slaves of African origin to be settled in Sierra Leone, at Freetown. Thirty years later a college, Fourah Bay College, was set up, to be Africa's first modern institution of higher education. It became a center for the spread of Christianity, as black missionaries went out into the region. The most important of these was a Yoruba, from what is now Nigeria, Samuel Ajayi Crowther (1809?–91), who became Anglican Bishop on the Niger.

Even before the main partition of Africa, missionaries were making progress, though the most famous white missionary in Africa, David Livingstone (1813–73), was more successful as an explorer than as a winner of souls (he only converted one person, who fell away). But during the colonial period there was specially strong activity in the translation of the Bible into vernacular languages, and this had a powerful influence on people. Christianity and education were closely connected, not just because in fact so many schools were run by missionaries, but because African societies saw the need for modernizing – if only often intuitively – and school was the main agency for this. And more than this: Christianity did supply something to rely on in a period of sudden and disturbing change. As classical African religion wilted, so Christianity provided an alternative.

The Bible seems to have had great potency. The missionaries were rather short-handed, and made much use of local catechists who were often poorly trained. But they could carry the Bible around with them – for most Africans the first and often the only book in their own language that they knew. Its power was the more spiritual in that it could bring forth the very sounds of language – it was a miraculous score from which the person who could read could play a wonderful set of musical pieces. Also, its themes rang true to the African condition. It spoke of circumcision; of the witch of Endor; of Mount Carmel and the contest in rainmaking; of prophecy, healing, and the sufferings of the people of Israel. With much of this the black African could easily identify.

As has happened at other times and places in Christian history the Bible was at odds with perceived practice. It had revolutionary potential. The mission Churches were almost completely in the control of whites until the end of the 1950s. It was not surprising, then, if many blacks saw in this some contradiction with the spirit of the Gospel. Part of the expression of black resentment at injustices was found in the independent Churches, which proved to be so potent a phenomenon in most of black Africa. It should on the other hand be noted that many missionaries supported independence movements. Still, there was until the 1960s a feeling of paternalism which was pervasive. Vatican II on the Catholic side, and various revolutionary changes "back home" among Protestants, altered this picture.

The Legacy of Missionary Activity in Black Africa

In a large part of Africa, Catholicism has come to be the majority religion, and not only in territories formerly colonized by, say, France or Portugal. But it is, in most areas, very short of priests. Similarly, Protestant Churches are short of trained people. The result is that much of African Christianity follows on with the use of catechists, as in the days of the missionaries. This has meant that even when the whites were in control at the top, at the bottom things were more fluid and not easy to keep a strict eye on. The strength of the system is that it leaves a lot to the work of the laity, and so it engenders a lot of active piety. Increasingly the leadership has become black, with six African Cardinals. South Africa, with many white Anglicans and Catholics, has black Church leaders, Archbishop Desmond Tutu, of Cape Town, being the best-known example. Such figures have begun to play leading roles in Church policy-making through ecumenical and other global organizations.

Some different strands of thought are evident in these Churches. On the one hand there is a greater interest in Liberation Theology, because of the struggle in South Africa and also elsewhere. More conservatively, there is interest in an African theology, which is the effort to make use of classical African categories in the statement of Christianity (see Chapter 11, pp. 249-54). It is the attempt to see in indigenous ideas something of a forerunner of the Gospel, and so to find in them an alternative or a supplement to the Old Testament. Some make the distinction between African theology and black theology, the latter being a version of Liberation Theology.

Modern Europe

The Challenge of Secular Worldviews

The new knowledge and the new methods of inquiry stimulated by the Enlightenment involved elements which were to prove a threat to Biblically-based Christianity. The use of history in a modern manner to probe the past rather than just to tell a story inevitably began to raise questions about the historical authenticity of the Bible. At the same time, the formation of Evolutionary theory was among the factors in greatly shaking confidence in traditional cosmology (which already had had to be modified in view of Newtonian physics).

The first of these strands in the intellectual challenge to tradition was in part sparked by the highly influential philosophy of Georg Wilhelm Friedrich Hegel (1770–1831). In his view the processes of existence are manifestations of one Absolute Spirit (*Geist*). One of his reasons for this was the breakdown of Kant's compromise. Kant thought that we project categories on the world of experience, but that experience itself is the product, in some sense, of "things in themselves" beyond the phenomena. Critics saw this as a weak point. In Kant's own view, categories could not be applied to that which lies beyond experience, and so one should use neither singular nor plural nor the notion of cause or existence in speaking of the "things in themselves." So

Idealists like Hegel, having scraped away objective reality from behind the world of experience, saw the world as experience.

Hegel's originality lay in seeing the Absolute as dynamic – as working, for instance, through the processes of history. And he saw these as following a logic, which he called the dialectic: a notion of profound influence on Karl Marx and so on the world. In history, according to Hegel's view, one movement (the thesis) is faced with its opposite (the antithesis); in the conflict between the two a synthesis is formed. This synthesis then becomes the thesis, which stimulates its own antithesis and a new synthesis; and so on.

Different religions are popular, imaginative, and intuitive ways in which human beings have tried to grasp the Absolute. In Christianity the Absolute is thought of as achieving self-consciousness. Ferdinand Baur (1792–1860) took up Hegel's dialectical view and saw Jesus as thesis, Paul as antithesis and Catholicism as synthesis. All this was a speculative trend, but stimulated much historical enquiry into the actualities of what we could know about Jesus. From this arose the great industry of modern critical scholarship directed at the New Testament and at the earliest Christianity. Such an industry flourished especially in the nineteenth century, in the Protestant faculties in German universities, and from there spread to Britain, the United States, and elsewhere.

Once the Bible was treated not as authority but as evidence, not as holy writ but as historical material, not as evidently true but as often woven together from theological desires and oral traditions, it lost its old authoritative force. This presented a clear crisis for the Churches.

This crisis was deepened by the publication of the Evolutionary theory of Charles Darwin (1809–82), published in 1859 in his book *The Origin of Species*. If Christians had before accepted physics, it was only because a sharp line was drawn between it and the study of living things. It seemed a great shock to Victorians (both to many scientists and to many but by no means all Church people) to think of humanity as descending from apes. Hitherto, animals had often been seen in a poor moral light, as witness the use of such words as "brutish," "beastly," and so on. Besides, Holy Scripture spoke of the direct creation by God of the species, not their slow and hungry evolution as Darwin proposed. Moreover it seemed that some of the strongest arguments people had had for belief in a good God were undercut by the theory – particularly the so-called argument from design. Now "survival of the fittest" could explain the cunning anatomy of the eye and the delicate artistry of the spider, without needing to evoke an all-seeing Creator.

History and Evolution – these ideas and much else besides called in question the literal accuracy and truth of the Bible. Adam and Eve would disappear among the monkeys. Jesus' sharp outline would melt behind the hot uncertainties of historical scholarship. Little could be depended on absolutely, and much of what was orthodox belief might have to be hedged with maybes. Was science becoming a cuckoo in the nest of theism? Was scholarship taking the backbone out of believers?

The doctrinal dimension: *Punch* here laughs at Darwin's evolutionary theory, often seen to be in conflict with Christian and Biblical orthodoxy.

Another, quite different, challenge was the uprooting of society which the new Industrial Revolution presented. Men and women flocked into sordid cities, where they were enslaved to great machines and tyrannized by clocks. If some turned to gin and prostitution it was not surprising. Meanwhile the country parish system crumbled, designed for a different age and another kind of life. So the established Churches everywhere felt themselves weakened, even though in England, for instance, Methodism was very active in the industrial era and there were gallant attempts to reshape religious organization toward the needs of the new society.

These three examples stand for all those forces of scholarship and philosophy, of scientific inquiry, and of social challenge that met Christianity in the Europe of the nineteenth century.

One response to all this was to embrace it. The quest for the historical Jesus and the new discoveries of science might weaken confidence in the literal truth of the Bible – but so what? It did not need to be either a textbook of history or a manual of biology. Science has to do with this world, while religion deals with this world seen in the light of the next world. Religion sees tigers and planets lit by the light of God and seen in the eye of faith. And the Bible is about the actions of God but is not itself a guaranteed recording of them. Moreover, Evolution is good news. It hints at how we have risen from earlier stalkings and screams in the undergrowth to our present moral stature: and in that elevation of humankind religion – above all, so the argument goes, the Christian religion – has played a crucial part. As for the sorrows of capitalism, yes, they should be mitigated: but human invention and energy are already fashioning a brighter world. We should be optimistic at rising toward the Kingdom.

In many ways the greatest of all exponents of this nineteenth-century liberal Protestantism was Adolf von Harnack (1851–1930). He saw Luther as having only partially reformed Christianity, freeing it of ritualism, hierarchy, and so on, but keeping the dogma uncritically in place. We need, in Harnack's view, a historically anchored faith which looks to the Gospel of Christ. We need a faith which stresses the love of God the Father, which we can experience, and the love of one's neighbor by the help of God's grace, but which takes a critical view of Christian tradition.

Another response, which I will describe more in detail when dealing with Christianity in North America, is to deny the force of liberalism and to go on affirming the literal truth of the Bible in the teeth of scientific skepticism. This fundamentalism often combined with a fervent evangelical zeal, and remained a dynamic force in the Christian tradition. Yet another response was to bolster the strength of faith by emphasizing the importance of the organization of the Church. Within Protestantism this kind of move occurred in effect as the Oxford Movement. This underlined the vitality of Catholic ritual within the Church of England, and revived high theories of the sacred authority of the Church – but some of its adherents, most notably John Henry Newman (1801–90), crossed over into the Church of Rome. This revival had its effects very much in the ritual dimension and material aspect of Anglicanism, being a stimulus to the revival of Gothic architecture in the large church building and rebuilding program undertaken for the expanding population of Victorian England. The Pre-Raphaelite movement in art helped, too, to present a revitalized late medieval style of religious painting.

But more important than all this was the reaffirmation of Roman Catholic Church authority, partly through the Council known as Vatican I, held in Rome in 1870. This Council asserted the principle of the infallibility of the Pope in matters of doctrine and ethics when he speaks *ex cathedra*, literally "from the throne," that is, in his sacred and official capacity. It was also reaffirmed through the crackdown in 1907 on what was called Catholic Modernism. A number of writers and theologians were exploring the liberal approaches which had had such impact on Protestantism. Biblical scholarship in the Catholic tradition, and certain philosophical lines of reasoning, were greatly restricted. This attempt to trammel the members of the Church was in the long run bound to end in failure, but it held the line until the Council known as Vatican II (1962–65), summoned by Pope John XXIII (1881–1963).

As to the challenge of the new social world, some Christians in Europe responded by adopting a version of Christian socialism. In Britain the Labour movement, with its trade union affiliations and leanings toward a socialist solution to economic problems, was greatly permeated by the spirit of the nonconformist Protestant denominations, such as Methodists and Baptists. Indeed, Methodism had been in the vanguard of social action from the early part of the nineteenth century. In the United States the movement known as the Social Gospel was important, and we shall come to that later (p. 160).

New Ideologies as Alternatives to Religion

Of all the new thoughts which were produced in the nineteenth century the set which had the greatest impact on the world was Marxism. It became the ideology of revolutionary groups who identified the troubles of the world with the capitalist system itself. Karl Marx (1818–83) had early in his career fallen under the influence of Hegel, but he took Hegelian categories in very different directions. After editing radical journals in Germany and Paris, he settled in the more tolerant atmosphere of London, in a year of great revolutionary activity in Europe, 1848. There in great poverty he wrote prolifically, helped financially by his rich friend Friedrich Engels (1820–95), and engaged in revolutionary organization.

His, and Engels', philosophy was materialist, as distinguished from the idealism of Hegel. The dialectic of history was to be seen in differing economic systems in collision and contradiction. Capitalism itself contained contradictions, because the interests of the bourgeoisie who owned the means of production demanded that they exploit the workers – their profits came out of the extra value imparted to materials by labor. Class conflict was bound to intensify, held Marx, and would lead to a revolution, then to the so-called dictatorship of the proletariat, and then to the establishment of a

The iconography of the Russian Revolution and its aftermath: Marx, Engels, Lenin, and Stalin.

classless society. It was a fine vision, backed with impressive economic evidence and theory, and gave confidence to revolutionaries, who were on the side of history. It was itself a form of secular prophecy, having some of the flavor of Messianism.

As to religion, that, to Marx, was a byproduct of the socioeconomic situation and a symptom of alienation. It was the cry of the oppressed and the opium of the people. The exposure of religion was the first intellectual task of all, and in his famous *Theses on Feuerbach* Marx showed his indebtedness to Ludwig Feuerbach (1804–72), another follower and critic of Hegel. Feuerback saw God as being a projection, by us, of essential human attributes such as reason and love. Marx took this "projectionist" strand and gave it an economic interpretation. It may be noted that projectionism – the theory that God and other supernatural entities are projected onto reality by human beings – is a powerful ingredient in modern thought, appearing in a different form in the thought of Sigmund Freud (1856–1939).

In many ways, Marxism itself was a worldview with a religious flavor, not directed toward a higher world but toward the transformation of this. For *doctrines* it had the writings of Marx, Engels, V. I. Lenin (1870–1924), and others. For *myth* it had the pulsating rhythm of history culminating in the earthly paradise of a classless society. For *ethics* it had the ceaseless pursuit of social justice and the maintenance of class struggle. For *practice* it had the need to realize theories concretely, in revolutionary activity. For *experience* it had the nurturing of ardor and of hatred toward class enemies. For *organization* it had the various Communist parties. When it became the official doctrine of various countries, these religious features were to be much accentuated.

Not all Marxists were Communists. There was also a more moderate strand of Marxian socialism which became important in Europe and elsewhere, and which tried to combine Marxism with a liberal-democratic idea of the state. For Marx himself had been skeptical of the importance of law and other means of preserving political rights. He despised some of the creations of the bourgeoisie as shams, and so the ideal of individual freedom did not, in a political sense at least, figure largely in his thinking. As it transpired, virtually all the Communist parties turned out to be totalitarian in outlook. Democratic socialism with Marxist ingredients was, however, an alternative option.

The rise of Marxism in the late nineteenth century stimulated some responses from Christians, probably the most notable being the Encyclical letter to the Church entitled *Rerum novarum* ("Of new things"), issued by Pope Leo XIII (1810–1903) in 1891. Leo had earlier condemned socialism as a plague, but he recognized that in the industrial age new forms of organization were necessary. In the Encyclical he laid the theoretical basis for the formation of Catholic labor unions and ultimately of Catholic political parties committed to democratic forms. He had also been prominent in the reform of Catholic education, and in his *Aeterni Patris* (1879) had made a revived form of Aquinas' thought, called Neo-Thomism, virtually mandatory for Catholic thinkers. As it happened, this was not a strong enough system to challenge easily the growing power of Marxist and secular thought on European intellectuals. Indeed, among European intellectuals in the early twentieth century, Christianity was no longer a predominant belief.

Various forms of secular ideology were influential. There were those who thought that Marxism was not based enough in realities and was too speculative. A more liberal and democratic way of thinking, such as the thought of Bertrand Russell (1872–1970), a kind of empiricism with humanist ethical values, was attractive to many. Russell was a notable representative of scientific humanism, which sees humanity as the highest value, love of fellow humans as the highest ethic, and science as the best way of relating to the cosmos. Humanism was an alternative to religion in the West. It was and is atheistic, though some humanists prefer to use the word "agnosticism" to characterize their position, meaning the lack of knowledge and evidence one way or another to assert or deny the existence of God. Later, humanism was given a more personalist tone and a grounding in dramatic human choice in the atheistic Existentialism of Jean-Paul Sartre (1905–80) and others. A form of scientific humanism came to dominate English-speaking philosophy under the influence of scientific empiricism and language analysis.

Partly under the influence of Hegel, who saw the state as a kind of incarnation of the Absolute Mind, right-wing ideologies appeared, which were hostile both to the liberal ideals of the Center and the revolutionary impulses of the Left. In Italy there was Fascism, espousing a corporate state which organized professional, union, and industrial life in the service of nationalist expansion and a return to the glories of the Roman empire, under Benito Mussolini (1883–1945). More serious and more devastating still was the Nazi ideology. This hypernationalist program presented an assertion of

German and "Aryan" superiority, and a plan for conquest and the elimination of inferiors, notably Jews. Though Fascism in Italy could live on reasonable terms with Catholicism, in Germany the Nazi ideology had a religious (and anti-Christian) character of its own. The parades, the Hitler salute, the uniforms, the flags, all gave it a strong *ritual* element. The *emotions* of being saved through the leader in the restoration of a fallen Germany were strong. Though its *doctrinal* and theoretical bases were weak, the *myth* of Aryan Germany was a powerful one. And the idea of the Thousand-Year Reich was a beguiling prophecy. The role of the Führer was religious too. Here was the plain German who had fought in World War I, now ready to transcend aristocrats and generals and lead the nation on the warpath (never mind that he was an Austrian!). Though Fascism and Nazism scarcely survived the death of their leaders, much the same tendencies can coalesce into the modern right-wing dictatorship, often military. Sometimes these tyrannies are in alliance with and sometimes in conflict with the churches.

Christianity in Twentieth-century Europe

The destiny of the religions was considerably affected by the secular ideologies which functioned as alternatives. In Russia, the Revolution of 1917 brought the Church into a new captivity. World War I, with its devastating power to kill mass armies, saw the collapse of that optimism which had been one ingredient of liberal Protestantism. The rise of Fascism in Italy tempted the Catholic Church into a new deal or concordat with the Italian state in 1929. This gave the Catholics certain rights over education and marriage law and the like. The rise of Nazism posed dilemmas for the German Churches, and brought agony to the Jews. Secular humanism came to be the prevailing ethos in most parts of Scandinavia and was strong in Britain. World War II, often thought of by the Western Allies as a struggle between good and evil, mobilized Christians on both sides, as usual, and ended with the extension of Stalin's Communist empire into Central Europe. The Spanish Civil War of 1936–39 saw bitter anticlericalism at work. Altogether the period up to and indeed beyond World War II was an unhappy one for the major religions, and for Judaism it was a catastrophe.

Two significant books were published in 1917 and left their imprint on the European religious scene. One was by Karl Barth (1886–1968), and was his commentary on the Epistle of Paul to the Romans. It heralded the production of his major work, *Church Dogmatics*. It was a statement of Protestant theology which cut against the optimistic liberalism dying along the Western Front. It kept to modern canons of scholarship but from a conservative angle. For him the "Christ-event," rather than the words of scripture as such, constituted the revelation. But he kept strongly to Paul's notion of grace, and restated this in a way which rejected all forms of natural theology. Only by revelation do we know anything of God. It was a hard-line position which made Christian revelation discontinuous with all other religious ideas and teachings. These were, just as Feuerbach had said, a mere projection of human concerns. Christianity has value only as the response of people to the revelation in Christ. This dogmatic position, narrow and nonrational, had great influence between the Wars both among Christians of the liberal wing and in the mission field. Its prestige was enhanced because Barth stood up against the Nazis and, with other members of the so-called Confessing Church which resisted Hitler, signed what became known as the Barmen Declaration of 1934.

The other book was Rudolf Otto's *The Idea of the Holy*. Otto (1869–1937) saw in the Holy the key category of religion and analyzed the experience of the Holy as spiritual, a mystery that both awes and fascinates. In so basing his philosophy of religion on a kind of experience, Otto revitalized an older tradition, but he did so very much in the context of the comparative study of religions. By the 1970s and 1980s, Christian theologians had at last begun to see with clarity that other religious traditions in the world represent a genuine challenge to old-fashioned theology and need to be taken seriously. The imperial age had not been without its fine Christian scholars who studied other religions, but the main tenor was of European and Christian cultural superiority. Otto, as one of the revitalizers of the comparative study of religion, was an important figure. It turns out that his emphasis on the spiritual is good in characterizing the feel of various kinds of theism, where God is the Other. It works less well, however, in characterizing non-theistic mystical experience, especially Buddhist. So we need to think of more than one basic type of religious experience. But that does not invalidate the approach which Otto was pioneering.

The Updating of Catholicism

Among the Christian Churches of Europe probably the most vital events since World War II have been those connected with the Ecumenical Movement – the founding of the World Council of Churches in 1948 – and the reforming Council, Vatican II (1962–5), which led to radical changes in Roman Catholic thinking and practice.

In *doctrine*, Vatican II saw the melting away of Neo-Thomism. In matters of *narrative* the winds of Protestant scholarship were allowed to riffle the pages of the Bible. In *ritual* the Latin tradition was abandoned and the Mass was simplified and translated into the vernacular languages of the world. In *ethics* a more open attitude prevailed, and renewed concern for the poor. In *experience* new experiments with devotion and charismatic ecstasies were initiated. In *organization* the Church was somewhat democratized. In architecture and the *arts* new forces of modernity were released. Ecumenically, the Roman Catholics became much less reserved, and now play a vital role in initiatives of Christian cooperation.

In short, Vatican II represented a vast source of change. For John XXIII it was an act of *aggiornamento* or "updating" the Church. Large numbers of priests and monks and nuns, however, about this time began to leave their vocations, though most remained loyal Catholics. New forces of rebellion were released in the Church, which consequently became highly dynamic and not always obedient to the dictates from the Vatican. A notable example is birth control, where many Catholics simply disregarded papal pronouncements against the use of artificial methods.

In postwar Europe there has been another force affecting the practice of Christianity. The fact that Church authority is largely unenforceable in pluralistic communities has led to a wide proliferation of new religious movements. Christianity and Judaism have also come face to face with other world religions on what they had come to regard as home territory. Many adherents of Islam, for instance, have come to work in Western countries, so that it is the third largest denomination in Britain. Young people have found much in Buddhism, in Hindu movements, and in new experiments in living. With the added fact that the majority in virtually all Western European countries are non-practicing and many of them reject traditional Christianity, there now exists a much more fluid picture of belief in Europe.

Reflections on Modern Europe

It may be noted that in Europe, more or less continuously from the reign of Constantine the Great until this modern period, Christianity in one form or another has had official status. It is now, for the European populations, more or less a voluntary matter. There is thus a new weakness and a new vitality in religion. The weakness is that the Churches appear statistically in decline – the strength is that voluntary religion is deeper than conforming religion. Further, we note that since the various postwar economic revivals – German, Italian, British, and so on – Western Europe is a consumerist entity. Choices have rarely been so abundant. And something similar is beginning to happen in religion; a kind of consumerism, with many new varieties being added as cultures cross and merge. Poverty remains, but more at the margin in the West. Therefore, Christianity looks increasingly to the global village to fulfill its role of serving the poor.

Oddly, though, despite the multiplications of new sects and religious movements, the currents of mainstream Christianity have greatly converged. The differences of *ritual*, for instance, have been greatly moderated since Vatican II and among the Protestant denominations. Nor are there quite such acute divergences of *doctrine*. Only perhaps on the *mythic* side is there acute division. Those who take the Bible more or less literally form a conservative movement cutting across denominations, and there is a corresponding movement of more liberal Christians who likewise have similar interpretations of the Bible. There are differences in *ethical* stance, for example over abortion, but somewhat at the edges. Martin Luther King, John Paul II, Mother Teresa, Allan Boesak, Archbishop Robert Runcie of Canterbury (now succeeded by George Carey), although of quite different historic pasts, have gained wide Christian recognition in this ecumenical age. But the center of Christianity has already moved southward from Europe, into Africa and Latin America and, in general, the so-called Third World.

CHAPTER 8

The Christianities of North America

A New Pluralism

The Christianities of North America, and particularly of the United States, have pioneered a number of new forms and circumstances. For instance, the division of Church and state in the American constitution was a novelty in its day, largely unprecedented at least among European nations. Again, it was in North America that some of the most vigorous revivalist movements of modern Christianity occurred. There are also religions born in North America, like the Mormons and Christian Science. Roman Catholicism and Eastern Orthodox Christianity had to take on a rather different flavor in the New World. And it was in America that the modern forms of Judaism were most extensively developed and in some cases created. Side by side with all this, we must contemplate the fate of the Native Americans. Their populations were greatly diminished by European diseases and bullets and their cultures greatly subverted.

North America is also vital for the history of modern religion because it demonstrates the ways in which great immigrations and a melting-pot of cultures affect traditions. All these facets of American religion give it great vigor. Very often the migrants became much more committed to their faith than they would have been had they stayed at home. This sometimes makes it difficult for Americans to appreciate the degree of religious secularization which has occurred in parts of Europe, especially the North.

In the twentieth century, too, North America has seen experiments in living, mainly from the late 1960s on, which have multiplied options and incorporated some Eastern religions into Western patterns of life. It has also had the vigor of black religion to refresh it, and this has incorporated Islamic elements, as well as the strongly emotional faith of evangelical Protestantism. In addition there has been migration, especially from the Far East, which has brought Chinese and Japanese, later Korean and Vietnamese, Buddhism (and other concomitant religious forms such as Taoism and Confucianism) into the North American picture, especially in California.

There are differing periods for us to look at. First there is the colonial period up to Independence; then there is the initial period of United States religion up to the mid part of the nineteenth century; then the period of rapid immigration, the opening up of the frontier and the Civil War; then there is the twentieth century. In Canada, roughly the same framework will work, since similar conditions prevailed, though without slavery.

The Religious Affairs of the Colonies

In the settlement of North America, Britain predominated along the eastern seaboard, especially after the fall of New Amsterdam to Britain, as New York, in 1664. The more southern colonies, notably Virginia and the Carolinas, were settled in principle by members of the Church of England. By contrast the more northern colonies, Massachusetts, Connecticut, Rhode Island, Pennsylvania, and west New Jersey, had a predominantly dissenting character.

The most famous landfall was that of the *Mayflower* at Plymouth Rock in Massachusetts in 1620. The New England colonies provided a refuge from persecution and social disadvantage in England and a focus for new religious aspirations to found a "City upon a Hill," a new Zion. The Puritans of New England did not necessarily extend to their members the rights of religious toleration. A new conformism became apparent in the colonies, which were substantially self-governing. New theocracies were built. However, some notable exceptions to this were not long in appearing.

One was the Rhode Island colony founded primarily by Roger Williams (1603–83). He was in his beliefs a Calvinist; but he was most vigorous for the separation of Church and state. He joined the Baptists, as conforming best to what he expected of a Christian group, and founded the first Baptist church in America, in Providence. He eventually secured a permanent charter for the new colony, of which he was president for three years, and there freedom of religion was assured. In retrospect he has been seen as a great pioneer of separatism and a forerunner of the later First Amendment of the Constitution, passed in 1791: "Congress shall make no law respecting an

The narrative dimension: the Puritan migration to New England has entered powerfully into the story of America's history. Puritans are seen here illustrating a ballad celebrating the Independents' voyage to New England, a journey from persecution, shown on the left, to a new life, shown on the right.

THE CHRISTIANITIES OF NORTH AMERICA

establishment of religion or prohibiting the free exercise thereof."

The Quaker colonies of west New Jersey and Pennsylvania also incorporated religious toleration. William Penn (1644–1718) played a leading part in efforts to secure the passing of the English Act of Toleration after the so-called Glorious Revolution of 1688. In Pennsylvania there were ethical restrictions imposed, such as the rejection of forts and armaments – the Quakers were pacifists – and the outlawing of slavery. Incidentally, full rights were accorded the Delaware Indians. So religious dissent had an important political message. This stemmed from the thinking of George Fox (1624–91). The movement which he founded, the Society of Friends, nicknamed Quakers, looked to inner experience and the "light that lights every person" as the source of true religion, and conscience as the source of true morality. They simplified worship to the meeting in which people awaited inspiration before speaking or leading the group in prayers. Their meeting houses were of the simplest. They were pacifists, and accorded each person equal dignity. It was the recognition of Christ in every person that took them on the path to a fine egalitarianism, which naturally extended to slaves and Native Americans. They became an important strand in Puritan thinking in America, but only in the very earliest days of the Pennsylvania colony did they have a majority role. For the most part, they have been a relatively minor group, though influential beyond their numbers. Both Quakers and Roger Williams made a point of friendship with the "Indians," in often bleak contrast to other white–Native American relationships.

Many of the New England Puritans were Congregationalists in their organization. Someone has referred to Congregationalists as decentralized Calvinists. Their government was through independent congregations, as the name implies, and they rejected the more complex and centralized Presbyterian system, for the most part (Presbyterianism was stronger to the south in the Middle Atlantic States). In their thinking they were often millenarian, and they saw a special destiny in the New England dream of a purified faith. Thus, Cotton Mather (1663–1728), famous son of Harvard and Boston preacher, defended the fusion of Church and state because he saw a redemptive role for society in New England. In this he followed his father Increase (1629–1723) – wonderful, these Puritan names! – who thought of New England as a place for the final consummation of the work of the Reformation. Cotton Mather thought that the Second Coming of Christ might take place in his time and in New England. Such shining hope and the feeling of a special destiny for the American colonies was to carry over into the optimism and sense of chosenness in the Republic.

Early on, the Congregationalists had paid good attention to education, founding Harvard in 1637 and Yale and other colleges a bit later. As a result America had much more investment in higher education than England, which till the early nineteenth century had only the two universities of Oxford and Cambridge. But though intellect was important in colonial American religion, the heart was, too.

The Great Awakening of the eighteenth century was a formidable revival, the first in a cycle to influence and stimulate American piety. Its onset in 1734 was experienced in the church of Jonathan Edwards (1703–58), perhaps America's greatest theologian, in Northampton, Massachusetts. The movement was passionate and charismatic, and was further spurred on by the preaching of George Whitefield (1714–70), English preacher and itinerant revivalist. His sermons were marked by great enthusiasm up and down the Atlantic Coast. He was looked at askance by the Anglican Establishment, though ordained a priest, but got a good reception from Congregationalists, Presbyterians, Reformed, and Baptists. Among other causes which he espoused was the opening of Dartmouth College in New Hampshire to Native Americans.

The Baptists benefited from the Great Awakening, for it made some of their doctrines and practices more relevant. Their separatism (that is, their rejection of an established Church) was made meaningful in an enthusiasm

A Mennonite assembly in America: note the simplicity of the meeting house and the prominence of the pulpit.

155

which saw true Christianity in the fruits of religious experience rather than conformity to orthodoxy. In addition, their itinerant mode of preaching was something which now became normal. They began to make great advances, and from that base were to be very effective as the frontier moved over the Alleghenies and into the wide beyond. More complex, established Churches found it hard to follow the shifting populations.

Moreover, the Baptists, with their warm and charismatic appeal and preference for conversion-experiences, had a special appeal to the blacks. For by the mid-eighteenth century there were already over 100,000 slaves in the South. The Baptists were on their way to becoming the largest religious denomination in America. In advocating adult baptism they followed the Anabaptist principle (see page 125).

Another important strand in American Protestantism was beginning to grow just before and during the period of the Revolution. It was Methodism, so called from the notion that one should live according to a "method" laid down in the Bible. This movement had started, through the work of John Wesley (1703–91), as a means of revitalizing the Church of England. But Wesley was much influenced by the Moravians, a mainly German group stemming from the work of John Hus (1369?–1415), the Czech reformer. Eighteenth-century Pietism, a warm devotionalism associated with the leader Count Zinzendorf (1700–60), also provided strong inspiration. Their warm feeling for Christ was appealing to Wesley. The Methodist movement was enhanced by the great hymns composed by Charles Wesley (1708–88), and was to make important strides in postcolonial America.

Mingled with emotionally oriented religion and the Puritan ethos were ideas derived from the Enlightenment – anticlerical Freemasonry, deism, feeling for the rights of man, and commitment to toleration. All these found their fulfillment, as far as religious organization went, in the First Amendment, which made a vital statement about the meaning of the American Revolution. So it was that Anglicanism re-formed itself, no longer as an Established Church, but as the Protestant Episcopal Church of the United States. In Virginia its endowments were lost, and many clergy left for Canada and the Bahamas. Nevertheless a vigorous Anglican tradition survived. The first American bishop, Samuel Seabury of Connecticut (1729–97) was consecrated by Scottish Episcopal bishops, who had no established status. Indeed, they were regarded at the time as being in schism with the Church of England.

Roman Catholics in Colonial North America

The most important area for Catholicism was not in the British colonies but in Quebec. There the Church became, in part, a sign of ethnic identity, especially after the fall of Quebec to the British in 1759 during the Seven Years' War, a disaster for the French. The Quebec Act of 1774, however, granted full citizenship to Catholics and allowed the Church to maintain its tithing system. The province was brought into the colony of Canada.

The position of Catholics in the British colonies to the south was much less favorable. Maryland had in principle been a colony for English Catholics, but a Puritan majority in the colony repealed the Act of Toleration in 1664, and Catholics were deprived of voting rights. Similar deprivation occurred in Rhode Island and Connecticut.

It was during the nineteenth century that American Catholicism made vast progress, because of the large numbers of migrants from Ireland, Italy, Poland, and other European countries with strong Catholic populations. We will come to that shortly.

The American Revolution and Beyond

The opening-up of the frontier into Kentucky, Ohio, and elsewhere beyond the Alleghenies had begun in earnest. In the new optimism of the young Republic a Second Great Awakening occurred at the turn of the century, with revival meetings in tents along the areas of new occupation. The mobile folk who were opening up American farmland were susceptible to evangelical fervor. So it was that the warmest type of preaching and religion – Baptists, Methodists, Congregationalists – made the greatest impression.

Meanwhile, in New England, there was a shift among many Congregationalists toward Unitarianism, which took over many of the beautiful churches of the area. This move into the Unitarian persuasion was in no small part due to the influence of William Ellery Channing (1780–1842), of Boston. His sermon on Unitarian Christianity in 1819 summed up what many already thought – that Christ, though morally perfect, was nevertheless subordinate to God. It was like the old Arian position (see p. 101), which made Christ noneternal, being himself created by God. It rejected the fullblown version of the Trinity doctrine which had been the hallmark of Christian orthodoxy. Unitarianism was to make strong advances among the educated elite of the period and the area.

It also had a frontier with the movement known as Transcendentalism, associated above all with Ralph Waldo Emerson (1803–82) and Henry David Thoreau (1817–62). Transcendentalism as a view emphasizes the presence of the divine in Nature, and the need of the individual to be true to himself and to work in harmony with Nature. It has affinities to Taoism and some aspects of the Hindu tradition, by which Emerson was somewhat influenced. Transcendentalism helped to stimulate interest in the comparative study of religions, and was one of the factors lying behind the famous World's Parliament of Religions in Chicago, 1893. It also had an influence on Christian Science.

It was in the first part of the nineteenth century that the first important homegrown American religion was created, by the prophet Joseph Smith II (1805–44), from upper New York State. Stimulated by visionary experiences and guided, he said, by an angel, he discovered at the Hill Cumorah some gold plates which he translated as *The Book of Mormon*. This claims to give

Brigham Young, the great Mormon leader.

the story of some of the peoples of North America before Columbus, some of whom were ancestors of the Native Americans, and who were migrants from the Lost Tribes of Israel. In 1830 the Church of Jesus Christ of the Latter-Day Saints was formed (the full name dates from 1838). The story of this new movement was tremendous. Smith and his followers moved to Kirtland, Ohio, and then further west, eventually setting up a fine city with its own temple in Nauvoo, Illinois. Near there, at Carthage, Joseph Smith and his brother Hiram were murdered in 1844. Their new theocracy was becoming too powerful, and some of the new teachings and practices (including polygamy) were scandalous to outsiders. Brigham Young (1801–77) led the main body of the Mormons, as they were nicknamed, to Salt Lake City in Utah. He set about establishing an empire there, the State of Deseret. But Congressional unease and pressure led eventually to the incorporation of Utah into the United States, with theocracy and polygamy abandoned, at least among mainstream adherents. Many converts, especially from Britain, went out on the hard trail to Utah. Mormon cohesiveness, puritanism, and family values had a strong appeal. Some of the doctrines – that God is material, that there are many Gods, and that human beings may become Gods – have been modified. In many ways, in fact, Mormonism is now a conforming evangelical kind of Protestantism, with the colorful additions of the *Book of Mormon* and the charismatic memory of the genial and masterful Joseph Smith.

The Effects of Mass Immigration

In the second half of the nineteenth century the processes of settlement and industrialization speeded up. This sucked into America large numbers of immigrants, many of whom were Catholic and Jewish, foreign to the prevailing Protestant ethos. Both groups were regarded with some suspicion. But up to the period of World War I these groups made their fundamental adjustments to the New World.

For Catholics the question was a double one of integration. On the one hand, how were the masses of immigrants of different nations to live together in one Church? There were Irish and Poles, Hungarians and Italians, Germans and Mexicans, to be blended together. On the other hand, how was Catholicism to be woven into the fabric of American life? The key to both of these operations was education, and Catholicism paid a great deal of attention to it. There evolved a system of parish schools and Catholic colleges and universities which made the transition into American life feasible without the loss of religious tradition. Such schools could weld together Catholics of various ethnic groups, and provide the skills necessary to give Catholics entry into many professions and crafts. Part of the task, too, was showing others that Catholicism was in no way disloyal to the American heritage. By prominence in games, such as American football, in cultural life, and appropriately in politics, Catholics could demonstrate their all-American character. The Church devoted most of its energies to social affairs, to building churches (most extensively and floridly), and to education. Catholic Orders were prominent; many engaged in these social and educational tasks.

For Protestantism the immigration brought North Europeans, especially Swedes, other Scandinavians, and Germans. All this added up to Lutheranism, which became especially strong in the Midwest and often provided a bridge between the national culture and the New World. In Canada a similar process of migration brought in many Scots and Northern Irish Protestants, as well as Germans and others. This gave its own flavor to the Protestant heritage in Canada, which became very strongly Presbyterian.

The period saw new chances for black religions to flourish, for the Civil War ensured that blacks would gain emancipation. Churches which had existed before now blossomed out. Moreover, Churches were about the only sphere in which blacks could be in control. Already in 1816 there had been formed an African Methodist Episcopal Church, following the lead of Richard Allen (1760–1831), who had formed the first black Methodist congregation. With emancipation there was a great exodus of blacks from white-controlled denominations to create new organizations for black Baptists and so on. The Reconstruction period saw the foundation of various important black colleges and universities. But it was followed in turn by a darker period of renewed oppression.

One option was to look to migration back to Africa. Freed slaves were settled in Liberia, which became independent in 1847. Africa remained a symbol for black Americans. Bishop Turner (1834–1915), a Methodist, said that it was necessary for black people to have a black God, and that only in Africa could black people exercise their full powers. The idea of a restoration of Africa's past glories by the action of those who had gone through the suffering of slavery was a not uncommon theme. In fact rather few blacks actually returned to Africa. But there was much dynamism in black Christianity, and even more from the time of World War I onward.

The spread of white settlement across the Plains to the far West was an unmitigated disaster for the Native Americans. From early days, the Native American experience of the whites had not been happy. Thus, in 1622 the Pamunkey Algonquians rebelled against their treatment at the hands of the Jamestown settlers in Virginia, and were defeated. With the coming of the whites across the plains and the reduction of the buffalo, various new religious movements emerged, which tried to deal with the problems of the Indians. The Ghost Dance religion of Wodziwob foresaw a time, imminently, when dead Indians would be raised up, the whites would go away, and a new life would begin again. A second wave in 1889 started from Nevada, under Wovoka, and spread across the Plains. Sadly, this culminated in the massacre of Wounded Knee, when Sioux had thought their sacred shirts would render them immune to bullets (a belief found in various parts of the world during the period of colonialism). The Native Americans were shifted, put into reservations, and reduced to a miserable state, ravaged by loss of morale, alcohol, and impotence in the face of white control. Nevertheless revival was on its way, during the twentieth century, with a reassertion of Native American values. To this we shall return in Chapter 9.

Christianity and the Social Gospel

In looking at the latter part of the nineteenth century and the early twentieth, we need to take account of the movement often labeled the Social Gospel. This was one of the major ways in which Protestantism addressed itself to the consequences of capitalism and the problems of modern urban life. It was stimulated chiefly by the work and thought of Walter Rauschenbusch (1861–1918), who worked in the Second German Baptist Church in New York for over a decade and was able to experience the sufferings of those who toiled at the bottom of the urban heap. The Churches were less fitted for the large modern city than for the easier integration of small-town life. In addition, Protestant Christianity often allied itself with social democratic movements.

More New Religions

In the latter half of the nineteenth century the creation of new forms of religion continued. Three characteristic and important ones are the Seventh-

Day Adventists, the Jehovah's Witnesses, and Christian Science – in the first and last of these, women played a crucial role. The Adventists were built up by Ellen Gould White (1826–1915) and her husband James. They arose from the disappointment of a prediction made by the Adventist group founded by William Miller (1781–1849), that Christ would come on October 22, 1844. Some time later, Ellen White, who had been injured by a rock thrown at her head when a child, and had been unconscious for weeks, had a vision. This taught her that the Sabbath, as the Bible says, is on the seventh day, namely Saturday, and that indeed a new era of judgment had started on October 22, 1844. As a result, she and her husband became the central figures in the creation of the Seventh-Day Adventist Church, which steadily grew. It also adopted health methods dictated by Ellen White's visions. After her husband's death she became matriarch of the group, and her theology shifted more toward an emphasis on grace, bringing the Adventists closer to mainstream evangelical Christianity. Her life, with its vision and its near-death experience, exhibited, in very modern form, themes of shamanism.

The Jehovah's Witnesses stem from the teachings of Charles Taze Russell (1852–1916) and of his dynamic successor Joseph Franklin Rutherford (1870–1942). Their name springs from the conviction that Jehovah is the proper Biblical name for God. They look forward to a wondrous restoration of the earth and the salvation of 144,000 souls who will reign with Christ in heaven. They pray to Jehovah through Christ; but their chief activity is publication and preaching. They consider that since 1914 Satan has been ruling over the world, and so they should not take part in state activities or fighting. For this reason, they are much persecuted for pacifism and insubordination. They forbid priesthood and the like, and refuse blood transfusions, being contrary to Jehovah's laws (Leviticus, 17). They have remained very energetic in mission work, and there is scarcely anyone in the West who has not been approached by them.

Mary Baker Eddy (1821–1900) was a product of New England Puritanism, but rebelled against Calvinist predestinationism. In her search for the truth the most decisive experience occurred to her in 1866, when she miraculously recovered from the consequences of a severe accident while reading an account of one of Christ's healings. She then set about trying to understand the world and the New Testament in the light of this. Nine years later she brought out her *Science and Health with a Key to the Scriptures*. For her God is All, and so matter, considered in itself, is unreal. We can be healed first of sin and then secondarily of sickness by yielding to God's grace or influence, and by seeing the all-pervasiveness of Mind or Spirit. There are echoes of Transcendentalism in her thought. But when she came to preach this message she found a lot of hostility from orthodox Christians. In due course she founded her own Church, and later recognized it as the First Church of Christ Scientist in Boston, in 1892, which serves organizationally as the mother church to all the churches round the world. Again, as with Ellen White, we meet the confluence of healing and the Gospel. In many ways it is a religion which has rediscovered a major aspect of original Christianity. In 1908 she founded *The Christian Science Monitor*, indicating her commitment to education.

These three are, with Mormonism, samples of the new American religions. They reverberate with differing parts of American religious dreams. Mormonism has the sense of moving west to the chosen land, also the sense of being the instruments of God's will, and seeking for a theocracy, alas in a land committed to the First Amendment. The Jehovah's Witnesses testify to the dream that Satan rules – there has often been a feeling of the great struggle between good and evil in the American heart. The Seventh-Day Adventists seek to figure out the end of history. The Christian Scientists look to salvation here and now.

Evangelicals and Fundamentalists

The Rise of Fundamentalism

We have noted already how liberal Protestantism played a dominant rule in Europe. Such liberalism of scholarship could not be far away from the American scene, with its high commitment to education. And yet so much of American religion was tied to the Bible. It was in America, therefore, above all, that the conservative reaction to liberalism took place. This was to be known as fundamentalism, a term derived from a series of pamphlets called *The Fundamentals: A Testimony to the Truth*. These broadsides appeared before World War 1, attacking modernist or liberal views of the Bible and defending "fundamental" doctrines, namely the literal infallibility of the Bible, the Virgin Birth of Christ, the Substitutionary Atonement (Christ's death atones by way of substituting for sinful human beings), the Resurrection of the Body, and the Second Coming. More loosely, fundamentalism means taking the Bible as "literal where possible" (for obviously the Bible itself contains metaphors). More loosely still, the term is applied to a strong antimodernist reaffirmation of any faith, for instance Islam. In the Christian context it is associated with evangelicalism – that is, the belief in the authority of the Bible, the claim that salvation can only come through close personal faith in Christ, the regeneration of spiritual life, typically through some conversion experience, and a transformation of moral life. Means to these ends include typically Bible-reading, prayer, abstention from specified wickedness (such as smoking, drinking, and promiscuity). Fundamentalism tends to be a branch of evangelicalism – not all evangelicals are fundamentalists. But since they all tend toward an authoritative and inerrant Bible, the lines are hard to draw.

In the nineteenth century the emphasis of fundamentalism in America became oriented toward a gloomier view of human nature and destiny through the doctrine of premillennialism. This is the view that Christ will come again after a dark period of strife and war in order to institute the millennium. The alternative, postmillennialism, is more optimistic. Human affairs are improving, and we will establish the millennium on earth before the Second Coming. A powerful figure in the premillennial movement was the great revivalist Dwight L. Moody (1837–99). Most fundamentalist and evangelical revival was involved in promoting personal, individual holiness, but not all. The Salvation Army, founded in 1865, was at the forefront of social work in the big cities of Britain and the United States. The group was organized on military lines, and hoped to save the derelict by setting a caring example to induce them to reform.

The evangelical movement comprised large denominations or parts thereof, such as the Southern Baptists and Missouri Synod Lutheranism, and much black Protestantism. So there were wide sympathies for the more strident affirmations of Biblical inerrancy by tough-minded fundamentalists.

The latter were also influenced by the method of interpreting the Bible called dispensationalism, associated with Dwight L. Moody, and expressed in a relatively scholarly way by C. I. Scofield (1843–1921), who published his *Scofield Reference Bible* in 1909. According to this way of reading the Bible, it refers to a succession of different eras or dispensations – for example the age of innocence at the start of the human story in the Garden of Eden, the dispensation of the Law from Moses to Christ, and so on. Human history nears its end, which will be marked by the Second Coming of Christ, the "rapture" of believers who will be taken up into the sky to meet him, a vast war, the conversion of the Jews, a thousand-year kingdom ruled over by Jesus from Jerusalem, and finally the Last Judgment. This theme is a powerful one for modern fundamentalists.

Twentieth-century Evangelicalism

For many evangelicals in America, the aftermath of World War 1 was disturbing. Already there was a sense that the older evangelical values which they thought were intrinsic to American nationhood were being submerged or swamped. Already the immigration before the War had deeply marked America with the Catholic (not to mention the Jewish) influx. Old bastions of New England Protestantism, such as Massachusetts and Connecticut, now found Catholic majorities in the major cities. The same went for some sizeable Midwest towns, notably Chicago. Then, the immediate ethos of the 1920s was culturally frivolous, or so it seemed. A new pluralism seemed to undermine mainstream values. It was partly in this mood that the nation had decreed Prohibition in 1919. As it turned out, this produced the speakeasy and enhanced the role of the Mafia, and it was done away with by President Franklin D. Roosevelt (1882–1945) after he came to power in 1933. But it was a powerful expression of evangelical values in American society.

Less effective, however, was the challenge to science mounted by the politician William Jennings Bryan (1860–1925). He acted as prosecutor in the famous Scopes trial in Dayton, Tennessee, when a teacher of that name was indicted for teaching Evolutionary theory. Bryan's position attracted much ridicule in the world press, and shortly after the trial, as it happened, he died.

The ritual dimension: an important ingredient in the proselytizing of the frontier was the evangelical meeting, here seen in modern form.

Periodically, to this day, there are similar legal challenges to the teaching of biology and of pluralist values in the public schools. Part of the problem lies in the dogmatic epistemology (or theory of knowledge) of the fundamentalists. They dismiss the idea that there might be legitimate alternatives to the interpretations that they place on the Bible – or indeed genuine alternatives to the Bible itself. This leaves a tension between their Christianity and the essentially pluralistic character of the American Constitution and way of doing things.

Fundamentalism withdrew into a period of regroupment in the 1930s. But evangelical religon remained a great dynamic, especially among blacks. It was out of this milieu that there came the most important Christian leader in the United States in the twentieth century. This was Martin Luther King (1929–68). Raised in Atlanta, and educated at Morehouse College and Boston University, he was influenced by Walter Rauschenbusch and sociological reading, by Thoreau and his line on civil disobedience, and by Gandhi. In Montgomery, Alabama, he led a bus boycott and in other ways campaigned nonviolently for civil rights, helping to alleviate the condition of Southern blacks, especially in education. He was assassinated in 1968. His was a liberal evangelical position, influenced by a touch of the Hindu tradition.

The more ecumenical wing of evangelical revivalism was represented by Billy Graham, a highly successful preacher and crusader, who opened out his campaigns to cooperation with all the mainstream Churches. But it was to be the arrival of television which created the most prominent type of preaching – the TV evangelism of such as Jerry Falwell, Oral Roberts, and Robert Schuller of the Crystal Cathedral in Anaheim. The last of these is really rather removed from mainstream evangelical preaching, stressing the credo of the power of positive thinking in a vaguely Presbyterian setting. The others, though, have a fundamentalist background, and it was in part the resources of TV ministry which powered the revival of the religious Right in the late 1970s. It was in 1979 that Falwell formed the movement known as the Moral Majority, and in this and other ways evangelicals entered strongly into the political process. President Jimmy Carter helped to make evangelicalism in general fashionable. But whereas he and other liberal evangelicals were not opposed to some fundamentalist legislation in the 1970s, the Moral Majority saw the times as decadent. Old American values were being attacked. There were Equal Rights, whittling away at the traditional family role of women; legalization of homosexuality; legalized abortion; new religious movements and cults; defeat in the Vietnam War (1965–73 for the United States); and Watergate. Since the new campaigning appealed to conservative ethical values, it combined easily with patriotism and attracted alliances with the Roman Catholics – which would have been unthinkable in the 1920s.

Dimensions of Evangelical and Fundamentalist Christianity

The Narrative Dimension

The stress is of course on the Bible – the story of Eden, Israel, Christ, and the coming of the Spirit. This vivid narrative can be arranged for interpretive purposes as a series of dispensations. There is division about the future story between those who look to Christ's coming as before or after the great harmonious and victorious period, the thousand years or millennium. The threat to their story posed by liberal or modernist readings of the Bible, and by such theories as Evolution, leads them to take a strong stance on revelation.

The Doctrinal Dimension

The doctrinal dimension affirms unequivocally the existence of God and the Trinity. It also seeks a philosophical position which will allow a literal interpretation of the Bible to live with most of science. The Evolutionary thesis is attacked (often not without some reason) as itself being overdogmatic and having difficulty over the methods of evolution (random gene shuffling plus natural selection do not seem adequately to account for quantum leaps in animal evolution). The fundamentalist wing of evangelical

165

Christianity has lately espoused a seemingly scientific alternative theory (that is, one using the jargon of science), known as Creationism.

The Experiential Dimension

The experiential dimension is of great importance, mainly because of the general evangelical espousal of conversion and being "born again," as the modern fashion has it. But it is also crucial because there have been fed into evangelical Christianity streams of Pentecostalism, both among blacks and whites. This encourages speaking in tongues and ecstatic experiences of the Spirit, in line with the accounts of Pentecost and the coming of the Spirit in the early Church. There was, for instance, the Azusa Street revival started in 1906 in Los Angeles by William J. Seymour, a black preacher. At first the various forms of Pentecostalism tended to be rejected by mainstream Christianity, but they gradually made their way in. Some of these motifs combined with faith-healing, which was also used in television religion in the 1960s and on. In any event, one way or another both white and black evangelicalism is fervent in its emphasis on personal experience of Christ.

Baptism by total immersion, but in a new key: this ceremony took place at an evangelical rock concert.

166

The Ritual Dimension

There is a strong emphasis on personal prayer, and preaching is probably the main form of rite, with hymn singing and Bible readings. The revivalists did much to stimulate hymn-writing, usually to Victorian tunes. The pastor or preacher has to develop his skills as a rhetorician, and this gives evangelical Protestantism a very fluid nature. People switch congregations because A is a superior preacher to B, and gathering a congregation is a vital task – its size is an index of evangelical success.

The Institutional Dimension

There is a tendency for the hardline fundamentalists to separate themselves off from evangelicals who are in their view too soft, or who co-operate with the wrong people, such as liberal Christians, Roman Catholics, and Jews. So there are networks of fundamentalist congregations. But as we have seen, there is a wider co-operation on the political front. Evangelicalism is heavily entrenched and possesses some notable seminaries, such as Fuller Theological Seminary in Pasadena, California.

The Ethical Dimension

There is a strong affirmation of what may be called conservative individualism. Society is made up of individuals, and its quality will reflect the life of individuals – who should be sober, hardworking, sexually faithful, patriotic, keeping the Sabbath, and so on. Some fundamentalists particularly dislike certain fashions which they identify with permissiveness – long hair, beards, and women's slacks, for instance. They are unsympathetic to liberal political causes, on the whole, though among evangelicals there are widespread social concerns.

The Material Dimension

Evangelicals are not much committed to the visual side of religion, being somewhat heirs to the old iconoclastic tradition. But it is characteristic for them to be keen on up-to-date methods of disseminating their message. The new-style television preachers are a case in point – all the most recent technology is used. It was reported, for instance, in the *Los Angeles Times* of March 11, 1978, that the Christian Broadcasting Network in Virginia Beach, Va., had acquired the use of the RCA Satcom II satellite and had ordered 12 million dollars' worth of earth stations. In an earlier age, Aimee Semple McPherson (1890–1944), the Pentecostalist evangelist and founder of the Foursquare Gospel Temples, had used radio dramatically (not to mention great choirs and theatrical techniques).

In many ways, then, evangelical Christianity can be nontraditional, but at the same time it claims to stand for older values that it feels may have been betrayed by the liberals. It represents one way of coping with the crisis in authority posed by the relation of modern knowledge to the Bible. But it flourishes because it represents a concrete way of life that it can identify as Christian and involves great intensity of experience and ritual.

Developments since World War II

The Religious Revolution of the 1960s and 1970s

After World War II there was a variant on the loss of satisfaction experienced by many Americans after World War I. This time the threat to the American way of life was perceived externally as the Communist menace. A somewhat Zoroastrian myth underlay foreign policy, of a cosmic struggle between good and evil. McCarthyism came in as an internal force to root out dissent. By the 1950s, during the Eisenhower years, America was comfortable and conformist. This was the heyday of the mainstream liberal Protestant Churches and of unreconstructed Roman Catholicism. It was followed by the hopeful Kennedy administration, which itself betokened a new living together between Protestants and Catholics. It was also the period when the United States was concerned most with supporting the new state of Israel. In the process, a genuine confluence of what were perceived as Christian and Jewish interests emerged. The new religious establishment was Protestant, Catholic, and Jew. But it was a period of relative harmony due for a big shake-up. The late 1960s saw the rebellion of many young people and the birth of the Counterculture. It was a rich and fruitful period, but a disturbing one. Ominous events were at hand: the assassination of President John F. Kennedy (1917–63) and the intensification of the Vietnam War (1965). At the same time, for Catholics there was the exhilarating but disturbing second Vatican Council (1962–65). For blacks the 1960s were a period of new opportunities, though the killing of Martin Luther King in 1968 was a reminder of the violence and prejudice still there in American society.

The revolt, partly against mainstream American religion, took various forms. One was a search beyond Western religion – a complex voyage into Eastern religions. Above all, this search concerned inner consciousness and the pursuit of mysticism. These features of religion of course existed within the Catholic and Orthodox traditions, but the latter was little known, while American Catholicism tended to be activist and in that epoch was in any case digesting the reforms of Vatican II. Monks and nuns were leaving orders, while the young sought mysticism in foreign traditions. It was an irony. Under the guidance of gurus such as Alan W. Watts (1915–73), who expounded Zen, and of writings such as those of Aldous Huxley (1894–1963), whose *The Perennial Philosophy* put mysticism at the heart of universal religion, and whose *The Doors of Perception* commended depth experiences created by mind-altering drugs, young folk took off into Eastern religious experiences. The Beatles sat at the feet of the Maharishi Mahesh Yogi in Rishikesh, India. Others experimented with LSD and other substances. The ethos was against the Protestant ethic and in some measure against the capitalist and technological world. Paradoxically, the young sometimes used the technology of drugs to overcome the technology of the outer world.

The Counterculture also had its violent strand, especially in those circles where Marxist-style revolution was adopted as the ideal. That Marxism could ever be fashionable in America after the McCarthy era was surprising. But the writings especially of Herbert Marcuse (1898–1979) became fashionable. Some of this revolutionary feeling was triggered by the Vietnam War, with its inequities and burnings. The pacifists increased, partly under Eastern influence. Hippies came to be seen as against war, holding up flowers, and chanting the slogan "Make love not war." A new antiwar activism stirred the mainstream churches. Mingled into these movements was a new concern for the environment. There was a large move toward sexual liberation too, and from that epoch stemmed the now customary cohabitation of people without marriage and the "coming out" of homosexuals. All this remains shocking still to many Americans, but it became widespread social fact.

Of the more permanent consequences of that era we can point to the rooting of Eastern religions, especially Buddhism, from Tibetan to Zen and from Mahāyāna to Theravada, on American soil; the stronger presence of the Hindu tradition, partly through the Hare Krishna movement; the survival of smaller so-called cults, such as the Unification Church of the Reverend Sun Myung Moon and the Children of God movement; the wider use of yogic and other meditation techniques among the wider population; the increased recognition by Christian and other mainstream religious groups that they need to take the challenging existence of world religions more seriously; the environmental movement, and increased interest in vegetarianism and animal liberation; and greater sexual permissiveness. Also given a boost, because of the advent of Black Power, was Islam among blacks (see p. 218).

The perhaps inevitable backlash against many of these movements and ideas came in the late 1970s and early 1980s. The Moral Majority was a

Many New Age beliefs stem from the growth of Eastern religions in the West during the 1960s and 1970s. Here American members of the Hare Krishna movement give devotion to their god, Krishna.

169

symptom of this. But the trends listed are here to stay. The Eastern emphasis among whites was reinforced by immigration from East Asia especially. In California, for instance, Anglo-Buddhists mingle with Asians of various nationalities, who enrich their experience of Buddhism. All this has brought into relief the great extent of American pluralism, and this makes it hard for those who wish to put the clock back to a more uniform Protestant era.

Meanwhile the radicalism of the 1960s and early 1970s encouraged new patterns of identity among blacks, Native Americans, those of Mexican descent, and others. It also helped to give great vigor to the women's movement, which had some strong effects in relation to religion.

Women in Christianity and Judaism

It was in the 1960s and 1970s that women most prominently began to conduct a critique of the Christian – and to some degree the Jewish – traditions. An example is Mary Daly's *Beyond God the Father*, which drew attention to the persistent gender discrimination in the Christian tradition, and the assumption that the male gender is primary. The language of the Bible is largely sexist. It does not take much reflection for us to see that gender as applied to God cannot be literal, except on some very strange assumptions about the material character of the Divine Being, which virtually all religions reject (for God is held to be a spiritual Being). God does not literally have hair on his (or her) chest, so any literal ascription of gender is nonsense. But when we see that gender is metaphorical, then it becomes important to use "she" of God as well as "he." Strictly God is neither male nor female, nor both, nor neither. The women's protest movement in Christianity drew attention to male supremacy as expressed not only in so much of the language of religion but – perhaps more importantly, and certainly more concretely – in the organizations of religion. Maleness has been largely entrenched in the hierarchies of episcopal religions, from the Orthodox to the Anglicans, and has been there in the other denominations too. The struggle for greater women's rights in these matters is far from over. In her *In Memory of Her* (1983), the writer and Biblical interpreter, Elizabeth Schüssler-Fiorenza, draws attention to the centrality of women's experience in the founding of Christianity. Here and elsewhere, the new discipline of women's studies gives a new and stirring perspective on the development of religions. Similar critiques and new slants have emerged in the Jewish tradition, and, while the women's movement is strongest among liberal Protestants, it has a sizeable presence in Roman Catholicism.

Eastern Christianity in the United States

Although a much smaller group than the dominating Protestants and Catholics in America, the Eastern Orthodox Churches have a presence through the migration from countries such as Greece, Romania, Bulgaria, the former Yugoslavia, and Russia, as well as from the Arab Christian Levant. While Greek Churches depend upon the Greek Ecumenical Patriarch, the trend in other nationally organized groups in North America is to join the so-called Orthodox Church in America, which was constituted under that name in 1970. There is also an independent Russian Church known as the Orthodox Church Outside Russia, which is based in New York. Arab Orthodox Christians look to the Patriarchate of Antioch. The swing toward co-operation and unity is assisted by the replacement of the vernacular languages by English. Orthodoxy has a significant if numerically small role to play in the total life of American religion.

Liberal Christian Theology in the Twentieth Century

Meanwhile amid the complexities of some of the developments we have noted, the dominant Protestant thought remained in essence liberal – in the scholarly though not always the political sense. The most important figure during the 1930s and on into the early 1950s was Reinhold Niebuhr (1892–1971). Having served for a short time in a parish amid the car workers of Detroit, he taught at Union Theological Seminary in New York, which was the most vital center of Protestant theology until the 1970s. Niebuhr's Detroit experience engaged him with political and moral issues. His stance was somewhat like Barth's, and he was often called neo-orthodox, although he disliked the term. In politics, for long, he was thought left-wing and for a time was a socialist. But with his Old Testament emphasis on linear history, his strong sense of the sin and frailty of human beings, and his emphasis on God's grace and love, he was far from holding any utopian views. He was, moreover, far from thinking that there were easy solutions to human social problems, as the title of his most famous book indicated: *Moral Man in Immoral Society* (1932).

Another Union teacher was the second overshadowing figure in Protestant theology, Paul Tillich (1886–1965). After holding professorships at Marburg, Dresden and Leipzig, he was removed by the Nazis from a teaching position in Frankfurt am Main, Germany, in 1933, and was at Union from then until 1955. His position was a twentieth-century reshaping of natural theology, but in the mold of Existentialism – that is a philosophy which takes seriously human experiences of the world. For him, religion was a pervasive aspect of all life – it was humanity's ultimate concern, that of the individual. We have to interpret religious symbols in this light. For instance, the story of Adam and Eve is ultimately about human finitude (and so about our sense of the infinite – which is symbolized as God). A person grasps the inner meaning of the story through her own experience of facing up to finitude and living in the presence of death. By his symbolic, emotionally anchored account of the Christian faith, Tillich managed to present it in a form which many found refreshingly modern and credible, especially in his *Systematic Theology* (1951–63). In his last days, part of which were spent in Japan and in California at Santa Barbara, he came to appreciate the vital importance of Christian dialogue with other religions.

But if Tillich was popular in the 1960s, new skeptical forces left him somewhat behind. New secularist emphases took a hold on much Protestant theology, in the thought of writers such as Paul van Buren and T. J. J. Altizer, known as the "death of God" school. In many ways the most influential of these writings was *The Secular City* (1965), by Harvey Cox (who later much changed his position at least twice). The death of Jesus was seen as a negation of the very idea of the transcendent God "out there," and these thinkers experimented with a kind of Christian atheism. This was the ultimate in the liberal attempt to keep Christian faith believable in an age of empiricism and science – it abandoned belief in favor of feeling and action.

This phase of theology did not – could not – last long, for now the tide of the 1960s, romantic, credulous, pluralistic, religious, washed across the nation. Partly because it was a revolt against the Vietnam War, it was transmitted rapidly into Canada where many young people had migrated in order to avoid the draft. This development did not at first affect Christian theology much, though methods of yoga and Eastern spirituality were often incorporated into Christian and especially into Roman Catholic faith. But both the work of Martin Luther King and the antiwar struggle by many Christians, including the Catholic Daniel Berrigan and the Protestant William Sloane Coffin, revitalized Christian pacifism.

By the 1970s the women's movement and other growing concerns stimulated a new view of the Christian and Jewish traditions; and there were influential attempts at minority theologies – Black and Red, for instance. Toward the end of the decade, as we have discussed in the last chapter, there was greater interest in so-called Liberation Theology from Latin America, which combined Marxist and Catholic (plus a few Protestant) motifs.

Among Roman Catholics, probably the most influential figure in these times was the Jesuit Karl Rahner (1904–84) who combined traditional and existential strands in his thinking, somewhat like Tillich. Also widely received in the United States was the Tübingen dissident Catholic theologian Hans Küng. His questioning of Papal doctrines and willingness to translate tradition into modern forms has a wide appeal. Increasingly since Vatican II, Roman Catholics in the United States have converged in their style and substance of thought with Protestants. So there is a broad stem of relatively liberal theology which has maintained its vigor, though probably it reached its greatest solidity during the 1950s and 1960s.

New Age "Religions"
Both in Europe and America, and elsewhere in such "Western" countries as Australia and New Zealand, there has been since the 1970s an increased interest in those phenomena which are loosely grouped under the head of "New Age." They are part of a wider trend to take items drawn from different traditions and sources, and to put them together as a personal response to the variety of spiritual traditions which face up to the experience of the modern world. Increasingly traditional authority has faded in

democratic countries, and the continuing rise of consumerism and political and social forms of criticism have strengthened individualism. That the majority of Catholics in Italy and the United States use artificial methods of birth control, contrary to the Pope's teachings, is significant in this light. And so it is that often Protestants "shop around" for the denomination or church of their choice. But, in addition, elements from other religions than Christianity may be woven into the fabric of piety – Hindu yoga, Zen practices, belief in reincarnation, and so on. But beyond such eclecticism there are many people who while affirming that they have spiritual beliefs may not be affiliated to any particular denomination or religion, and yet are drawn to a range of practices or ideas which are called "New Age."

A number of different trends have come together in the New Age. The late nineteenth century saw the rise in the West of greater interest in Eastern religions and spirituality. One of its most significant manifestations was the founding by Helena Blavatsky and Colonel Henry S. Olcott of the Theosophical Society in 1875, which combined motifs of Eastern wisdom and spiritualist practice. Another, more modern motif, is connected with various strands of the Counterculture of the 1960s – the use of astrology, consciousness-raising drugs, new forms of psychological therapy in the quest for personal fulfilment and happiness, as well as environmentalism, including treating mother Earth as a kind of goddess, Gaia.

The psychotherapeutic aspect of New Age includes what is often called the Human Potential Movement. This sees the development of the self, conceived as radiant and creative, and a kind of inner "god," as the central spiritual goal. Because of its individualism New Age comprises a great range of ideas, often marginal to the major mainline traditions of Christianity and Judaism. They are appraised by individuals, often with no tried and tested traditional criteria; but the large attention paid to New Age in a wide range of bookstores is evidence of its widespread popularity.

To summarize, the New Age is the manifestation of a growing trend in the West to pick and choose among spiritual practices and ideas.

Some Secular Forces

Meanwhile the wider context of the different religions in the United States was itself pluralistic. For many people it was not traditional religion, nor even new religious developments, which catered for their spiritual needs. Some were humanists, and others sought a solution to religious problems in some new therapeutic trends based on meditation techniques – such as *est* (Erhard Seminars Training) and in other movements concerned with human potential. These continue to exist alongside older institutionalized mental health movements, such as Freudian, Jungian, and other types of psychotherapy. On the whole, organized political ideologies which have often functioned like religions, like Marxism and Fascism, have had little importance in the United States. Marxism has, however, sometimes blended in with other worldviews, as in Liberation Theology and Black Power.

Reflections on American Religion

We can see several patterns emerge. First, liberalism, industrialization, capitalism, pluralistic democracy, individualism, and modern science and technology have arisen from within Western civilization, and indeed partly under the stimulus of Christianity and especially Protestantism itself. But Christianity has still had to cope with them as if they were external forces. The question has been: How much of beloved tradition could one persist in maintaining? How far was a revolution forced on the various denominations?

Second, the dominant Protestant ethos in America, while of course favorable to democracy, was eventually faced with the dilemma that pluralism was in conflict with its civil religion of trust in God, manifest destiny, and a working ethos. The 1960s and 1970s underlined the pluralism – both moral and religious – within American society. The contradiction was not so evident in slower-moving Canada, with its establishment leanings. But the United States Constitution built into itself a pluralism which was at odds with maintaining the traditional Protestant dominance, at least ideologically.

Third, there was a strong reaction in the fundamentalist movements against the attempt to synthesize liberalism and science on the one hand and Christian belief on the other. The mainstream Protestant Churches made adjustments to doctrine and reshaped myth, but left much of the ritual and organization in place. Interestingly, while denouncing Evolution, revivalist Christianity took individualism, capitalism, and technology increasingly seriously – the preaching was and is set firmly in the marketplace, and it uses up-to-date technological methods, it often discards established Churches and denominations, and it concentrates on the experience of the individual. Instead of rooting faith in a Bible that most Christians could agree was revelation, the fundamentalists turned the very basis of faith itself into an article of faith. Commitment had to be to both Jesus and Bible, often more to the Bible, and interpreted as literally as feasible. The cost lay with the doctrinal dimension, for the question of whether you did not really have to sacrifice science and humanistic history in all this could be acute. Also, the epistemology or model of knowledge, based in faith and authoritarian in tone, was at odds with pluralism. Fundamentalism, therefore, tended to cling to a form of civil religion and patriotism, especially after the traumatic blow to national pride after the Vietnam War.

Fundamentalism is usually called conservative, which it may be politically – but in fact it takes the Bible out of its ancient milieu and uses it today as if it were a contemporary newspaper. It is what may be called neofoundationalist, taking the foundation epoch of Christianity (its own version of Biblical Christianity) and using that as the exclusive norm.

Meanwhile, and fourthly, the Catholics have undergone their overdue attempt to update the faith, which means to synthesize with modern historical and scientific knowledge, to make the liturgy more immediate and simple, and so on. The Roman Catholics have changed through all the dimensions, but have retained the basic characteristics of organization. For it is through the framework of the *organization*, relatively stable, that they have been able to achieve great experimentation. In *experience* there have been experiments with pentecostalism and a revival of the mystical tradition. In *ritual* there has been the move into the vernacular language. This has welded together Catholics with differing ethnic identities. In *ethics* there have been divisions, with generally speaking a loosening-up. In fact, most American Catholics do not heed papal pronouncements on birth control, though on the other hand anti-abortion sentiment has led to an alliance on this and some other issues with conservative Protestants. In *doctrine* there have been new attempts at updating, especially through the lowering of resistance to Evolutionary thought. In the *narrative* dimension the Bible has come fully under modern scrutiny among Catholic scholars, since modernism is no longer condemned as it was at the beginning of the century. In *organization* there has been stability, as I have said; but house meetings and other ways of intensifying study and devotion are not without significance.

Altogether, with similar Jewish reactions playing their part, modern America has a much more pluralistic and diverse aspect today than before. It foreshadows a world situation of intermingling and experimentation, of consumerism and searching in religion, of individual choice. It is an exciting and creative period, doubtless, but one which leaves many people naturally perplexed. Maybe this is why the appearance of certainty in preaching and in tradition is attractive.

Are there discernible patterns in American moves into modernity? Surely. Where the social and organizational dimension was strong enough, as in the Catholic tradition, it was possible to resist liberalism, to moderate individualism, to mount social programs to cope with industrialization, and to make necessary but perhaps not excessive concessions to nationalism. But in the long run, most groups have made powerful accommodations to modern life.

CHAPTER 9

Early, Classical, and Medieval Islam

The Significance of Islam

The three most influential and enduring religions of the West have been Judaism, Christianity, and Islam. They form a kind of sequence, each building on elements of its predecessors. Islam is regarded by believers as the culmination of faith. Muslims see their Prophet as the last and most valid of the prophets, and they seek, among other things, to correct what they see as errors which have crept into the forerunners of the religion. Muslims have, historically, been emphatic in their drive to create not just a religion, but a whole civilization. And although Islam fell upon tough times during the colonial period, when virtually the whole Islamic world came under Western domination (from such powers as the Soviet Union in Central Asia, Britain in South Asia, the Netherlands in Indonesia, France in North and West Africa, and Britain and France in the Middle East), it did in fact create a glittering world, rarely unified politically but nevertheless reflecting Muslim values. We shall see below how rapid was the initial extension of Islamic rule under the leadership of the Arabs.

All this gives Islam an ambiguous relationship with Jewish and Christian culture. While it recognizes great figures from the Jewish and Christian past, such as Adam, Abraham, Jesus, and Mary, it nevertheless transcends Jewish and Christian belief. It is a universal faith and political program, which are not confined to any Chosen People; and it denies that Christ is God incarnate. For Muslims the notion that any human is divine is blasphemous, calling in to question the infinite superiority and power of God or Allah. If anything corresponds at all to Christian belief in the Incarnation it is the Islamic treatment of the Qur'an, as a pre-existing embodiment of God's word. The magic cadences and wondrous teachings of the Qur'an are woven deeply into Islamic daily life. In modern times many Muslim reformers wish to go back to a pure Qur'anic faith, sweeping away certain developments within religious practice which have arisen during the intervening ages and which have been thought to weaken Islamic spiritual and political power. These so-called "fundamentalists," as Western media often dub them, represent an increasingly energetic force in a Muslim world which seeks to restore its pristine vigor.

Though the Prophet Muhammad cannot for a moment be thought to be divine by the committed Muslim, he is nevertheless a paradigm of human behavior, and stories related to his life are a constant source of inspiration to the pious. As the vehicle of revelation chosen by God and as specially aided by Him, the Prophet's example is supreme.

As Islam developed it took varied forms, as we shall see. The most important divide is between the Sunni or traditionalists, who dominate much of the Arab world and much of the East, and the Shī'a, prominent in Persia (Iran), Iraq, parts of the Levant and the Indian subcontinent. The latter believed in the legitimacy of the succession to the leadership of the Muslim community of 'Alī (murdered in 661 C.E.) and of later *imāms*, or spiritual leaders, who had the true interpretation of the Qur'an. Their succession would end in a hidden *imām* who has disappeared from the visible world but who will return at the culmination of history. While often a minority group, the Shi'is came to dominate Persia in the sixteenth century and to bring about the revolution of 1979, which turned Iran into a theocratic state.

Another major strand of Islamic piety was the Sufi movement, which cultivated mysticism and the practice of meditation. Sufi orders organized themselves, and began making inroads into the spread of Islam, notably in India and Indonesia, where Hindu influences gave populations a sympathy for the selfless examples of Sufi saints.

Finally, by way of introduction to this highly successful faith and political system, we may note the inherent discipline of Islam in demanding prayer five times daily and the performance, if possible, of a pilgrimage to Mecca at least once in a lifetime. These practices confer on the faith a degree of unity which helps to combat the geographical spread of a worldwide religion embedded in a large variety of differing cultures. The ideal of a unified community still remains, despite Islam's divisions.

The Spread of Islam

Islam, the religion of Submission (as its name indicates) to the one God, took off from the northwest part of Arabia in the seventh century and rapidly spread north and west. It went north into Palestine and Syria, Iraq and Iran, and into Central Asia. It went west into Egypt, Libya, Tunisia, Algeria, Morocco, Spain, and Portugal. Beginning with Muhammad's migration from Mecca to Medina in 622, the political rule of Islam expanded with amazing rapidity. By 664 the new empire had taken Kabul in Afghanistan and by 670 Kairouan in Tunisia. By 732 it was beyond Bukhara and Samarkand in Central Asia, and fighting at Poitiers in France (where however it was defeated). This first phase, till the establishment of the Abbasid dynasty and the shift of the capital to Mesopotamia, may be called the early period. From 750 to 1258, the time of the Abbasid rule over all or part of Islamic territories, was what may be termed the classical period. Then from the mid-thirteenth century C.E. until the impact of Western powers in the colonial experience – until roughly the eighteenth century – we have what may be called the medieval or premodern period.

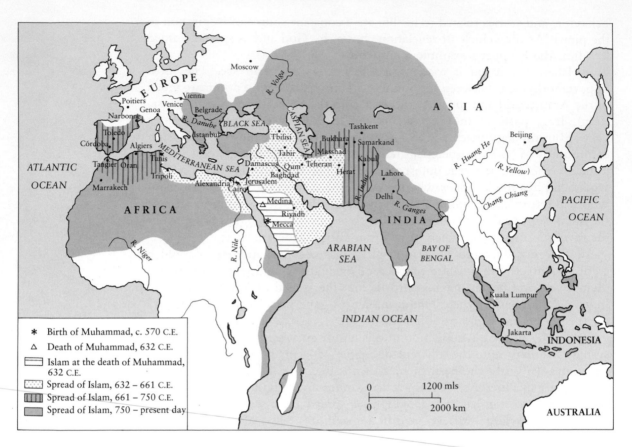

Map 7 The Spread of Islam, *c.* 570 C.E. to the present day.

Altogether Islam became the dominant religion over the whole of the Arab Middle East, along the shores of North Africa, across the Sahara in northern West Africa, through much of East Africa down to Kenya, through Iran, Afghanistan, and the Central Asian republics of the former Soviet Union, in north and northeast India, in Malaysia and Indonesia, in Turkey and a part of the Balkans. It is a significant minority religion in the Indian subcontinent as a whole, and in Thailand, the Philippines, China, Madagascar, the former Yugoslavia, and Tanzania. Broadly, it stretches in a crescent from the eastern tip of Indonesia to West Africa. Though the religion has strong Arab cultural ingredients, above all in the use of Arabic for the Qur'an, the majority of Muslims come from other cultures. The most populous Islamic countries are in South and Southeast Asia: Indonesia, Pakistan, Bangladesh, and the Republic of India.

Islam established its main outline very rapidly, partly because it had a single founder, namely Muhammad, partly because it had a foundation document, namely the Qur'an, and partly because in having a political aspect it had to take rapid decisions on organization in view of its great success. The story of the religion turns very considerably, of course, on the life of the Prophet, and with that we begin.

The Life of the Messenger of Allah

The Prophet Muhammad was born in Mecca, which at that time, probably in 570 C.E., was a highly prosperous place. This was because of its strategic position across the routes from the eastern Mediterranean, and from such rich cities as Damascus, to the ports which served the trade to India and Sri Lanka. It was also even then a sacred city, for it contained the sacred building, the Ka'bah. Accordingly it was the scene of annual pilgrimage from the tribes round about. The area round the Ka'bah was a sanctuary during certain months, thereby moderating the impact of tribal warfare. The dominant tribe in Mecca, to which Muhammad belonged, was the Quraysh. His father and mother died when he was young, and he was raised by relatives. As a young man he found himself without the capital necessary to engage in trading. But a wealthy widow, Khadijah, employed him and subsequently married him. Though he became active in trade, he had had opportunities for reflection – he is said to have spent a month each year meditating in a cave near Mecca.

It was in 610 that he began to have some striking religious experiences which set him off in his career as a messenger of Allah. To begin with he mentioned his revelations only to his family and close associates. After about three years, however, he began his public career. His message was not altogether welcome for at least two reasons. First, in attacking polytheism, which he came to do with increasing clarity, he threatened the livelihood of those who depended on Meccan shrines – and in any case people tended to be conservative in such matters. Second, the ethic he pronounced was not fully in accord with the money-making policy of the rich merchants of the city – everyone would have to appear in the end before the judgment seat of the mighty God. Later, too, Muhammad would be involved in conveying revelations which altered the legal shape of society, especially in regard to marriage.

His message made little headway at first in Mecca, though he accumulated some fifty loyal followers. In 620 and 621 he received feelers from the city of Medina to the north, and in due course, in 622, he was invited to migrate there and take up the leadership. The city and area had been in a state of faction for a number of years, and the hope was that Muhammad with his diplomatic skills and unifying message would be able to bring harmony to Medina. This he did and came to control its political affairs. Then began an armed struggle against the Quraysh and the people of Mecca, and in 624 he defeated them in battle at Badr. After a few years of intermittent struggle Muhammad entered Mecca and became its leader. A battle shortly thereafter, at Hunayn, disposed of some of the outlying tribes, and Muhammad was master of a large slice of Arabia. Already he had plans for conquests in Syria and Iraq. But in June 632 he died.

He was a considerable military and political leader, magnanimous and decisive, and had behind him the assurance of faith, as a result of his prophetic experiences. To Muslims he is an ideal figure, someone to be admired and followed, and seen as virtually perfect – the finest of human beings, to whom Allah entrusted his final revelation. Muslims are, of course, much opposed to any attempt to deify Muhammad – for that would be to set up another god beside God, which is the deadliest sin. In practice, however, he is seen as the supreme ethical ideal and more closely followed than Christ, partly

Shi'a Islam allows some human-type representations, as is this manuscript illustration of the archangel Gabriel, who revealed the scriptures to the Prophet Muhammad.

because of the accumulation of biographical stories about him. These traditions, or *hadīth*, are carefully sifted according to traditional methods, and constitute in effect a secondary source of revelation after the holy Qur'an.

The Prophet and His Experiences of Revelation

Muhammad seems to have started his religious career as Prophet in part because of his first experiences, which were of a supernatural character. There was a mighty being, on the horizon, whom he thought of as God but later concluded must have been the archangel Gabriel. The archangel made him recite from a book (though Muhammad is said to have been illiterate). He was commanded, according to surah (section) 96 of the Qur'an "Recite in the name of the Lord ..." This was probably the first surah to be revealed. At other times the Prophet felt certain words in his heart, which he took to be revealed by God. All these utterances were brought together in the Qur'an, a collection which is of very great power and beauty, in resonant and compelling Arabic. How, say Muslims, could an illiterate person create such a masterpiece? At any rate, the supernatural experiences of the Prophet are reflected in the tremendous and mysterious tone of the Qur'anic words.

There was also the famous night journey of Muhammad to the Temple Mount in Jerusalem, now marked by a mosque, from where he ascended to the seventh heaven. On his way he saw Moses, Abraham, and Jesus. Among other things the five daily prayers were supposed to have been revealed on this occasion. This experience was no doubt a visionary episode, but later piety often makes it into a literal journey astride Muhammad's winged horse Buraq. This interpretation was part of the tendency to surround Muhammad with miracles and to make him even more than a Prophet. He was supposedly prevented by God from sinning, for instance. But the orthodox theologians insist that one miracle was enough: the creation of the Qur'an. Or rather, not its creation – for it was with God forever – but its presentation to the human race.

The Qur'an

From a human point of view the Qur'an looks like a miraculous achievement of sublime artistry. In any event, being written down so rapidly during the lifetime of Muhammad, and being pretty much consistent in its teachings and prescriptions, it has not created the problems encountered in looking at the New Testament, which came into being through different hands over a much longer period, and has undergone great editing.

It is easy to think of the Qur'an simply as a book and to say that the Muslims have faith in the words of a holy book. But this does not convey the centrality and power of the Qur'an in Muslim eyes. If you were to look for a rough equivalent to the Christian Incarnation (the divine nature of Jesus) in Muslim piety, it would be the Qur'an. It is divine thought and divine law

The Transcendence and Immanence of God: Qur'ān

God is the Light of the heavens and
   earth;
   the likeness of His Light is a niche
   wherein is a lamp
   (the lamp in a glass,
   the glass as it were a glittering
   star)
   kindled from a Blessed Tree,
   an olive that is neither of the East
   nor of the West,
   Whose oil wellnigh would shine,
   even if no fire touched it;
   Light upon light;
   God guides to His Light whom
   He will.
And God strikes similitudes for
   men,
   and God has knowledge of
   everything.
In temples God has allowed to be
   raised up,
   and His Name to be
   commemorated therein;
   therein glorifying Him, in the
   mornings and the evenings,
   are men whom neither commerce
   nor trafficking diverts from the
   remembrance of God and to
   perform the prayer, and to pay
   the alms,
   fearing a day when hearts and eyes
   shall be turned about,
   that God may recompense them
   for their fairest works and give
   them increase of His bounty;

and God provides whomsoever
   He will, without reckoning.

And as for the unbelievers,
   their works are as a mirage in a
   spacious plain which the man
   athirst supposes to be water,
   till, when he comes to it, he finds
   it is nothing;
   there indeed he finds God,
   and He pays him his account in
   full;
   (and God is swift at the reckoning)
   or they are as shadows upon a sea
   obscure
   covered by a billow
   above which is a billow
   shadows piled one upon
   another;
   when he puts forth his hand,
   wellnigh he cannot see it.
And to whomsoever God assigns no
   light, no light has he.

Hast thou not seen how that
   whatsoever is in the heavens
   and in the earth extols God,
   and the birds spreading their
   wings?
Each – He knows its prayer and its
   extolling;
   and God knows the things they do.

incarnated in words. It is mysterious sound which has everlasting life and existence, an emanation from the one Divine Being. One of the attributes of God is speech, and the Qur'an is God's eternal speech. Of course, recitations or written copies of the Qur'an are all created. But as divine speech what lies behind and within the Qur'an is eternal. All this gives it a much deeper meaning and a much higher status than that of the Bible.

Also, the Qur'an must be alongside the claims made by the faithful on behalf of Muhammad. He was not just the greatest of the prophets, in a line stretching from Abraham and Moses through Jesus to himself. But he was also the final Prophet, the "Seal of the Prophets," the *khatm al-anbiyā*. It was he who delivered the definitive expression of Allah's speech.

All this implies a divine plan. Abraham and the rest are God's means of communicating with the human race, and are part of his education of human beings in the process of *islām* or submission to his will. But it should be noted that the very process of looking back at previous religious heroes as being in the line of prophets made them exemplary figures also. Islam could in this way claim to have ancient roots, though it was the last of the great religions to be revealed. It gave Islam a positive view of Judaism and Christianity, though this could also seem to adherents of those faiths to be somewhat patronizing. Muslims considered that Jews and Christians had tampered with the messages of the prophets – Christians by looking on Jesus as divine, which was blasphemous. This retroactive acceptance of elements of the other two traditions could be made concrete in very particular claims, for instance that the Ka'bah was built by Adam and then rebuilt by Abraham and Ishmael (Isma'il). Whatever others may feel about the validity of such a claim, Muslims will see in this something which is part of the very fabric of their faith, and so undeniably certain.

The revealed and everlasting nature of the Qur'an gives Islamic faith a great strength, especially because the book when translated is no longer the real Qur'an. It is only in Arabic: there can be no non-Arabic Qur'an, for it is primarily sound. The writing is like the music score from which you perform. The non-Arab may use paraphrases as a kind of commentary to help her or him. But the true Qur'an remains the Arabic Qur'an. In this sense, God thinks in Arabic.

The Dimensions of the New Faith

Therefore, built on the rock of Muhammad's career and the revelations of the Qur'an, there arose the great edifice of a new faith. It helped to define a new civilization, which was for long a glittering challenge to its neighbor Christendom. What were the dimensions of this faith?

The Ritual Dimension

Above all, the Muslim has the duty of praying five times daily, facing toward the Ka'bah, according to certain formulae of words and bodily postures: before sunrise, early afternoon, late afternoon, straight after sunset, and before retiring. (In Shī'a Islam, note, the requirement is three times a day.) One should also keep the fast during the holy month of Ramadan, which is the ninth month of the lunar year: between dawn and sunset there should be no eating, drinking, smoking, or sex. And one should try to perform the pilgrimage to the Ka'bah at least once during one's life. These three rules constitute the second, third, and fifth of the so-called Pillars of Islam. The first is a duty to commitment: one should recite the credo in public: "There is no god but God and Muhammad is his messenger." The fourth is to pay

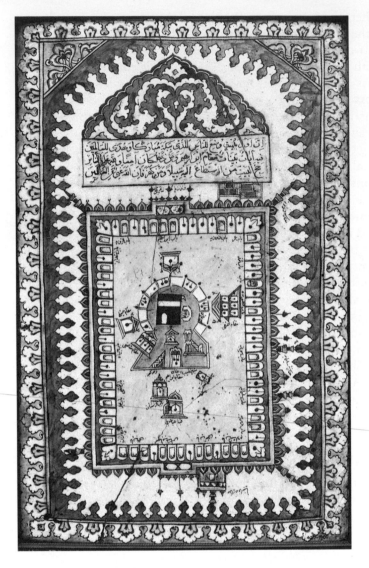

The ritual dimension: a plan of Mecca rendered on an 18th century Turkish tile.

the alms tax, or *zakat*. Therefore the community should look after the welfare of the poor. Friday is a special day of prayer, with congregational worship and preaching in the mosque.

The fact that Muslims have to orient themselves toward the Ka'bah and are urged if at all possible to go there on the great annual pilgrimage (*the hajj al-akbar*) means that there are continual reminders of the unity of the whole community, however much from time to time it may be torn apart by political or religious conflict.

The Experiential Dimension
Obviously the Prophet's own visions and the spiritual power of Allah left

184

their stamp not only on the Qur'an but also on the community's sense of the tremendous nature of God. The deepest sin known to Islam is in accordance with this sense: it is *shirk*, setting up some other god beside God. So we have a sense of the overwhelming presence of God, who yet in his mercy communicates with human beings to lead them on the right path. Later on, as we shall see, a different, mystical sort of experience appears – the sense of that which lies within, gained through the practice of contemplation. This was due to the Sufi movement.

The Ethical Dimension

We have to see that morality for the early Muslim was thoroughly woven into the political task of founding a good and just society under the guidance of God. Throughout the history of Islam there is recognition of the central place held by the law or *Sharī'a*. The obedience due to God should lead to the recognition of human equality. Rights may vary, as with men and women. But in principle all are equal before God. Social legislation and the payment of *zakat* stress our religious duty to the poor. Kindness should be cultivated,

---

Islam some key terms

Allah The one true God.

Hajj Pilgrimage to Mecca, urged on all Muslims.

Imām Prayer leader, and in Shī'a Islam one of the twelve great leaders of the community, the last having gone into hiding or occultation, to return at the end of history.

Jihad The struggle for Islam, interpreted either as righteous war or as a spiritual striving.

Nabi A prophet, among whom are some of the great figures of the Jewish tradition, and Jesus; the final one is Muhammad.

Qur'ān The sacred revelation or word of God, being eternal, and revealed to the Prophet.

Salat Worship or prayer, enjoined on Muslims five times daily.

Saum Fasting, especially during the month of Ramadan between sunrise and sunset, enjoined on all Muslims.

Sharī'a Islamic law.

Sufi A mystic within Islam, typically belonging to one of the various *tariqas* or orders.

Umma' The whole Muslim community.

Zakat Giving alms to the poor. One of the pillars of Islam, with the profession of faith, prayer, pilgrimage and fasting.

---

especially by husbands toward wives. Polygamy is allowed, but only four wives per man; and the rights of women are protected by the dowry system and legislation regarding divorce. The Prophet himself can be followed as an example, and the *hadīth* are a vital source of moral inspiration.

The Institutional Dimension

Islam organized itself as a state to start with, and only gradually did the total community – the *umma'* – break up. In theory this should be unified under a leader, or successor to Muhammad, known as the *khalīfa* or Caliph. From time to time in later Islam the Caliphate was revived. As for religious institutions more narrowly conceived, there were prayer leaders from early days, and later professional exponents of theology and law.

The Doctrinal Dimension

The single most important strand in Islam is the unity of God, who is creator of the universe. He has human beings as his regents over the earth, which was made for their ultimate benefit. Though varying emphasis in the Qur'an can be found, the trend is to think of God as determining each person's destiny. As we have seen, the Qur'an was believed to be the eternal speech of God. The Muslims were strong in condemning what they saw as the tritheism, or three-God-doctrine, of Christianity. But God can be addressed through the rich notion of his Ninety-Nine Names, beginning with *al-Rahman*, "the Compassionate." Among other people names are *al-Hafiz*, the Preserver; *al-Haqq*, the Real; *al-Qadir*, the Powerful; and *al-Rashid*, the Director.

The Narrative Dimension

We have seen that the Islamic story implies a chain of prophets from Abraham, and indeed before that from Adam, down to Muhammad. The coming of the last Prophet is, of course, central to the whole narrative understanding by Muslims of human history. The amazing success of the community in its early days, and the mighty conquests, were a sign of Allah's grace and mercy. Eventually the final hour of the world will come with various signs, the descent of Jesus, and a fire which will drive people to the place of judgment.

The Material Dimension

Islam began soon enough to have its houses of prayer. It was only later that they became a glory of Islamic architecture. Since the ban on any concrete representation of God was, for the main Sunni tradition, extended to cover God's image in the human face and form, much came to be made of calligraphy as an art. But in the early days the chief material aspects of Islam were the cities of Medina and Mecca, and above all the pilgrimage sites in and around the latter. There were, for instance, the valley of Mina to the east of Mecca, where pilgrims spend a night, and the mount of 'Arafat, where Muhammad had his first visions.

The Formation of Classical Islam

The early decades after the death of the Prophet were marked with dissension over the leadership. Muhammad's father-in-law Abu Bakr was first appointed. He died after two years and was succeeded by 'Umar, who organized the growing Arab empire along fairly simple lines. The Arabs looked after war and religion, and non-Arabs – and these were for the most part non-Muslims – paid taxes but rather lighter ones than they had been used to. 'Umar was followed by 'Uthman. His assassination led to the first civil war within Islam, when 'Ali's succession was opposed. 'Ali was assassinated in 661, and in 680 his surviving son Husayn was ambushed at Karbala in Iraq; he was to become the prime martyr figure for the Shi'i movement, which we shall come back to later. Under Mu'awiyah and his successors (661–750), the Umayyad dynasty, centered in Syria, carried on the highly successful policy of military expansion.

In the end, a revolution in 750 brought the 'Abbasid dynasty to power at Dar-es-Salaam, a new capital constructed at Baghdad in Mesopotamia. A glorious new cultural phase of Islam was thus entered, though disintegration occurred later through the establishment of rival Caliphates, in North Africa and Córdoba in Spain. The Islamic community was divided, but it was a fine period of Islamic civilization. There were stresses, one of them being the disaffection of the Shi'i party, who were loyal to the descendants of 'Ali and who opposed the status quo.

New religious forces were entering the body of Islam. One was the effect of Greek learning, and in particular philosophy, on Islamic theology. Another was the mystical movement, the Sufis, who brought contemplative methods into the practice of Islam. Meanwhile the law or *Shari'a* had to be interpreted, and diverse schools had been growing up.

The Development of Islamic Theology

One of the major movements in the second and third centuries of Islam (*c.* 700–900 C.E.) was that of the Mu'tazila, great systematizers of *kalam* or dogmatic theology. In their pursuit of a rational worldview they took over atomism, but gave it an extension beyond that of Greek philosophy. They saw the world as a succession of instantaneous and atomic (separate and indivisible) events, including human actions. God gives a person strength through an instantaneous empowerment before a person acts; but the choice is later and is still that of the individual. The Mu'tazila also did not want to make God's attributes something other than God, so it was no use saying that the Qur'an was God's speech as something eternal. It was produced by God and was not everlasting.

Their doctrine of free will was founded in the thought that God is just. So it is inappropriate to believe in any form of predestination. In such ways the Mu'tazila defended a rationalist position, and they were for a time patronized by the court in Baghdad and adopted as the official line. But there were elements in their thought which were not popular, notably the denial of the eternal character of the Qur'an. Moreover they were intensely against anthropomorphism (seeing the non-human in human form), and saw the statements in the Qur'an as being metaphors, when God is said to have hands, or sit on a throne.

It was al-Ash'ari (873–975) who most decisively formulated the Sunni or mainstream tradition. He argued that anthropomorphic expressions apply to God literally but in a manner which we do not understand. The Qur'an he defended as eternal, being an attribute of God, who has attributes in a mode different from created beings. And he held that God is all-powerful and determines human actions, but individuals acquire responsibility for their actions. In effect this left as the mainstream Islamic position a form of predestinationism. Men and women are predestined to good or to bad actions, and to heaven or hell (including purgatory, the fate of true believers who sin).

The Spread of Sufism

The movement which is known as Sufism (from *suf* meaning the coarse wool worn by ascetics) was an attempt to introduce into personal life a kind of spirituality which would compensate for the excesses of Islamic culture after its notable successes. Sufism was involved with austere training, but it issued ultimately in mystical contemplation. Sufis aspired toward that purification of consciousness which leads to the feeling that ordinary consciousness, with its dualism (the distinction between me as subject and God or the world as object), disappears. They therefore often came to speak of union with God, and even being merged with or becoming God. Now this was not at all to the taste of mainstream orthodoxy. In Islam there has always been a very strong emphasis on the radical difference between God and human beings. Some Sufi claims could be thought blasphemous. The Sufis seemed to think that by the annihilation of their egos they could make a place for God and so in some sense become God. It was not surprising that the orthodox would resist such ideas.

The Sufi movement started with groups who would co-operate in the cultivation of piety. There grew up the custom of having a leader or *shaykh* who would act as a spiritual teacher and master. The groups not only pledged themselves to simplicity of life, but engaged in forms of meditation – very similarly to the contemplative orders in Christianity and to much in Indian mysticism. Perhaps the most famous of all Sufis was al-Hallaj, who illustrated some of the tensions in the situation. An admirer and follower of Jesus (also of course an Islamic prophet), he reportedly said "I am the Real – *al-Haqq*," which was taken as tantamount to saying that he was God. In his teachings he spoke most of the love of God, and he openly referred to his divine experiences. As a result he was accused of blasphemy and executed on the cross, in 922 C.E.

Famous teachers were eagerly anticipated by Sufi practitioners: Persia is the setting for this sixteenth-century illustration of a sermon. The women and children occupy a separate gallery at the bottom.

Sufism was important in the spread of Islam. The holy person commands respect in many societies. In North Africa the *barakah* or mysterious power of the saint, in Central Asia features of shamanism, in India the prestige of the yogin – such manifestations were taken over by the Sufis. They had much, too, to do with the spread of Islam into Malaya and Indonesia.

The Nature of Sufism

In part Sufism was a communal movement, since it formed itself within the wider social embrace of Islam. Moreover, it formed fraternities in which individuals gathered together to pursue jointly the spiritual life. But it also brought to the fore a number of famous individuals. We shall look at six of these persons to illustrate different phases of the general movement.

An early figure of some importance was Hasan al-Basrī (642–728), whose austere mode of life was so strong that it helped to promote the inward search for God in a world-negating frame. He considered the world to be evil (indeed like a snake – poisonous, but smooth). His attitude to some degree reflected a similar motif among early Christian ascetics and mystics. Now that the Arab empire was no longer centered in Medina but in opulent and decadent Damascus there was a need to re-affirm the element of "giving up." In the same way, the creation of a Church–state alliance and, as a result, new laxity among the clergy, suggested to early Christians that true witnesses to the faith should renounce worldly things.

Another theme in Sufism is illustrated by Rābi'ah al-'Adawīyah (713/4–801), the first prominent woman mystic in Islam. While she stayed single, she emphasized a sublimated love of Allah as the focus of both her inner search and her asceticism, which she thought of primarily as a means to an end. In using the image of love between the saint and God, she set the tone for a vast amount of Sufi attitudes and philosophy. As elsewhere, mysticism often seemed to obliterate in experience the distinction between subject and object, and so suggested a merger between the soul and God. But was this like the entanglement of lovers, who are intimately united and yet remain distinct beings? Or was it like the obliteration of the distinction between the one and the other? The latter question suggests the root of al-Hallaj's claim, which brought about his downfall. If the mystic and God are merged or are really one, then the mystic is divine. And for that matter, conversely, God and the mystic are one, so that is why he or she easily gets worshiped by the populace. The cult of saints has its logic, though in modern times it has been heavily criticized for causing superstition among the masses.

If a certain hatred of the world was Hasan's main motif, and the softer image of love was that of Rābi'ah, the metaphor of annihilation was that of Abū Yazīd al-Bistāmi (d.8.874). As the mystic ascended to God he lost his self and the "I" became identical with the "He." The soul was subjected to obliteration (fanā'). This re-enactment of the Prophet's so-called "Night Journey," in which he mysteriously rode up to heaven, was a psychic parallel to what was seen by most Muslims as a kind of external, historical event. Anyway, Abū Yazīd's language naturally scandalized the orthodox.

This dialectic between the outwardly spiritual and the inwardly mystical strands of Islam became a recurrent theme in the whole of Sufi and indeed Islamic history. Islam espouses a powerful religion of the numinous and embraces, at the same time, an inward journey, culminating in the purification of the consciousness and intimate union with the Divine. This very duality was a source of richness. It showed a vital and generous openness to two major kinds of religious experience. But, as elsewhere, the duality caused problems. After Abū Yazīd there were two main categories of Sufis: the "drunken," as the image had it, and the "sober." He represented the former – but the latter held a more moderate view, conceiving of the God–mystic relationship in terms of intimate union but not merger.

The tension was resolved in a way by al-Ghazālī (1058–1111). A great philosopher, it was during his time at the university of Baghdad that he underwent a spiritual and mental crisis. He saw (or thought he saw) the emptiness of ritual and law, and doubted his ability to arrive at religious truth. He gave up his teaching career and tried Sufism. When he returned to teaching he was also able to provide an orthodox interpretation of Sufism. He produced a highly consolidating and influential work, *The Revivification of the Religious Sciences*. He saw Sufism as sometimes involving a "drunken" interpretation in which the mystic, carried away by ecstasy, thinks that he or she is merged with God, but actually is different, though united intimately. Provided the duality was maintained then the orthodox could be satisfied. Even today, it is still a matter of debate among analysts of religion as to whether there is some fine difference between God and the mystic. My view is that if a religion has a God or ultimate Being, then the question of duality or non-duality will inevitably arise. I believe that in such a faith the non-dual merging idea destroys the meaning of worship and devotion, which require the Other. But in faiths like Buddhism which have no ultimate God or Being, then non-dualism is the better interpretation, because in the mystical experience subject and object typically vanish. For this very reason, in God-centered religions, mysticism is often regarded as a problem, and

The experiential dimension: the slow, revolving dance of the Mevleli order of Sufis, here performed by young recruits, helps to create higher states of consciousness, while being a ceremonial ritual in its own right.

191

with suspicion. On the other hand, it is an enriching strand of religious experience: and in some religions, notably Theravada Buddhism and in Sankara's Advaita (Non-Dualism), dominant.

Jalāl ad-Din ar-Rūmī (1207–73), often known as Rūmī, was the dominant Persian (Iranian) mystical writer and founder of the influential Mevlevi or Mawlawīyah Order (known as the 'Whirling Dervishes' in the West, because of their solemn dance spinning slowly as part of their ritual). His book became the greatest Persian mystical writing. If there is a dominant image it is that of music: God in creating set off a dance of being out of non-being. This brought the unfolding of the beauties and wonders of the cosmos. The faithful in performing the mystical dance symbolize their self-sacrifice and death in order to rise to a higher life.

Finally, among our exemplars of Sufism, we should briefly mention Ibn-al'Arabī (1165–1240), whom we will discuss more closely in our depiction of Spain in the Middle Ages (p. 201). He was born in Spain but eventually, after extensive travels, settled in Damascus. His chief focus was the concept of the unity of being. Ultimately there is the indefinable, ineffable One, in which the soul of the individual is fused and disappears. It is the 'no god but Allah,' as in the confession of Islamic faith. At a lower level the unknown, unknowable God manifests itself as God who breathes out the cosmos. We suffer from the illusion of independent existence, but through the mystical path we can ascend to the knowledge of the One, and thereby extinguish our earthbound ego. In many ways Ibn al-'Arabī's thought is like that of the Hindu Advaita Vedānta, and it has more than a passing resemblance to the Neoplatonism of Plotinus. It is a wonderful deduction from the concept of unity, and in a way is highly consonant with much of early Islamic theology. But its flavor is universal.

These, then, are a few Sufi themes: withdrawal (Hasan), love (Rābi'ah), annihilation (Abū Yazīd), richness (al-Ghazālī), self-sacrifice (Rūmī) and unity (Ibn al-'Arabī).

The Dimensions of Sufism

Doctrinally, Sufism shows great variation, yet also tends to stress the impersonal, ineffable side of God: most markedly in Ibn al-'Arabī. As for the narrative dimension, there is considerable drawing on the character of the Prophet, himself seen as a mystic. There is Abū Yazīd's likening of the mystical ascent to the Night Journey of Muhammad as we have seen. A crucial utterance in the Qur'an (7: 172) describes how God even before the universe was created made a contract with the souls of human beings. (God had drawn forth from the loins of Adam the seed of humans and caused them to testify before him.) This is seen as a kind of affirmation that God and human beings had a pre-cosmic union which the mystic recalls in experience.

As to the *ethical* dimension, Sufism involves, typically, a rigorous "giving up" (though normally Sufis remain a part of society and married). But the rigorous following of the *Sharī'a* is an outward sign of an inner meaning and an inward following of the path to union and purification of consciousness.

The *experiential* dimension is central to the Sufi path, and we have seen some of the images used to hint at it. Sufi texts are often manuals which analyze and describe the different stages of the inward life and the conquest of the lower psyche, or *nafs*, seen as spiritually incorporating arrogance, greed, and deception, which of course have to be overcome. So there is a subtle and refined psychology of the progress toward the higher levels of religious experience.

As to the *ritual* or *practical dimension*: various common exercises of prayer and (in the case of the Mevlevi Order) dance are important, often under the direction of a *shaykh* or spiritual leader. The Bistāmi order is highly individualist, practicing its prayers and meditation in private. Typically there is a chain of lineage among spiritual leaders (reminiscent of the Hindu tradition). Two vital functions are characteristic of the orders: *dhikr* (remembrance, that is, of God), through the repetition of set phrases or names of God, the practice of breath control, silent meditation where *dhikr* is internalized; and *sama'* (listening or audition), that is, the use of music and dance to trigger off mystical experience. Such music is often accompanied by poetry and chanting, usually from the Qur'an.

The *material dimension* is represented particularly by the *ribāt* or training center (there were also individual hermitages). Also of growing importance were the tombs of *shaykhs*, which through much of the Islamic world attracted considerable popular attention and local pilgrimage. As time went on there was a tendency for Sufism to lose some of its spiritual meaning for the mystic and become identified with popular forms of religion. It provided an outlet for trends in popular piety. It was in part for this reason that in modern times there has been a move against the cult of tombs and the like, since this is supposed to cut at the purity of Islamic faith.

The Development of Islamic Law

As the Islamic community expanded, and as times and cultures changed, it was necessary to expand the interpretation of the law. In general it was important to have criteria for deciding. Four main roots of the law were evolved. The first is the Qur'an itself. If a law is clearly stated there then it is indeed obligatory. The next root is the tradition or *sunna*. This is where the collection of *hadīth* about the life and sayings of the Prophet is important to the system. Third, there is analogy, to be thought out by relevant reasoning or *ijtihād*. Fourth, there is *ijma'* or consensus.

By the tenth and eleventh centuries the main structure of Islamic legal thinking had been put in place. The effect was ultimately somewhat deadening, and it was said that the "door of *ijtihād* is closed." The main schools had been established, and it became customary to use a system called patchwork to arrive at legal changes – by taking a ruling from one school when that of another proved too severe or not severe enough, and so on. The various schools prevail in different parts of the world: the Hanafi in the Indian subcontinent, Central Asia, Egypt, Syria, Jordan, and Iraq; the Maliki in North Africa; the Shafi'i in Southeast Asia; the Hanbali in Saudi Arabia; the Ja'fari (Shi'i) in Iran; and the Kariji in Oman and East Africa.

The law covers all topics, from morality to civil law and from criminal law to courtesy. It is interesting that five classes of action are recognized: those which are obligatory, those which are recommended, those which are prohibited, those which are disapproved, and those which are indifferent. This five-fold distinction helps to give Islamic law a great deal of subtlety.

The material dimension: one of the glories of Istanbul is the famous mosque adapted from the previous Christian church of Santa Sophia.

Muslim Daily Life and the Law

We have already seen how the duty to pray punctuates and defines the day for the pious Muslim. Moreover prayer is directed towards Mecca, so that the whole Muslim world feels a kind of unity through being focussed on the main scene of the Prophet's activities. But because in its heyday the Muslim world was a civilization under (at least in theory) a single leader, the *khalīfa* or Caliph, daily life was suffused with values which ultimately sprang from a single source. The systems of law laid down what was correct behavior. The ban on alcohol ultimately led to the great development of coffee-making and the café as social aids to friendship and discussion. Such public life, however, was virtually all-male. At different periods there were differing modes of segregating men and women: a common practice came to be the wearing of the veil or *burqa*. Some attribute this to the fact that because interpretation of both the scriptures and the law was virtually an all-male preserve, a system which gave inferior status to women was developed, even though this is not strictly the teaching of the Qur'an. Nevertheless, gradually there came to exist two spheres of activity: that of the man to whom public life (including that of the mosque) was accessible; and that of the woman, which was largely domestic (including the paying of visits to the homes of friends, relatives, and neighbors).

The external dress of women was designed to shield their appearance from males other than husbands and children. The assumption was that women were too attractive, and so dangerous. But it is also part of the spirit of the law that there should be standardized means for distinguishing categories; and the gender difference is the most significant for daily life. But though the veiling of women could be thought to reinforce the submissive status of the female, it also conceals the fact that women had property rights, protection against unreasonable divorce and from bad conduct by husbands, as well as a degree of independence unknown in pre-Islamic Arabia. The veil could also be seen as a protection from unwelcome public molestation. Moreover, modern critics of Islamic law in regard to women are using contemporary criteria to discuss ancient arrangements. Muslims often make the point that traditional Islam was much in advance, regarding women's rights, of traditional Christianity, which did not have the elaborate arrangements of *Sharī'a* to protect women's status.

Classical and later Islam was enhanced by the contributions of those who lived as protected minorities, notably Christians and Jews. In early medieval Spain there was a rich symbiosis of cultures, in which philosophers and artists mingled in producing one of the most glorious periods of dialogue and interaction.

Also highly significant was the evolution of the Islamic calendar, which provides a pattern of events through the year, including such feasts as the celebration of the Prophet's birthday, or sacrifices of animals at the time of pilgrim's return from the *hajj*, or pilgrimage, from Mecca. There is, above all, the fasting month of Ramadan, when food, drink, smoking, and sex are banned between sunrise and sundown. The month ends with the joyous celebration *'Īd-al-Fiṭr*. In Shi'a areas the whole cycle of rituals associated with Muharram and the death of Husayn is most vital, although mourning, but on a much lesser scale, also occurs among Sunnis. And so by the punctuation of the year with solemn occasions, the Muslim is reminded of his or her faith and commitment.

Further Aspects of Islamic Law

As the community became established in political units there had to be authority to determine what was the *Sharī'a* or law. For even if the life of the Muslim was in a particular social and political context his or her ultimate destiny was personal and outside time. The judgment which God would in the end impose inevitably concerned individuals not collectivities. This by the way gives a unique dynamic to Islam: while so much of it is public and legal and communitarian, at its heart it is a religion of the individual.

Law in the Islamic context came to be seen as exclusively based upon the Qur'an and *hadīth*, that is upon the traditions of the Prophet's life. There were ways of testing traditions about his actions – based on fairly sophisticated principles. For it was inevitable that the traditions, or *sunna*, would play a vital role in the formation of the law. After the ninth century the certified traditions of *hadīth*, giving insight (so it was hoped) into the values of the Prophet himself, were compiled with the Qur'an, and both sources were shortly to become the twin foundations of the law.

The development of the law depended greatly on the process known as *qiyas*, which means "analogy." New forms of behavior may not be covered by an existing law, but may become forbidden because of their similarity to those covered by previous rulings. But ambivalence can reign for a time: if alcohol is forbidden, then what about marijuana? Another criterion concerns *ijma'*, or consensus. This was often a matter of hot debate. And so on: the formulators of Islamic jurisprudence, or legal philosophy, discussed in depth a whole series of criteria for developing the law. It is notoriously hard to develop general principles which can adequately deal with specific cases. Such cases needed to be examined with clear-sighted rationality, and, on its own terms, Islam has been very successful in laying down workable rules and resolving ethical disputes.

The system also depended on judges, or *qafi*. Though appointed by the ruler, these judges would, theoretically, be independent. However, judges were held responsible by the government to punish offenders, and so their independence was severely curtailed. Despite this, Islamic law functioned effectively on the whole, partly because judges were seen not just as people who could execute the law but also as spiritual advisers. At the same time any judge could refuse an appointment if he felt that the ruler was governing in a non-Islamic way. Otherwise, it may be noted that the differing schools were tolerant toward each other. If a ruling in one school clashed with that of a different school, both could be accepted by the whole Muslim community. Also, there came to be a laxer regime of law for those Muslims who lived in an environment where the majority was non-Muslim. On the other hand, the aim was to see to it that the vast majority of Muslims lived in Muslim-controlled territory.

The law had a strong moral content, both controlling personal affairs – penalties are meted out for such offences as adultery – and enforcing a general ban on alcohol. Commercial transactions, however, were also overseen by the court; these might include such issues as the levying of interest rates.

Jihad or Struggle

An aspect of Muslim law which is important historically is the notion of the duty to struggle on behalf of the faith, and indeed to fight on its behalf to expand the territories over which the faith dominates. It became customary in the classical period to divide the world into two spheres, the *Dar al-Islam* or Abode of Islam and the *Dar al-Harb* or Abode of War. The Qur'an looks on it as a duty to fight against polytheists, and against Christians and Jews till they pay the *jizya* or tax as an acknowledgment of the supremacy of Muslim rule. This in turn guaranteed protection to the People of the Book. Non-Muslims were exempted from serving in the army, though they could serve as volunteers. The duty of struggle, *Jihad*, is sometimes counted as the Sixth Pillar of Islam. The doctrine of a duty literally to fight has been softened in many ways. It can be argued that early wars as mentioned in the Qur'an were conducted in self-defence. It is also held that there is a greater struggle than that of literal warfare, and that is the inner war on behalf of faith, to eliminate temptations and obstacles to true obedience to God. This is a particularly Sufi teaching.

Shi'i Islam

While Sunni teachings and interpretations of the law are dominant in Islam, in some areas Shi'i practices still prevail. The name derives from the *shī'at 'Alī* or "party of 'Ali." 'Ali was leader or caliph from 656–661 C.E. and in origin the movement was the party which supported him and upheld his right to the Caliphate during what came to be known as the First Civil War within the Islamic community. In theory, from a Shi'i (or Shi'a – lots of Westerners tend to use the noun "Shi'a" rather than the adjective "Shi'i" to describe this wing of Islam) point of view, the Prophet himself appointed his cousin 'Ali as his successor, though in fact the community recognized Abu Bakr. Anyway, the Shi'i party maintained opposition to the Umayyad Caliphate in Damascus, being themselves based in 'Ali's capital at Kufa in Iraq. 'Ali's son Husayn was martyred at Karbala in 680, dying at the hands of an army from Kufa mobilized by the Umayyad forces. It was out of these events that the Shi'a emerged, commemorating the tragic death of Husayn and denying the validity of the succession of Caliphs beginning with Abu Bakr.

The most important branch of Shi'a came to be the so-called Twelvers or *Ithnā 'Asharıyah*, who believe in twelve spiritual leaders, or *imams*, beginning with 'Ali and culminating in Muhammad al-Mahdi, who is supposed to have gone into "occultation" in 941 C.E.. This means that he disappeared from human view, though he is due to return as a messianic figure to restore Islam. This *imam* is a most potent focus of spiritual experience and prayer, who intercedes between God and human beings, and who up to a point fulfills a role not unlike that of Christ in the Christian world. Indeed, the Shi'a expectation is that the coming of the future Mahdi will usher in the arrival of Christ, and this will be the culmination of history.

In the latter part of the eighth century the theory of the Imamate was evolved. This postulated that humanity needs a divinely appointed teacher to lead it and to ensure the continuance of the world. It came to be held that this teacher is infallible and free from sin. Such epithets had been applied to the Prophet himself, and were extended to his daughter Fāṭimah, wife of 'Ali, increasingly the object of veneration in the Shi'a world.

Because of the tragedy of Karbala, and because they were the political losers there, the followers of the 'Ali succession withdrew into a quiet phase, continuing their teachings but often under the surveillance of the dominant Abbasid administration. But their spiritual message was increasingly congenial, particularly in Persia and in South Asia (India). In addition, they had influence in Egypt, Syria, and elsewhere. In the thirteenth century the devastating Mongol invasion of the Islamic world dramatically weakened Sunni ruling power, and in the aftermath the Shi'a took an increasingly political role. During the Safavid dynasty in Persia it was supported by the state. But at the end of that regime, in the late eighteenth century, Shi'i scholars or *"ulamā"* tended to readopt a very passive (though devout) role. Under the Pahlavi administration (1925–79) the influence of the scholars declined somewhat, partly because of secularist modernizing which the Shahs undertook. But this in turn stimulated a backlash, in which a new role for the formulator of the law was advocated, most of all in the thought of the Ayatollah Khomeini, who led the Revolution of 1979. He was thought, by some, to be the Hidden Imam returned to this world. But, at any rate, he articulated a new political role for the Shi'i leadership, which culminated in the notion of an Islamic Republic. This policy meant adopting modern economic and social policies while at the same time saturating civil society with the Islamic Sharī'a.

The Dimensions of Shi'a Religion

The Narrative Dimension
The narrative aspect of Shi'ism is highly important, since it highlights not merely the history of religion up to the foundation of Islam under the Prophet Muhammad, but also the tragic aftermath at Karbala, with the death of Husayn. It also importantly includes the story of the succession of holy

leaders, or Imams, up to the disappearing from view of the Hidden Imam in 941 C.E. But also vivid is the sense that Muhammad al-Mahdi will return. During this period the Mahdi is simultaneously hidden and ever-present to the faithful, and ruler of this world. All this represents a more elaborate story than that which is told among Sunni Muslims. It also gives a measure of authority to the Islamic scholars who carry on the teaching of the Hidden Imam. Also, the sayings of the Imams are included in the collection of *hadīth* or traditions (of the Prophet himself in Sunni Islam, but here extended).

The Doctrinal Dimension

Doctrinally, there are at least two important and distinctive items in Shi‘a. One is the belief in the perfect knowledge possessed by the Imams, so that they know both the inward and outer aspects of the meaning of scriptures. The Imams are also seen as gates to the divine and living proofs of God's existence and mercy toward the world. Second, Shi‘i theology insists on the need to penetrate to the esoteric meaning of both texts and rituals within Islam. There has always been an esoteric side to the Shi‘a, bolstered up by the notion of obscure interpretation or *ta‘wīl*. As a result, Sufism found a warmer home in orthodox Shi‘i interpretation than it did in corresponding Sunni circles. Shi‘i thought also developed important philosophical schools, typically stressing the importance of free will in human life.

The Ethical and Legal Dimensions

As to the ethical and legal side of Shi‘ism, we have noted that there were long periods when the Shi‘a favored quietism rather than a direct link to state or royal power. On the other hand, in most recent times new formulations of the law have emphasized a religion-centered form of government, notably, of course, in Iran. As for the pattern of private and family law, the Shi‘a has the concept of temporary marriage as a possible arrangement alternative to long-term marriage – for use by students, for example. This is not in vogue among Sunnis – indeed it was banned in the early evolution of Islamic law. Generally in the interpretation of the law the Shi‘a rely not merely on canonical collections of the sayings of the Prophet and of the Imams, but also upon *ijtihād* or legal reasoning. The gate of *ijtihād* was closed in Sunni Islam a thousand years ago, thus preserving more traditional ways of expounding the law.

The Ritual and Experiential Dimension

As to the ritual or practical dimension of Shi‘a Islam, there exist relatively minor differences with the Sunna in the practices of daily prayer and procedures during the *hajj* or pilgrimage to Mecca. In addition, there are many vital pilgrimage places in the Shi‘a world, most notably Karbala and Kufa in Iraq, as well as the tombs of the Imams and their descendants. Other sacred places are important university towns, most famously Qum in Iran. In Cairo the head of Husayn is interred, and this is the focus of both Sunni and Shi'a devotion. Probably the most striking festival of Shi'a Islam is the replay of the martyrdom of Husayn, celebrated on the 10th of the month of Muharram. The preceding ten days are typically spent in subdued spiritual remembrance of the tragedy. On the great day, in Iran and India especially, colorful processions are taken out, with ten mobile and finely decorated structures representing the tombs of the Imams. The faithful perform such acts as self-flagellation with chains. The procession includes a beautiful white horse which both commemorates the mount of Husayn and which will serve as the steed of the Hidden Imam when he emerges from his hidden realm.

Traditionally widespread in Shi'a was the practice of Sufism – the inner search which reflects the meanings of all the outer rites prescribed daily and throughout the year.

The experiential and emotional dimension of Shi'a remains vital. The faithful are supposed to reflect in their inner feelings the doctrines and law of Islam. Sometimes, as during Muharram, sorrow and the elevation of martyr's vital role are evident. The idea of dying for God is something which lies as the heart of Sufi imagery; but, at a less spiritual level, it can be invoked by the Islamic Republic to mobilize its sons to military service.

The Organizational Dimension

While the priestly lawgivers are important, having attained their status by learned reputation, Shi'i states have also recognized up to a point the legitimacy of secular rulers, assuming they allow the practice of Shi'a and rule justly. But since the nineteenth century a growing movement has recognized the clergy as possible secular rulers. This is the ultimate basis for the role of the Ayatollah Khomeini in the Iranian Revolution of 1979. In earlier days, the secular sultan was not seen as the real ruler of the world or of part of it, since this is, by definition, the Hidden Imam. But learned men can be his representatives here on earth.

The Material Dimension

Materially, the greatest significance is attached to the pilgrimage centers of the Shi'a world, as well as cities which have blossomed with Persian and Indian architecture. Also noteworthy is the increased use of pictures among Shi'a Muslims, especially of sacred persons in the tradition. Such representations were severely banned in much of Sunni Islam.

Medieval Islam

At the start of the tenth century the claim by the Abbasids of Baghdad to have universal rule over the Islamic world was seriously faltering. Already breakaway reforming dynasties, of Shi'a persuasion, had established themselves in North Africa. An Ismaili group, the Fatimids, came to establish themselves in Tunisia, Egypt, and Syria. At the end of the eleventh century and the beginning of the twelfth, the First Crusade led to the setting up of

Latin States in the Eastern Mediterranean, most notably in Jerusalem. The wars between Christendom and Islam led to a legacy of suspicion and bitterness, which constrasted with the more cooperative relations in Muslim Spain. In the East, the Seljuq Turks overthrew the Abbasids. But, meanwhile, Islamic rule was expanding into India.

While the concept of a unified community disintegrated, and in some degree Arab cultural dominance waned, Islam by this early medieval period was benefiting from its mixture of cultures. There remained wide trade contacts across the Islamic world, despite the disruptions. If we now select Spain as an example it is primarily to illustrate the creativity of a civilization which had reached maturity.

It was during the Middle Ages that we can see the consolidation of the Shi‘a tradition, and the high point of Sufi mysticism. There were offshoots too of Shi‘a, such as the Ismaili denomination, and the Druzes, who incorporated varied esoteric teachings into their philosophy. Though not too widespread today, they had a wide influence, notably on the Fatimid dynasty in Egypt from the tenth century onward.

Islam in Spain: Ibn Rushd and Ibn al-‘Arabī

Two of the most widely known Islamic writers, one a philosopher and the other a Sufi, came from Spain. This itself is testimony to the riches of the blended Hispanic and Islamic civilization which flourished in Spain especially in the twelfth and thirteenth centuries. Ibn Rushd (1126–98) was educated in Córdoba, chief intellectual center of western Islam, and much of his life was spent as a judge there and in Seville. He was commissioned by his Sultan to write summaries and commentaries on the works of Aristotle. He brought to the attention of scholars elsewhere, including Aquinas, features of the Aristotelian position which were highly controversial from a Christian point of view, and indeed also from the point of view of usual interpretations of the Qur’an. These were doctrines such as that of the everlasting or eternal nature of matter, and the blending of individual souls in the one Active Intellect upon death. This seemed to deny individual immortality. He wrote a famous reply to Ghazālī’s distinguished book *The Incoherence of the Philosophers*, which he entitled *The Incoherence of "The Incoherence."* Though by all accounts a good Muslim, he and some fellow students of Aristotle were indicted for irreligion in his last years, and he was sent into exile.

Ibn al-‘Arabī (1165–1230) studied extensively in Seville, and also came into contact with Sufi teachers living there, to whose style of life he was attracted. During a visit to Córdoba he is said to have had an encounter with Ibn Rushd, and he supposedly got the better of him in debate. But the climate was not too good for someone of his mystical inclinations, and intolerance, as the case of Ibn Rushd has shown, might restrict his writings and reflections. He therefore left Spain in his thirties for the Middle East. He visited Mecca and the Ka‘bah and ultimately settled down in Damascus. During his years in Spain he had met Fatima, a famous and, by then, old Sufi woman, whose

During the medieval period, Córdoba was the chief intellectual center of western Islam. The city's remarkable Grand Mosque, built in the eighth century and later taken over by Christians, is a glittering monument to the civilization that the religion had produced.

visage he had seen as if bathed in light. In Mecca he had a similar experience, but in relation to a young beauty, Nizam, daughter of a Sufi master from Persia who had befriended him. He wrote a wonderful poem about her, called "The Interpreter of Warm Longings," which attracted criticism as being libertine. But the poem had a deeper meaning, for she was a symbol of the divine *Sophia* or Wisdom. Throughout his later writings he insisted on the importance of what are called depth hermeneutics – in other words, we should not interpret texts, including the Qur'an, by their surface sense alone.

As a result of his experience he formulated a controversial philosophy of the One, in, among other writings, two particular books, *The Meccan Revelations* and *The Jewels of Wisdom*. In the experience of the One, the soul of the individual experiences complete disappearance, *fanā'*. There is only the One, and all subject–object consciousness disappears. When he returns to the world the mystic experiences *baqa'* or "survival," in which he sees the Many in the light of the One. The One manifests itself as a determinate God and as the world of creation. There are resemblances between Ibn al-'Arabī's system and that of Advaita Vedānta in the Indian tradition, and he was to have an influence on Dante Alighieri.

As well as the poetical, philosophical, legal, and other riches of the Spanish Muslim tradition, there were great architectural achievements, such as the Great Mosque in Córdoba and the wonderful Alhambra palace in Granada.

Developments after the Mongol Incursion
The thirteenth century was a terrible era of devastation, because of the

eruption of the Mongols, initially under the leadership of Genghis Khan. In the first years of the century the Muslim centers of Central Asia were destroyed, along with much of the Persian empire. In 1256 Hülegü Khan, Genghis's grandson, sacked Baghdad and slaughtered large numbers of Muslims. The Mongol successor state in Persia, the Il-Khan principality, was eventually won over to Islam, so that the Mongol rulers began to favor the faith. Later, Turkish power under Timur caused devastation across Central Asia and into India, where the Muslim capital of Delhi was sacked. But a descendant of Timur, Babur, established his rule in Delhi and founded the Mughal Empire, which turned out to be a great patron of both Islam and the arts.

Meanwhile, though the Mongols had struck at the rising Ottoman regime, the latter was to make its way in Asia Minor. Turkish in texture, it ultimately conquered the Byzantine empire and established rule over most of the territories formerly ruled by it, in a kind of alliance between Muslims and Christians. In the fifteenth century, although Islam was driven out of Spain, in much of the rest of the world it underwent a renaissance. It was penetrating deeply into Indonesia and Malaya. It made its way through the patronage of the Mughals in India. It was busy crossing the Sahara and moving into black Africa. Though the Middle Ages of Islam brought it into conflict with rising European power, it was nevertheless a constructive period. In Central Asia, in India and in Ottoman territories, rich varieties of architectural style, calligraphy and painting flourished.

The Dimensions of Medieval Islam

The Ritual Dimension

There remained an essential unity – one maintained during the entire history of Islamic civilization – through the performance of the acts of daily prayer. This was virtually universal across the length and breadth of Islam, from India (now being absorbed into its sphere of influence) to West Africa, and from distant Bukhara in Central Asia to trading posts down the East African coast. Some of the dominant dynasties, as well as many lands, that were under the spell of the religion were now non-Arab. These dynasties included the Berbers of the North African region, the Seljuq Turks and the rising Ottomans, as well as the Mongol dynasties in Iran and India. However, learning that applied to the ritual aspects of Islam, such as the recitation of the Holy Qur'an, remained Arabic. With the rise of the Sufi saints, there were many localized sacred places, such as their tombs, which could be the focus of pilgrimages. The *hajj* remained as a vital duty, even if the demands of medieval travel were huge – so that sometimes secondary centers, such as Bukhara, could substitute for Mecca. It was above all in the Middle Ages that the duties of the Muslim year consolidated themselves. Within Sufi circles, prayer turned more inward and developed into methods of meditation not unlike those of Christian mystics and Indian yogis.

The Experiential Dimension

Some tension remained between those who saw Islam in terms of orthodox prayer, directed toward a supreme and infinite God and those who saw the faith as a pursuit of the inner light and the purification of consciousness. The mystical experience drew upon a sense of unity within, while the external experience of Allah relied on an essential dualism. But both strands of feeling are to be found in the Qur'an, where God is said to be closer than the neckvein – a strong image.

The Legal or Ethical Dimension

The medieval world saw the main lines of Islamic law and morality already in place. It became clearer than ever that ethics and law were to be treated as one in Islam. Morality was, and still is, defined within the framework of, for instance, the personal and family law of the tradition. Because Islamic law took the question of the intention of the actor very seriously, it was not possible to divorce the ethical from the legal. Moreover, because by now the project of building Muslim political power was well grounded in the Islamic imagination, morality could not be something free-floating – it had to be integrated into the general social and political obligations of the citizen. Law was something which developed its own impetus and professionalism, so that centers of learning such as al-Azhar in Egypt came to have great prestige, as with analogous centers like Qum in Shi'a Persia. But there were antinomian techniques, that is, tendencies to flout morality and the law as publicly conceived, in branches of the faith oriented toward inner meaning, such as the Ismailis. Sufism also emphasized new kinds of asceticism for the pious Muslim who has a vocation for the inner life.

The Doctrinal Dimension

In philosophy, there were enormous riches between the tenth and fourteenth centuries, as expressed in the positivism of al-Ash'ari and in the questionable ideas of Ibn Rushd, following Aristotle. The period witnessed a fruitful synthesis of Greek and Qur'anic ideas, and a fertile period of interplay between Christian and Jewish scholars. Islam was greatly responsible for transmitting Classical Greek philosophy to the Latin West. Sufi elements too were vital in new philosophies, such as that of Ibn al-'Arabī, who in turn influenced Dante.

The Narrative Dimension

Here, the major divergence was between the Shi'a interpretation of the role of the *imāms* and the traditionalist Sunni story of Islam and its mainstream succession. Again, the very fact that vital splits could occur over the succession to the Caliphate indicates the close integration between social, political, and religious concerns in Islam. But concern with narrative could have its more historical manifestation. The famous Islamic writer Ibn Khaldun (1332–1406) could give a balanced history of the world as he knew it, together with a good evaluation of the nature of the Caliphate and of the dispute about when and how the end of the world might occur.

The Institutional Dimension

Though medieval Islam had its political divisions, these were mostly counteracted by its transpolitical institutions – the *hajj* or pilgrimage, the *madrasahs* or expert religious colleges, the universal practices such as prayer. The various movements created leaders of varied kinds – *imāms*, Sufi saints, jurisprudents – and these were not officially appointed persons, but ones who depended on reputation and prestige. The framework of Islam, however, defined by orthopraxy (or correct practice) was sufficiently strong for a general Islamic culture to persist despite regional and political differences.

The Material Dimension

In terms of art and architecture, the Middle Ages are Islam's greatest period. The greatest monuments to architecture are found – the wonderful buildings of Spain, the mosques of Samarkand and Isfahan, the beginnings of the Indian style, the Fatimid creations in Cairo, and so forth. These achievements prepared the way for the brilliances of the Ottoman Empire in Turkey and the Mughal Empire in India. There was also the burgeoning of figure painting in Persia and India, a style that contravened Islam's ban on icons of humans and, above all, of God. But such restrictions were overcome in varying ways. Yet the medieval period was also a prelude to the downward spiral of Islamic submersion under the tide of Western colonialism. Having driven Islam from the peninsula, Spain and Portugal were preparing a new, ship-borne imperial era, which was destined to humiliate Islam and which rendered the region unstable from that point on.

Beyond the Middle Ages

While medieval Islam had its remarkable riches, it was, as we have noted, soon to be faced with new challenges. These did not become obvious immediately. The Ottoman Empire captured Constantinople in 1453 and began penetrating into Europe. But meanwhile it was being bypassed. The European powers were going round Africa to the East, and, indeed, it was eventually sea power which proved the dominant factor in history. The Mughal Empire in India succumbed eventually to the British. Egypt, eventually, had to face an invasion by Napoleon in 1798. The Islamic crescent, stretching from Indonesia to West Africa, was beginning to crumble.

The Middle Ages was the most glorious period of Islamic civilization and yet, being politically split in various directions, it was weakened. Furthermore, Muslims had to face a much deeper challenge than they had ever encountered in medieval Europe or Russia. These had been perceived to be inferior civilizations. But the Europe of the Renaissance and of later industrialization was different: it had an unnerving air of superiority. Was it right to think that way? And would the Muslims have to think that way too?

CHAPTER 10

Islam in the Modern Era

Setbacks and Responses

The Reversal of Islamic Fortunes

The year 1683 marked the high tide of Ottoman expansion into Europe. The forces of the Turkish empire failed to take Vienna, which was relieved by an alliance headed by the Polish king, John Sobieski (reigned 1671–96). During the next century large parts of the Balkan possessions of the empire were taken by the Austrian Habsburgs – Hungary, a large part of Romania, Serbia, and other lands. Originally a small principality in Anatolia, the Ottoman empire had risen through its conquests of land formerly belonging to the Byzantine empire to a power which stretched from Central Europe to Kurdistan and south to Egypt. It stretched over most of the Arab lands, including the Holy Land, and considered itself to be the heir to the great early civilization of Islam. But European techniques of warfare had gotten better, and the Ottomans had stood still.

It was not only in Europe that troubles were besetting the Muslim world. The Mughal empire in India was in complete disarray by the end of the eighteenth century, and by the middle of the nineteenth the subcontinent was dominated by Britain. During the seventeenth century the Dutch were extending their hold over mainly Muslim Indonesia. In the nineteenth century Malaysia was taken over by the British, and Islamic North Africa by the French, save that in the early twentieth century Italy gained Libya. The British dominated Egypt and the Sudan. In Central Asia the Russians were advancing into the mainly Muslim areas. Greece freed itself from Turkish rule, and the rest of the Balkans was liberated from the Ottomans, during the nineteenth century.

After World War 1 the Ottoman empire was broken up, and the Arab countries came under the rule of Britain and France through a League of Nations mandated territories scheme: Iraq, Transjordan (later Jordan), and Palestine to the British, and Syria and Lebanon to the French. Britain controlled the small Gulf States. Saudi Arabia was independent under its monarchy and system of Wahhabi Islam (of which more below). But Persia was intermittently under Western dominance. So virtually the whole of the Muslim world found itself occupied by the West. It was a traumatic experience for a once proud and glorious civilization.

Wahhabism and the Saudi Royal Family

The eighteenth century was a period of restlessness in Islam, and there were attempts at the social and moral reconstruction of the faith. Such restlessness was in part sparked by the recognition of the weakening of the Islamic world in the face of Europe. But the Wahhabi movement started in one of the least affected areas – Arabia – which was then seen as so poor and barren that it was little regarded by the marauding Western sea powers. Ibn 'Abd al-Wahhab (1703–92) started his studies in Mecca and Medina, where he was inspired with the task of renewal in Islam, and instructed in the Hanbali school of jurisprudence. Later he studied in Basra and began his preaching career calling for the purification of the religion.

After his return to Arabia he formed an alliance with a local ruler, Muhammad ibn Sa'ud, and after his death with his successor. The Saudi state came to control most of Arabia, but the Egyptian governor was ordered to suppress it, which he did in 1818. Later on the Saudis made a comeback and a second state was established, which fell apart, however, by the 1890s. However, in 1902, a dynamic leader from the Saudi family, one 'Abd al-'Aziz, usually called Ibn Sa'ud (1879–1953), captured Riyadh, and the third, and most important, Saudi state was established, which saw the country develop its fantastic oil riches, and so become a leading power in the region. Wahhabism remained the choice of the royal family and is the official ideology of the state.

The teachings of Wahhab were a call to reform and to go back to the original doctrinal and legal basis of Islam. Wahhab above all preached *tawhid*, or the Unity of God, and condemned those forms of practice which for him signified creeping polytheism. A key example of this would be the veneration of saints at their tombs, which was common popular practice among Sufi-oriented people. His major writing was called *Kitab al-Tawhid* or the Book on the Unity (of God). He was radical in his interpretation of this, since anything which might come in the way of faith in the one God – anything which ascribes ultimate concern to something other than God – is polytheism in principle and so to be condemned. He rejected many parts of medieval law and custom as being innovation and went back to a more strictly Qur'anic law. He also revived the notion of *ijtihād* or informed reasoning as being a source of guidance. Such reasoning had to be directly based on the Qur'an and the early tradition or *sunna*. He used it as the basis for rejecting many of the opinions of medieval jurists. In short, his renewal movement was more or less what we have described as neofoundationalist – going back to the basics of Islam and sweeping away much in medieval practice. The Wahhabi movement regards itself not as a denomination of Islam but as a call to reform, and yet it has come to accept the name (originally used by opponents) as if it were a denomination. It rejects Sufism, which has come under fire from a number of different directions in the modern Islamic world.

The alliance between Wahhabism and the Saudi royal family is institution-alized in the system by which Wahhab's descendants are made the chief religious advisers: they are the "family of the *shaykh*." Ibn Sa'ud used religious fervor in forming an organization of soldiers who were bonded together as the Brotherhood or Ikhwan. In 1929 they revolted, because the state had adopted a fairly pragmatic style which offended against their commitment – but the rebellion was put down. It may be said that in subsequent years a rather pragmatic style has continued to blend with the revivalist conservatism of the Wahhabi ideology. This is especially true since World War II, when the Saudi royal family has had to struggle with the thrills and problems of large oil-based riches.

It may also be noted that Saudi Arabia holds a special place in Islam because of its control of the holy places and the *hajj*. Though Wahhabism has a somewhat fundamentalist air, it does represent in its own way a revived mainstream Islam. It expresses a thought. Namely, if Islam is suffering ravages from other civilizations this is because it has not remained true to its tradition. The flagrant wealth of Saudi Arabia argues the converse. If a country prospers it is because it has remained faithful to the dictates of God and the spirit of early Islam. But its critics may find fault with it for having made too many compromises with Western modernity and for ruling through a royal family – a concept not welcome to many Muslims of more traditionalist yearnings.

In fact what the Saudis have done, in a way largely unparalleled elsewhere, except in Kuwait and some of the Gulf States, is to institutionalize a vast family of three thousand members or more. This skeleton within the flesh of the nation keeps control of most of the important functions of the state. So family and national loyalty are fused in this elite. They also have hired many people to work in Saudi Arabia without giving them political rights. So it is a system of layers of elitism: the elite of the family; the wider family; the nation; and the guest-workers. But the fidelity of the family to Islam is not in doubt, for the constitution of the country is the Qur'an.

Ideologically, too, in accordance with Wahhabi ideas, the country is strongly opposed to willful ignorance, of which a prime example was the atheism of the former Soviet Union. It is strong, therefore, in its anti-Communism. It does not follow, however, that it is sympathetic to Western values, which furnish many examples of *shirk* or polytheism by putting things other than God before God. We will later look at some other forms of conservative revivalism within Islam, which became one option in the face of the West, and need not preclude technological modernization. Briefly, such a conservatism depends on the feeling that nations will be brought down because believers have not been faithful enough to its pure form.

Modernizing Islam

Egypt was part of the Ottoman empire, which was nominally at least the main representative of the Muslim community or *umma'*. But it was easily detached by the West, and the opening of the Suez Canal in 1869 showed that France and Britain had a continuing stake in the region. Anglo–French

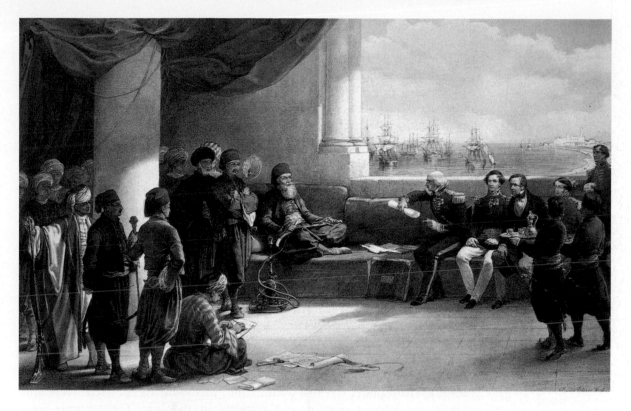

joint rule followed, and after a rebellion in 1881–82 under Arabi Pasha, in which the British fleet bombarded Alexandria, Britain took direct control. It was through this period that Muhammad 'Abduh (1849–1905) lived and worked. Probably the greatest modernist of nineteenth-century Islam, he was educated at al-Azhar, the famous medieval university in Cairo.

He also came under the influence of another reformer, Jamal al-Din al-Afghani (1838/9–97), a colorful figure who professed pan-Islamic ideals. Al-Afghani thought that the prime weakness of Islam was its disunity, and during his travels in India he deeply disapproved of those Muslims who accepted British rule. Against them he wrote a powerful tract. His own position was that of the medieval Ibn Sin'a. People have through reason a natural means of the knowledge of God, but such a use of reason is not easy. For the masses the prophets – and above all the Prophet – have therefore given forth revelations couched in rich symbolic forms. This illustrative approach could adjust easily to the advance of modern knowledge. As our understanding of the world increases, so will our way of seeing the Qur'anic revelation change. Al-Afghani was a great preacher of pan-Islam, and he hoped to revive the universalist aspirations of the Muslim community in the face of the advancing West, particularly the British.

Muhammad 'Abduh partly agreed with these views. His involvement in the revolt of 1881 led to his exile. In Paris he and al-Afghani published

The most successful Muslim modernizer of the nineteenth century was the Egyptian leader Muhammad 'Ali Pasha. He built factories, combated disease, improved agriculture and constructed the first railway between Cairo and Alexandria. He is shown here conferring with Western engineers.

together a radical journal calling for revolution and social reform. Later he was able to return to Egypt, became a judge and in due course *mufti* of Egypt and chief interpeter of Islamic law. From this position he engaged in the reform of Islamic law and the system of religious endowments.

In his thinking he attacked various elements which in his view had wrongly crept into Islam, such as fatalism, and the blind acceptance of tradition. He was influenced by early Islamic rationalist thinking and underlined the importance of free will in human life. As for science, this had developed in the West in part because of Islamic contributions, and there was no incompatibility between faith and modern knowledge. It would be fatal if Muslims rejected modern knowledge for wrong reasons, since it would condemn them to backwardness. So he wished to promote a purified Islam which went back to early days, without such additions as obsolete medieval knowledge and the cult of saints. He was, however, somewhat influenced in this theoretical work by Sufism: the inwardness of religion showed the spiritual compatibility of faith and science; like other mystics he tended to veer away from literal interpretations of the scriptures. He saw early Islamic institutions as pointing toward legislative democracy. For him (in response to Christian missions and claims to civilizational superiority) Islam is the perfect religion, which takes up and universalizes what is good in the Jewish and Christian traditions.

It was under the influence of such modernism that many Islamic states, emerging from under colonial domination, including Egypt itself, were able to combine Islamic religion and reforms in the law, for example over polygamy and in areas such as banking and charitable trusts. The main planks of modernism were as follows. First, Islam must rid itself of medieval accretions, including Sufi rituals. Second, the Qur'an and the tradition had to be interpreted according to the spirit rather than the letter of the teaching. Modernism was influenced by the Wahhabi example in going back to beginnings, but it was liberal and antiliteralist. Law was to be seen under the light of reason, which included arguing by analogy and taking account of the general wellbeing of the community. Such practices as wearing Western dress and eating meat which was not ritually slaughtered were allowed by modernist decisions. Third, Islam was seen as a system which was to be realized in this world. To build a modern Islam was to do much more than preach heavenly rewards.

Following on from 'Abduh was the work of Muhammad Rashid Rida (1865–1935), from the Lebanon, whose magazine *Al-Manar* (The Lighthouse), which he published out of Cairo, had wide influence. Though he was against what he thought of as innovations in belief and worship brought in since the time of the *salaf* – the first generation of the Prophet's followers – he was for change in regard to social norms. He thought of the Qur'an as laying down general principles rather than legal details of right action and the proper organization of society. Because of his appreciation of the central place of the Arabs in Islam, because of the language, he was somewhat identified with the Arab nationalist movement between the World Wars. Nationalism, as it happened, was a special problem in the Islamic context, which had the theory of a single Islamic community and a central leadership or Caliphate.

Nationalism and the Islamic Anticolonial Struggle

It was clear to intelligent observers that nationalism was one of the ingredients of the Western mix and much bound up with the process of modernization, in Europe and abroad. But when applied in the Islamic context it had mixed results. The Indian *khilafat* movement (1818–1924) was based on something wider than nationalism, namely Muslims' loyalty to the Caliphate (*khilafat*). The Caliphate had been maintained in a weak form by the Ottomans, and after their fall was kept on briefly as a religious office in Turkey and then abolished, which caused the collapse of the movement. Still, it did represent one strand in Islamic response to Western imperialism, a pan-Islamic movement. Modernism, however, did move in a nationalist direction, and it was possible to blend national loyalty into the wider framework. Thus the slogan was already used in Algerian Muslim schools before World War II: "Islam is my religion; Arabic is my language; and Algeria is my fatherland."

In the run-up to World War I and in its aftermath, Arab nationalism was widespread, but aimed in the first instance at the Ottoman empire. This blended in easily enough with modernism. But there were also some attractions in Arab socialism, as a concept which battled somewhat against what were seen as the socially disruptive effects of Western ways. Some movements such as Ba'ath socialism, which achieved power in Iraq and Syria in the 1960s, were explicitly secular movements.

Turkey and the Nonreligious Solution

The most spectacular response to events was in Turkey, which under Mustafa Kemal (1881–1938) went the whole way in dealing with the problem of the West. The revolution in Turkey in 1923 followed the bitter war with Greece, which finished in 1922 and ended with the mass transfer of populations and the abolition of the Sultanate and the Ottoman system. The Ottoman empire had modernized itself in a mild way during the so-called Tanzimat (Reordering) period from 1838 onward, and before World War I briefly under the movement known as the Young Turks. But it was Mustafa Kemal, who renamed himself Kemal Atatürk (meaning "Father of the Turks"), who decisively institutionalized a major antireligious and secular revolution from 1923 onwards.

First, a Western-style constitution was introduced, in which (in theory) sovereignty was vested in the people. Second, secular education was introduced, in the Turkish language, and the old religious schools were abolished. Third the *Sharī'a* (revealed law) was done away with and replaced

211

with civil law. Fourth, the Sufi orders were suppressed, saints' tombs were desacralized, clerical garb was for the most part banned, as was the fez head-dress, Arabic was no longer used, Arabic script was abolished, and the language was romanized. Women were discouraged from using the veil, polygamy was stopped, and other apparent forms of discrimination against women were made illegal. Marriages were secularized.

All this profoundly shocked religious traditionalists. But, superficially at least, it turned Turkey into a European-style country. Nothing more drastic has happened in the rest of the Muslim world, except in those few Muslim areas which became Marxist: Albania, the South Yemen, and the Central Asian republics of the former Soviet Union. The Turkish experiment has not been wholly successful, in part because the promise of constitutional government has been marred by military dictatorships. A revival of religious interests has occurred, and some of the harsher Atatürk measures against religion have been modified.

The Muslim Brotherhood in Egypt and Beyond

Egyptian nationalist hopes were in part pinned on the evolution of democratic government after World War I, but this was hampered by the monarchy and by foreign control of the country. As an alternative to a moderate modernism, the Muslim Brotherhood emerged as another option, also modernizing but not in a modernist way. It was founded by Hasan al-Banna (1906–49), who was a primary school teacher. He wished to have a vigorous revival of Islam in the Salafiyah tradition – that is, rooted in the religion of the first generation of Muslims, the *salaf*. We have seen how Rashid Rida made use of this concept too (and it was a theme which became prominent in North African reform movements). Al-Banna had been attracted to Sufism, and though the Muslim Brotherhood which he formed eschewed much that has been added to Sufism through the centuries, it did hold to the Sufi stress on individual piety.

The Brotherhood was a society which embraced a variety of activities: it was interested in politics and economics, as well as athletics. It was a typical modern urbanized religious movement in these ways, not owing much to tradition. But it was radically neofoundationalist in its doctrine and prayer practices, and it worked for the liberation of Muslims from foreign control. The Muslim Brotherhood (*al-Ikhwan al-Muslimun*) rapidly became a highly effective organization in Egypt, with about a million members by the beginning of World War II. By its conferences, its preaching, its publications, and its general activism it made its mark. It also trained secretly in violent and revolutionary tactics.

The creation of the state of Israel provided the group with both opportunity and tragedy. Many young Muslim Brothers took part in the fighting. But on the armistice the Egyptian police chief was assassinated by a Brother, and a while later the Prime Minister. In 1949 Hasan al-Banna was himself killed, probably with official approval. The movement was proscribed by the government. Many fled to carry the organization into other Arab countries, notably into Syria. In 1951 it was legalized again, and had great expectations when the "Free Officers" under Gamal Abdel Nasser (or Nasr, 1918–70) came to power. But the Brotherhood was suppressed again. Later it was allowed to operate again under Anwar el Sadat (1918–81). An extremist version of the movement was behind his assassination in 1981. Again, the problem was Israel: Sadat's peacemaking efforts were viewed as a betrayal of the Arab cause.

In Syria in the city of Hama, a center for the Brotherhood, as many as ten thousand are thought to have been killed. Similar events took place in other major cities in Syria, in 1982. They were regarded as a threat to the Alawi regime, which was based on a small sect, and secular in its ideology. It may have been offshoots of the Brotherhood who seized the main mosque in Mecca in 1979, when much bloodshed followed. So in various parts of the Arab world the group are active, and are regarded as a threat to existing government. They are, as one might expect, as severe on those Muslims whom they consider to have betrayed Islam as they are on the Western threat to Islam (as they see it), often made concrete by the state of Israel.

Though the members of the Brotherhood are modern in their methods of organization and propaganda, they are not modern in their attitude to education and the state. They consider it their duty and their destiny to struggle for the restoration of the *Sharī'a*. A pluralistic state in a Muslim country is a betrayal. A truly Islamic state would have the Qur'an as its constitution. This hard line on the law is important and calls into question the possibility of Islamic modernism. And because they advocate the proper implementation of the law, they would no doubt agree with the dictum of Lord Cromer, who wrote in 1908: "Islam reformed is Islam no longer."

Colonel Gamal Abdel Nasser, a popular Arab nationalist, here being mobbed by supporters.

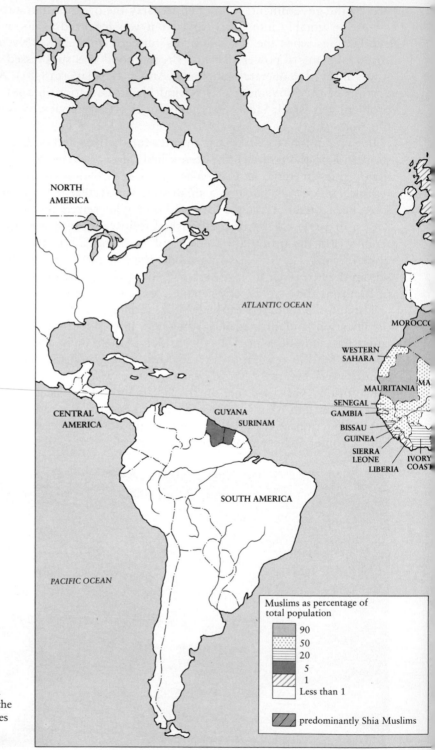

Map 8 Muslim
population of the
world (estimates
based on 1976
figures).

FORMER USSR

EUROPE

FORMER
YUGOSLAVIA

BULGARIA

ALBANIA

TURKEY

ASIA

TUNISIA

Cyprus

SYRIA

AFGHANISTAN

LEBANON
ISRAEL

IRAQ

IRAN

JORDAN

ALGERIA

LIBYA

EGYPT

KUWAIT

QATAR

PAKISTAN

SAUDI
ARABIA

U.A.E.

NIGER

CHAD

SUDAN

OMAN

INDIA

UPPER
VOLTA

YEMEN

SOUTH
YEMEN

BANGLADESH

NIGERIA

DJIBOUTI

INDIAN OCEAN

BENIN

GHANA

CAMEROON

ETHIOPIA

AFRICA

UGANDA

SOMALIA

TANZANIA

Sumatra

Borneo

INDONESIA

Celebes

MALAWI

Comoro Islands

Java

MOZAMBIQUE

AUSTRALIA

Madagascar

0

0

3000 mls

5000 km

215

The Main Themes of Islamic Modernism

The modernists were keen to bring Islam into line with modern thinking and indeed social reform. There were numerous efforts to revive the notion of *ijtihād*. This was an old principle literally meaning "effort," as applied to one's own interpretation of the law. It stood for the right to original thinking, though within a more general respect for *ijma'* or consensus. But by the beginning of the Middle Ages and the formation of the major recognized schools it was declared that the gates of *ijtihād* were closed. This declaration was challenged by many modernists in the nineteenth and twentieth centuries. They were stimulated by the impact of European colonialism, which brought important challenges to traditional doctrine and law.

On the whole the modernists were critical of many medieval and traditional conclusions and methods. They wanted to emphasize the role of reason in theology, going back to the old Mu'tazilah school. Moreover, they strove to find meeting points for modern science and traditional belief in Allah – not difficult since new cosmology and evolutionary theory could be seen as expressions of God's creative methods. In regard to social institutions the modernists were legal revisionists. They wanted new ideals of social justice, which could be gleaned from the Qur'an, though not necessarily in the provisions of the traditional schools of *Sharī'a*. They were critical therefore of the conservative '*ulamā* and sought revisions in the traditional educational process. Also, modernists were strongly influenced by modern democracy, which, despite obvious Western influences, remained resolutely anti-colonial in flavor. Democracy was seen as a strong motif in early Islam. Politically, too, the modernists had a love–hate relationship with the emerging elite in such countries as Egypt and India (and, in due course, Pakistan). These new potential rulers were Western-educated and seen as decadent, despite the fact that they were, in part, bearers of the values that were cited by modernists to criticize traditional Muslims, who were allegedly bringing the faith into disrepute.

While modernism has been a genuine attempt to synthesize modern thought and traditional Islamic values, it has had only limited success. Partly this was because of questions to do with the theory of knowledge – how we know what we know. By taking on board modern science and certain strands in modern philosophy, modernists must assume a critical stance toward knowledge. Science constantly revises and criticism is the engine of change and advances in knowledge; new theories knock down old ones if they can, and so on. But many of the newer modernists, such as the Muslim Brotherhood, subscribe to a very different theory of knowledge: truth, essentially, springs from the Qur'an. So it was not possible to be liberal and critical in the Western sense. Though such "new Muslims" subscribed to many of the modernist criticisms of the '*ulamā* and of traditional learning, they were also rigidly adhered to the Qur'an. So here was a kind of modernism, in method and intent, which was however "fundamentalist."

Both older modernists and the newer, more militant groups are critical of Sufis, even though Sufism is in many ways congenial to contemporary Western thought and science. It is easier to blend Sufi philosophy within the framework of a modern cosmology and ethos. But Sufism is somewhat contaminated, in the eyes of modernists and fundamentalists, with older superstitions: miracles, Sufi saints, relics, tombs and so on.

No doubt, these currents and cross-currents of thought will continue to develop. At the present time liberal modernists are rather out of favor, despite the achievements of Muhammad ʿAbduh and Muhammad Iqbal, among others.

Palestine and Israel

The question of how Muslims should respond to the West has been further complicated by the contradictory promises made by Britain about a Jewish homeland in Palestine and the subsequent foundation of the Jewish State in 1948. This has sharpened Arab nationalism and a sense of solidarity with the Palestinian Arabs. Separate wars in 1948, 1956, 1967, and 1973 have kept up a strong sense of hostility.

An added religious tension comes from the fact that Jerusalem is regarded as a holy city by all the three great religions, and some pious Muslims vow not to rest till they have got back Jerusalem for the Islamic cause. Moreover, it is traditional in Islam to distinguish between the *Dar al-Islam*, the "House of Islam," and the *Dar al-Harb* or "House of War," with the latter being the scene for armed struggle or *jihad*. The state of Israel is like a painful intrusion into the territory properly belonging to Islam, and it is the duty of Muslims therefore to struggle against it. From the Islamic angle, then, Zionism is like a dagger thrust at the heart of the faith. It is also a continuation, from the point of view of the Arabs, of Western colonialism. Without United States support the state of Israel, they argue, would collapse. So there remain many sources of bitterness and strife.

The Islam of North Africa

To the west of Egypt the major part of the North African coast and its hinterland is the so-called Maghreb, from Morocco to Tunisia. It is sometimes regarded as including Libya. The religion of the area came to be dominated by the marabout (*murabit*), a holy person who had wondrous powers as a saint. Such holy men came to be rallying points for centers round which brotherhoods would congregate, and with the brothers the women and children of their families. In many areas the whole population would belong to one center or brotherhood or another, and many people to more than one. All this became very much the standard religion of the Maghreb. The saint's holy power persisted beyond his life, and his tomb would be credited with the same force of *barakah*. It was a North African version of a widespread Sufi phenomenon; and the marabouts were important too in the spread of Islam across the Sahara and into West Africa.

An Egyptian vendor sells tracts and scriptures in a Cairo street. In the last twenty years, Islam has undergone a revival among students and others.

But with the coming of French rule over the region (and, later, Italian rule in Libya), there was less influence of such religion. The reformist Salafiyah movement came to be the more dominant perspective among the new middle classes, on whom nationalism as an ideology began to take a grip. The Salafiyah's explanation of how the Maghreb had been taken over by foreigners was that the religion had been corrupted and divided by the brotherhoods. The Salafiyah was a general movement in the Maghreb, and combined with anticolonial nationalism. But when the various countries achieved independence, religion came to be subsumed under the state, whether in royal Morocco, in socialist Algeria, or in more capitalist Tunisia. In Libya there was also a neofoundationalist critique of the brotherhood. In due course Colonel Muammar Qaddafi (b. 1942) introduced his Green Revolution, which was thoroughly modernizing and socialist in emphasis, and with a strong faith in the Qur'an alone rather than in the traditions which had accumulated in Islam. In all these countries the 'ulamā became subordinated to the state. More recently, though, in Algeria, the government has had difficulty containing Islamic revivalism.

Islam in North America

In the United States, black Christianity had been powerful in the 1960s and had achieved much. But at the same time there were attractions in seeking identity by an alternative route, and the chief of these was Islam. The story of black Islam is a fascinating one, as we will see, because of its move from unorthodoxy to orthodoxy. Blacks in America, generally speaking, did not have much contact with worldwide Islam, though of course quite a number

218

of slaves had originally been Muslim. In the 1920s some Ahmadiyah
missionaries from India came to America, and a number of black converts
were made. But much more significant in the next forty years was the so-
called Nation of Islam.

A peddlar called Wallace D. Fard came to Detroit in 1930 and began
preaching and organizing, but disappeared in 1934. His chief minister was
Elijah Poole (1897–1975), renamed Elijah Muhammad. He declared that
Wallace D. Fard was Allah, and that he was his messenger. He taught that
human beings were originally black, but a bad scientist created an evil race
of whites who were allowed by Allah to rule for six thousand years, after
which civilization would collapse in chaos, to be replaced by a new world
ruled over by blacks. The moral was that blacks should segregate themselves.
Purity of life was to be followed – no alcohol, no smoking, no drugs, no
pork, no movies, no cosmetics.

Eventually the most articulate spokesperson for the movement came to be
Malcolm X (1925–65), who rejected Martin Luther King's nonviolent

219

A crowd raises its hands in response to the preaching of Malcolm X, a major leader of black Islam in America.

approach. However, he went on a pilgrimage to Mecca in 1964 and saw that, in fact, the teachings of Elijah Muhammad were incompatible with those of true Islam. When he returned, he broke with his erstwhile mentor. He was killed in 1965. Ten years later Wraithuddin Muhammad, son of Elijah Muhammad, took over the movement on his father's death and moved in the direction set by Malcolm X. He became Orthodox, opened the community to whites, changed the name to the American Muslim Mission, and stimulated the membership to take part in political life and social action and not cut themselves off from the mainstream of American life. Some of the Nation of Islam predictably stayed faithful to the older vision, under the militant leadership of Louis Farrakhan. Meanwhile Muslim communities from other parts of the world have settled in the States and have been joined by American blacks. The Muslim population of greater Los Angeles is rapidly overtaking the Jewish population, for instance. It is obvious that black experience of Christianity has often been negative, in times of slavery and segregation and persistent racial prejudice, and this constitutes a main reason for seeking brotherhood in Islam.

Other Muslims in North America
Before World War II there were relatively few Muslim migrants into North America. Many of those were from the former Ottoman empire, including Turks, Kurds, Arabs and Albanians. But since that war there has been a larger influx, yielding a total population of some three million in North America. These include significant numbers of Arabs, Iranians, and Turks. Their lobby

is already proving to be of some influence, giving U.S. politics a somewhat different slant from its traditional pro-Israel leaning. Gradually there is an increase in mosques in virtually all large cities of North America, and as these communities begin to coalesce and organize there are increasing opportunities for Islamic education. Though on the whole Muslims are less influential in North America than they are in France, Germany, and Britain they are beginning to have a significant voice in American affairs. On the down side and particularly in the wake of the Gulf War, the media have generally given a less than flattering portrait of Islam, which disturbs Muslim Americans.

Iran and the Backlash against Modernization

In Iran, under the Safavid dynasty, from the sixteenth century, the Shi'a position was consolidated, and it became the official religion. Under the reign of Shah Abbas (1527?–1628, reigned from 1587) the culture flourished greatly, with the building of beautiful Isfahan. Religion was beginning to be enforced, however, and his reign marked the start of a period of intolerance, which nevertheless had the effect of entrenching Shi'a Islam. Eventually, in the eighteenth century, the Safavid dynasty collapsed, and a period of shifting fortunes began. By World War 1 Russian, including Bolshevik, and British intervention was an unsettling feature in the affairs of Persia. In 1921 a coup by Reza Khan (1878–1944), who later took the title Shah of Shahs, led to a fairly stable regime which lasted until 1979.

Reza's policies followed those of Kemel Atatürk. He abolished religious schools, modernized education, discouraged the veil for women, and set Persia (or Iran as it was called from 1935) on a path of Westernization, at least in the cities. Because of his sympathies with Hitler he was deposed in 1944 by the joint action of the British and Russians, who occupied the country. But his son Mohammad Reza (1919–80) succeeded him and took further steps, especially in the 1960s and 1970s, to aid modernization and the huge building up of the armed forces, paid for by massive oil royalties.

The Iranian Revolution of 1979 was both a traditionalist backlash against the changes, and a reaction to the police repression with which the Shah imposed his regime. The opposition forces were a variety of movements – the Tudeh party which was Communist; liberal Muslims; Islamic socialists; and the neofoundationalist Shi'a movement headed up by the Ayatollah Khomeini (1900–89). He had been arrested and then deported in 1963, living first in Iraq, a major Shi'a center, and then in a suburb of Paris, France. His message was a rather new one: he wanted the establishment of an Islamic republic.

Khomeini's Islamic republic would conform to the dictates of Islamic law, and certain constitutional safeguards for this were to be built into the system. It was to be democratic, with a parliament. Though this was a somewhat conservative program, it was also radical in relation to the Iranian past, which had been dominated by kingship. Its purpose was, in the name of Islam, to

221

The Ayatollah Khomeini, shortly after his return to Teheran at the time of the Iranian revolution, which he led in 1979.

remove tyranny and worldly pretensions. It was also radical in demanding an experiment in Islamic living: the law was to apply to banking and the processes of capitalism as well as to marriage arrangements and family living. It was to Islamicize the universities and the whole system of education. It was to make public life obviously and consciously pious.

Negatively, the Islamic republic was to struggle against the twin Satans of Soviet atheism and the irreligious materialism of the West. It was also to struggle against atheist tendencies in the Muslim world, as in Iraq, with its Ba'ath (Renaissance) party regime. The new republic, it was hoped, would be able to export its revolutionary impetus beyond its borders. And indeed in many countries and circumstances Muslims, though they might disagree with Khomeini's postrevolutionary regime, admired the way it re-established a kind of Islamic independence over against the West.

Baha'i: A New Religion from within Islam

Khomeini's Iran was not a tolerant place. It was natural that with this revivalist ideology certain groups would be hounded, notably the Baha'i. For they were regarded not as a separate religion but as Muslim heretics, to whom there could be shown little mercy. The Baha'i movement has become a worldwide religion, with its American headquarters in Wilmette, Illinois, and its world administrative center in Haifa, Israel. But it can also be seen as a radically modernizing movement from within the compass of Shi'a Islam.

222

It follows the teaching of Mirza Husayn Ali Nuri (1817–92), known as the Glory of God or Baha'Allah. He was a follower of the movement known as the Babis, who followed the Bab or "Gate" to the truth. Identified as the Gate was one Sayyid 'Ali Muhammad (1819–50), who was born in Shiraz in Persia. Eventually, when his followers, who looked on him as a link between them and the Hidden Imam of the Shi'a tradition, were involved in rebellion against the regime, he was executed by a firing squad in Tabriz. His teachings involved a symbolic interpretation of the Qur'an, and looked for the coming of a savior figure.

It was with this figure that the Baha'is identify Baha'Allah. When he came to declare his prophetic status, after having a dramatic religious experience when in prison in Tehran, most of the Babis followed him. Exiled to Istanbul, he was later banished with his followers to Palestine by the Ottomans, and settled in Acre. They are another group that looks on the land of Palestine as the Holy Land.

His eldest son, Abbas Effendi (1844–1921), also known as 'Abd al-Baha (Servant of the Glory), carried on with the work of mission and organization, and visited Egypt, Europe and America. In his will he appointed Shoghi Effendi Rabbani (1899–1957), the eldest son of his eldest daughter, as his successor. Since *his* time the movement has been run by a council.

The Dimensions of Baha'i

The *doctrines* of the Baha'i are evolutionary in tone. The various religions of the world, and they were thinking primarily of the three Western ones, are not obsolete or wrong but are stages on the way. Therefore it is all right to think of Muhammad as the "Seal of the Prophets," but only in the sense that he has completed the work of his predecessors. Even the Baha'Allah will in time be superceded. There is much emphasis on the inherent unknowability of God, but his Logos or Word (a kind of rational manifestation of God) makes itself known. Doctrinally, then, the Baha'is are keen to point to the relatively of religious truth and the underlying unity of all religions.

From a *narrative* point of view the Baha'is see the Baha'Allah as setting in motion a new age in which the community of the human race will become the main arena of action, moving toward world government and stressing the equality of all humans and of men and women. A world language (English) is favored, as is nonviolence. *Ethically*, therefore, the movement stresses brotherly love, abstention from alcohol, and service to humanity.

Ritually, the movement asks for daily private prayers, and certain periods of fasting, but it is not a heavily ritualized tradition. The Baha'is, because of their commitment to the underlying unity of religions, are concerned with different forms of religious *experience*, including the development of meditation. *Organizationally*, they have an elective system which is nevertheless theocratic. As for their *material* expressions, the various great temples, such as the one in Wilmette, are huge and impressive structures which contain in their decorative motifs the symbols of the various world faiths.

In brief, Baha'i arose from within the matrix of Shi'a Islam and makes uses of its prophetic themes, latching on to the idea of the Hidden Imam. However, it has evolved into a quite different faith with its own distinctive and modernizing characteristics. It is an example of a spiritual revolution which intuitively recognized the global state of world culture before its time and gave religious preparation for this unified world.

It is thus attractive to people around the world, especially reflective folk who are dissatisfied with the rivalry of the more traditional religions. It experienced great growth in South Asia, and in Africa, where its Islamic coloration but outward-looking message has made it attractive. In Iran it is the largest religious minority, but currently, because of the Iranian revolution, under a deep cloud. Its world membership may amount to about two million.

Islam South of the Sahara

During the colonial period Islam continued to spread into black Africa from the north. Important agents of conversion were the various Sufi orders and the marabouts, who played a leading role in West Africa especially. One of them, from Senegal, Ibrahim Niass (1900–75), was especially important in stressing the universal character of Islam in contrast to the particularist trends which often emerged in the blends of Muslim and local cultures and values. But it was especially the Salafiya movements, led by men who were educated in Cairo and in North Africa, who introduced the more radical anticolonial and anti-Western impulses. They were highly critical of marabout and Sufi leadership in tending to play upon the ignorance of the masses. They wanted a reformed, neofoundationalist Islam firmly rooted in the Qur'an. At the same time, they saw this Islam as able to stand up to the West both in values and in intellectual strength.

In East Africa, Islam played little political role. But Swahili culture was important: the language itself reflected a mixed and fluid Afro–Arab culture. This society had established itself in various centers along the coast and inland, partly as a result of the vigorous trade in slaves conducted by the Arabs in the nineteenth century. Islam got a foothold in Uganda, too, among the Baganda nobility, and this was one area of fierce struggle between Islam and Christianity. Because they were aided by the British, more power went to the Christian missions.

Reflections on Modern Islam

We have looked at Islam in the areas of the Western world where it is dominant. We have seen that modernism and neofoundationalism have been the dominant motifs, and in these movements there is some distancing of Islam from the past. Sufism, despite its popularity in some circles in the West, has been heavily criticized, especially by neofoundationalists, though it has

made a vital contribution to the life of Islam in the former Soviet Union. It was also of great importance in the conversion of large areas of South and Southeast Asia, since it supplied a kind of bridge to pre-existing religions and folk cults.

Gradually, Islam is consolidating itself through reform movements and becoming more unified. This is partly due to the fact that modern air transport makes the *hajj* to Mecca much easier than it was, and this helps to cement Islamic unity. On the other hand, clashes of interest are promoted by nationalism. The break-up of the Islamic world into sometimes conflicting entities can result in bitter conflicts, for example the war which started between Iraq and Iran in 1980. This was partly based on different ethnicities, partly on differences of religion, and more on differences of ideology – between the secular thought of the Iraqi regime and the Iranian revivalism of Khomeini's government.

Despite such obstacles to Islamic unity, at least the infrastructure is being laid. More areas of the world are taking up a renewed Islam, going back to

The ritual dimension: pilgrimage to Mecca has vastly increased with the coming of the Jumbo jet. The circling of the Ka'bah, or Tawaf, is captured by this continued-exposure photograph, with people swirling round the sacred site through the night.

the early days, and thinking about or implementing the rule of Islamic law. But there does remain a gulf between the religious revivalists who want to go back to early foundations and the more radical adaptors of the faith who aspire to some version of Islamic modernism. The signs are conflicting: as Islam spreads into Europe and America and reaches more places where it is in a minority, the greater is the pressure for modernism. But where it has control of the majority of the population, the greater the pressure for a revivalist imposition of the Law. And we still wait for some answer to the question posed by Lord Cromer: Is a reformed Islam Islam any longer?

Dimensions of Revived Islam

Despite the importance of the Iranian revolution, it may well be that the future lies more with the revival movements within Sunni Islam, such as the Brotherhood. At any rate, in a number of countries, such as the Sudan, Pakistan, and Malaysia, there is the pattern of Islamic law being required. There are calls in a whole range of countries for similar legislation. This spirit of revivalism seeks to restore practice to what it was; but often its mission is conducted in most up-to-date terms. We can discern some of the dimensions of this Islam as follows.

Doctrinally it has a tendency toward more, rather than less, literal interpretations of the Qur'an. It is not hostile to science, but it rejects some of the philosophies of medieval and premodern Islam. As far as its *narrative dimension* goes, it of course accepts and focuses on the career of the Prophet. But it also sees Islamic culture as having betrayed the spirit of true Islam through various innovations. It is because of all this that Islam has fallen into its relatively sorry current state. *Ethically and legally* it calls for the revived application of the *Sharī'a*. It is strict about such matters as alcohol and the conduct of women: it usually favors the use of the veil. Since it is traditionalist but not quite traditional (for it arises from the very situation in which tradition is being challenged and overridden), its espousal of tradition is a matter of self-conscious commitment, so that there is a great emphasis on being "converted" to true Islam. It has a much more notable evangelical fervor than would be typical of simply traditional Muslims. *Experientially*, therefore, it is vigorous: but it is not much oriented toward the mystical meditation of the Sufis, since Sufi practices are often what has brought Islam (in its eyes) into disrepute. *Organizationally*, revivalist Islam is much indebted to the methods of Christian missionaries, while it also lays stress on Islamic education. *Ritually*, it is pious in reaffirming the importance of regular public prayer worship. *Materially*, it is often at the forefront of the building of new mosques, especially where the Muslims are a minority. As a result, in the lanes of Sri Lanka and the backstreets of Liverpool, England, new structures will be found, often subsidized by oil money. Islam is at a vigorous global stage.

CHAPTER 11

Classical and New Religions in the Americas, the Pacific, and Africa

The penetration of Christianity and of Western culture generally into the Americas, the Pacific and Africa, was mostly disastrous for native peoples, as discussed in Chapter 7. The different tribes and civilizations, faced with such an onslaught, devised various means, through religion, of expressing new forms of a worldview. These found their basis in indigenous values, while often drawing, at the same time, on Christian ideas. In the Americas, new kinds of prophetism arose; while in Africa, sizeable new religious movements have grown out of missionary teaching; and in Oceania, as well, new forms of Christian faith have come to prominence. But at the same time there have been revivals of the ancient, classical religions in these regions. In this chapter we will concentrate mainly on these classical religions which, in important ways, express older traditions, while at the same time presenting a multiplicity of values for the modern world to contemplate and absorb.

The Americas

It seems probable that all or virtually all the ancestors of the Native Americans in both North and South America migrated there from the Asian landmass by a northerly route, via what is now the Bering Straits. There may be some slight influence of Polynesian settlement, and it could be that in the period before Columbus there were Chinese landings. We also know of a small Viking presence. But, given the relative sameness of a largely Asian immigrant population (and even there, as today, there may have been great variations), the patterns of culture which were created in the regions of the Americas are extremely diverse. Among other achievements was the creation of some great urban civilizations in Central and South America.

Civilizations of North America

Some indigenous cultures of North America are based on sedentary agriculture, with maize being the central product. Notably, there are the Pueblo peoples of the southwestern States, who used irrigation techniques to shape their intensive agriculture. There are other groups, such as the Apache and Navajo, who blend agriculture and hunting; and some peoples who are still very much hunters and gatherers. To the west, in California and the Pacific Northwest, there is a variety of cultures, some very much oriented toward the sea and the catching of the abundant sea life of the area. In the Southeast there is rich agricultural land lining the alluvial rivers, and the region was broken into chiefdoms, some sizeable. Life in the Northeast had a predominantly hunting character, where the area was rich with life in luxuriant woodlands. But there too was the cultivation of the "three sisters" – maize, beans, and squash.

In the Plains, reaching up into what is now Canada as well as the great central part of the United States, the introduction of the horse by the Spaniards considerably altered the economy as it facilitated a new and effective way of rounding up and hunting the buffalo. Before that there was a mix of horticulture and nomadism, involving hunting and gathering. The various groups in the area were somewhat more co-operative than elsewhere, in so far as they developed extensive trade and a sign language which enabled interlinguistic communication. Finally there are the varied groups of the Far North including the ingenious Inuit of the Arctic, who had mastered a highly problematic environment.

Now it is obvious that with so varied an economic spread, and so many different language groups, the cultural variation is immense. But it might be useful just to consider four of the groups as a sample: the Hopi of the Southwest; the Iroquois of the Northeast; the Lakota of the Plains; and the Inuit of the North. In the Hopi I shall emphasize the *social* organization of religion and the *material* dimension, in the Iroquois the *experiential, doctrinal,* and *ethical* dimensions, in the Lakota the *ritual* dimension, and in the Inuit the *mythic* dimension.

Hopi Society

In this exposition the Hopi can stand as an example of the wider group of people settled in small towns and villages (*pueblos*) and known as the Pueblo peoples. It is interesting that they are organized, for ritual purposes, in a rather domestic manner, through the existence of a number of different societies each of which has to realize a particular type of ritual. In each of these groups there are priests and lay folk, and because their presentations are integrated into an annual cycle it means that a certain degree of cheerful competition ensures a high level of ceremonial. The ritual societies themselves are at different levels, so that a young person may graduate through them to senior status. At sixteen, males are initiated into the four main male groups, and the women into the women's society. There is a more exclusive male society which organizes the highly complicated and important ceremonies at the winter solstice. This is the time when the direction of the sun needs to be changed, and plants, animals, and human life need to be renewed and re-integrated in the general cosmic harmony.

Central in Hopi concerns is, of course, maize. Corn is the substance of life, and corn meal is sprinkled as a sanctifying force, much as water is used in

Kachina masks in operation among the Hopi of the American Southwest.

Christian ceremonial. Prayer is accompanied by the sprinkling of corn. When a child is born it is presented with two perfect ears of corn. And so on.

One of the most important features of Hopi ritual life is the *kachina* or mask, with accompanying clothes and body paint, through which a Hopi "performer" mediates the spirit inherent in the mask. It is a kind of icon animated by a dancer. The *kachinas* embody a whole range of supernatural spirits, the dead, and clouds (seen in their own way as spiritual beings). In this way it is possible to enact the sacred narratives of the people, make social comment, celebrate the gods, and bring blessings on the people. There is a special period, from the winter solstice onward, which is the *kachina* period. Afterwards, the sacred masks and other paraphernalia are returned to their home in the mountains until the next season comes round. In this way the material and iconic side of religion is given a living form, since the masks themselves become operative only when they are worn by individuals who, during the ritual, are possessed by the spirits assigned to them. It is a kind of sacred ballet, and requires material manifestation through the masks.

Iroquois Cosmogony, Experience, and Ethics

For the Iroquois the world was the creation of twins, one good and one evil. The Good Twin not only made that which is beneficent in the cosmos, but he also laid down human customs, which were modeled after the excellences of the sky world. The Bad Twin created what is distorted and horrid and against life. He is like ice, hard and cold. Both Twins made spirit forces which exist, both good and bad, in the world. It is the thrust of Iroquois religion, therefore, to fend off the effects of the Bad Twin and to promote the good forces which the Good Twin has made.

These spirit forces can be experienced directly, and for this reason great attention is paid to visions and dreams. Dreams especially are regarded with great seriousness and attention, for they may reveal some of the good and bad things that are in store for the individual or for the group. In this connection, as elsewhere in North and South America, shamanism is important. The shaman is simply a person with extra insight and dream-capacity. Through dreams an individual will come to be related to some spirit who will act as his friend or guardian. It is important to stay in a good relationship with such a force. Very often, illness is the consequence of a disruption of the friendship. It may also be the consequence of alienation within the individual between his body and his spirit. Dreams could be a clue to the secret desires of one's soul, and these have to be fulfilled. So their diagnosis is important, and is the subject of dream-guessing rituals.

Iroquois lived in longhouses shared by a group of families. This made for a strong emphasis on co-operative enterprises. It is perhaps not surprising that on the larger scale there was the formation in the eighteenth century of the League of Six Nations among the Iroquois (Mohawk, Oneida, Onondaga, Cayuga, Seneca, and Tuscarora). The dualistic cosmogony also emphasized the importance of moral values, as being on the side of life, and evil and bad intentions, on the side of death. There was, as with many other Native Americans, a sense of the harmony of Nature and humans as something which needs to be promoted and enhanced. Something of the ethical feeling underlying this is revealed by the fact that most of the Northeast woodlands people apologized to Nature for killing animals or cutting plants. Apologies would be directed at the animal killed, or rather to the collective spirit which the individual animal manifested, and similarly to the tree-spirit when one cut down a tree.

The ethical outlook of the Iroquois is further revealed by the fact that their most basic form of worship centrally involves thanksgiving directed to a spirit or force. The good manifestations of the Sacred Power which pervades the world must be thanked for the fact that they bring blessings on human beings. By contrast the evil use of ritual through sorcery is to be opposed.

The sense of community is enhanced by rituals for the dead. For instance, at the annual Feast for the Dead food is shared with the ghosts, and song and dance are put on to entertain them. There is a sense of the sacramental character of sharing food. Apart from such a high feast there are numerous family meals for the dead.

Ritual among the Lakota

The Lakota originally dwelt in western Minnesota, but moved further west to the Plains in the first part of the eighteenth century C.E. This was a period of great movement and disruption among North American groups, especially in the Northeast and Plains regions. As a result of their move their economic life changed: they were now mainly concerned with hunting buffalo on horseback. The transition from a settled lakeside existence to this nomadic life led to alterations in their cosmology and values. However, they retained their seven great rituals, some of which are importantly representative of kinds found much more widely in the North American scene. I shall describe three in particular.

The first of these is the Sweat Lodge ceremony. The Sweat Lodge is a small domed structure built of saplings and covered with skins, which also represents the shape of the Lakota universe. Heated stones are placed in it, and the water poured on them turns to steam. The person who sits in the structure is greatly heated up, and so he sweats. At the same time this revitalizes his spirit and he is visited by supernaturals and given visions which provide clues to communal or individual concerns. So a medicine person may gain the understanding which can lead to cures of the sick individuals in his or her care.

Not unrelated to the Sweat Lodge ceremony is the concept of the Vision Quest, the second of the Lakota main rites. A person sets forth and stays on a hillside in a shallow hole for a few days, without food or water. He is typically given a vision which is then interpreted for him by a medicine man.

The third ceremony is the Sun Dance, which is the most significant of the Lakota rites. A tree is ceremonially cut and used as the central pole of a lodge which represents the universe. During a whole day the dancers move round the edge of the lodge gazing at the Sun as continuously as possible. Some of them are given hooks which are tied to the central tree and planted in their chests. They are encouraged in their sacrificial act by the martial songs and drumbeats of musicians. The families and groups from various tribes are seated round the lodge to participate in the sacred spectacle. The symbolism

---

Sacred Song of the Shaman (Kwakiutl Indians)

"I was taken away far inland to the edge of the world by the magical power of heaven, the treasure, ha, wo, ho

Only then was I cured by it, when it was really thrown into me, the past life bringer of Naualakume, the treasure, ha, wo, ho

I come to cure with this means of healing of Naualakume, the treasure. Therefore I shall be a life bringer, ha, wo, ho.

I come with the water of life given into my hand by Naualakume, the means of bringing to life, the treasures, ha, wo, ho."

Then Lebid sang his other sacred song:

"He turns to the right side, poor one, this supernatural one, so as to obtain the supernatural one, ha, wo, ho.

Let the supernatural one be the life bringer, the supernatural one, ha, wo, ho.

That the poor one may come to life with the life bringer of Naualakume, ha, wo, ho.

The poor one comes, this supernatural one, to give protection with the means of giving protection of Naualakume, ha, wo, ho."

of the affair is important, and is connected to fertility, for which the sun is a source. The central axis of the lodge (the *axis mundi*) has phallic meanings. The dancers bind themselves to the heart of the cosmic mystery, in preparation for the great midsummer hunts which will replenish the food and life of the whole group. The ceremony is also a great coming together of nomadic groups – or was in the old days – and so has a cheerful social significance.

These ritual themes of Sweat Lodge, Vision Quest, and Sun Dance have a much more general manifestation among Native Americans. They have a shamanic undercurrent: a pervasive theme throughout the Americas.

Myth among the Inuit

The life of the Inuit of the Arctic regions was traditionally a difficult one, which had to be closely interwoven with the seals and other sea animals on whom their living depended. So it is not surprising that among at least the Eastern Inuit there is the widespread story of the Mistress of Sea Animals, or the Sea Woman. Here there is a strange tale of how the sea animals, such as seals, whales and walruses, originated. The Sea Woman, when still a girl, had been tricked into marrying a Petrel who took her off to his land, where she was miserable. Her father went off to rescue her and, bringing her back in a canoe, was threatened by the Petrel who stirred up a big storm. To quiet down the Petrel the father threw his daughter overboard, but she clung to the side of the boat, and he began cutting off her fingers – first the tips, then when she clung again at the next joint and so on. The bits of finger became the various species, small seals, bearded seals, and so forth. The Sea Woman sank to the sea bed, where she still lives.

The moral of the story is that if you do anything offensive to the Sea Woman she will withhold your catch of animals. Sometimes it was thought that the transgressions of humans would create dirt which would lodge in the Woman's hair, and because she had no fingers she was unable to comb it, and it would become uncomfortable. A shaman would be needed to go beneath the sea to her abode. After a struggle with her he would comb her hair and she would release the animals. In some Inuit cultures there were also symbolic sacrifices to the Sea Woman every year to ensure a good harvest.

A shaman's mask from the Tlingit of Alaska.

Such a myth as that of the Sea Woman attests to the idea that behind a species or a set of species (the animals which the Inuit hunted) lies a Spirit. It follows, then, that we have to enter into good relations with that Spirit if we are to have success in the anxious business of getting food through the year. Here as elsewhere, the shaman is important.

If anything is close to being a universal theme in the Americas it is that of shamanism. The sacred center of Tenochtitlán and the pole erected in the Sun Dance both attest to the symbolism of the *axis mundi*. The Sweat Lodge and the drugs of ancient Peru both attest to the Vision Quest. The figure of the priest and healer who also has the secret of fertility is one of the great symbols of the archaic world.

The Revival of Native American Religion

The twentieth century has seen some success in the Native Americans' struggle for recognition of their rights. In some degree this has furthered and been furthered by a pan-Indian ideology. To start with there has been the spread of practices and ideas across cultural and national boundaries. Notable among such is the peyote cult, focusing on the sacramental use of the peyote cactus. This had been in use in Mexico before the present century, but it gathered force in the 1890s, spreading through the Plains. The rituals are conducted under the loose canopy of the Native American Church, which has had a powerful struggle to gain recognition (the combination of missionary prejudice and the fact that they used a mind-altering drug placed special obstacles in their path). The central ceremonial, to commemorate special occasions, takes place in a *tipi*, and is conducted according to a fairly complex pattern. The ceremony culminates in singing under the influence of the peyote, which brings a feeling of nearness to God (often conceived in Christian terms). All this has helped to give a sense of – if not pan-Indian – at least cross-Indian solidarity.

Further in this direction of Native American unity is the use of a combination of traditional rituals, from peyote to the Sweat Lodge and from the Sun Dance to the Ghost Dance, in order to promote health and well-being. Politically, this loose pan-Indian religiousness is fast becoming a primary underpinning of struggles to regain sacred places. In this the activist American Indian Movement has been a major force. At the same time, in higher education, increasing attention has been paid to Native American religions, a consequence of the great growth of Religious Studies as part of the new flow of ideas in the 1960s and the 1970s. To some extent this revival links with the struggle of Americans of Mexican descent to establish their rights and dignity, since there is a similar concern with some of the ancient religious traditions of Mexico and Central America.

Civilizations of Central America

The Maya

The classical civilization of the Maya in Southeastern Mexico and in Guatemala and Belize still survives in a fragmentary way, not only in the great ruins of the area, such as at Chichén Itzá and Mayapán, but also in the cultures of people who still speak Mayan languages. Their cultural achievements in art, writing, and mathematics were considerable. They also invented an ingenious calendrical system which was used to calculate and foretell auspicious days. It was based on units of 20, and so on a 360-day year, being the closest multiple of 20 to the real length of the year. Years were calculated according to a Short Count of 256-year cycles or a Long Count which started at the year 3114 B.C.E. The use of the Short Count persisted among the Maya until the eighteenth century, one of a number of long survivals of the culture after the Spanish conquest.

The ethical dimension: A Mayan relief from Yaxchilan in Guatemala, showing a penitent mutilating his tongue before a priest. British Museum, London.

Time became the fundamental preoccupation of Maya culture, and this was tied, of course, to the revolutions of the Sun. The Sun God became the main focus of religion – he was also the creator and the first priestly figure who invented writing. The cosmos was arranged vertically in seven layers of heavens and below the earth were the five layers of the underworld, which was the realm of the dead. At the centre of the cosmos stood the First Tree, the *axis mundi*. This is reminiscent of many other cultures, and may reflect the fact that some shamanistic motifs had entered into early Maya thought. But it seems that the sacred character of time which could be calculated by an esoteric arithmetic was the chief occupation of the priestly class.

The Aztecs

For the Aztecs their wonderful capital, Tenochtitlán, was the chief marvel of civilization. In its immense size and beautiful architecture it was modeled on the older Toltec city of Teotihuacán, the "Abode of the Gods," about thirty miles to the north, and in its division into four quarters it reflected the Aztec understanding of the cosmos. These four directions, together with the center, are the typical five directions of Central American (as of Chinese) cosmology. The cosmos had its axis or invisible center in the vertical line which ran through the City, with thirteen heavenly levels arranged above and nine layers in the underworld. The number five was also important for time as well as space. The universe has five major periods, each ending with various calamities. In modern times, we are now embarked on the period of the Fifth Sun, when the sun rises in the East.

But the universe is gravely unstable, for the continuation of order requires continuous sacrifices. Indeed, before the start of the Fifth Sun the gods had to combine to energize the Sun, which did not rise above the horizon, by sacrificing themselves collectively. This myth provided justification for the continuing sacrificial cult which was centered in Tenochtitlán. The Aztec emperor was also the highest priest. There fell to him the task of maintaining not only the order of the empire but the order of the whole cosmos as well. So the Aztecs had this rather haunting and terrifying thought that indeed the Sun might not rise tomorrow, that the onward harmony of the world was something which was for ever in jeopardy. There was, therefore, a deep resonance between the cosmic and human worlds. The Sun requires human blood: this was the ideology of human sacrifice, itself a great stimulus to warfare, which was waged to capture fodder for the gods.

The central rites of the empire, then, presided over by the emperor himself, were human sacrifices in which a victim's chest would be opened and the still quivering heart torn out and presented to the gods. It was a grim rite, and we may be blinded to the beauty of the city itself, in its fertile valley amid lakes, with towering mountains in view, its hanging gardens and intense cultivation of vegetables and fruits, its geometric layout, its white houses and great pyramidal temples, and its ready sunshine. Its weakness lay in its centralization and its commitment to warfare, which was bound to bring countervailing military forces to bear sooner or later.

Civilizations of South America

The Religion of the Incas

The Inca religious system of the fifteenth century was an amalgamation of earlier cults, and in a way that emphasized and organized imperial rule. Roughly, the empire was a centralized federation in which local chiefs were summoned periodically to the capital Cuzco (or "Navel," that is, center of the earth). The central Temple of the Sun at the junction of the rivers may also have been linked to the Milky Way, also seen as a river. At any rate, here was the center of empire. From here radiated theoretical lines along each of which was placed 428 shrines. There were reciprocal relations between Cuzco and the approved sanctuaries of the provinces (but many local cults were suppressed, no doubt through having supported resistance to the greatly expanding Inca empire). The imperial ideology represented the emperor (the

Inca) as responsible for the welfare of the empire, and so he was the chief point of intersection of his subjects and the great gods. He had to preside over earthly affairs during the present cosmic cycle. He was thus himself a god, the offspring of the Sun, which was the great deity at the heart of the ritual complex at the temple of Cuzco.

Doctrinally, some great store seems to have been set by the binary oppositions of the cosmos: male–female, Sun–Moon, and so on. Likewise, villages were divided into two halves, and the whole earthly and cosmic system was seen as both in conflict and capable of being harmonized. It was the Inca's chief function to contribute to this harmony, by relevant offerings and by the maintenance of the cycle of public rituals. There are echoes of the Chinese search for harmony amid the polarities of Yin and Yang.

The glories and complexities of the ritual year must have been great. The ceremonies at Cuzco were dazzling, with the Inca on a gold throne presiding over sacrifices in the gold-plated halls of the temple. The ability to control so large an empire depended in part on these rites. But it also must be remembered that everywhere in the villages and homesteads of the vast region men and women celebrated their divine ancestors and had relations to lesser *huacas* to help them with their gardens and food-growing, and in the fight against illness and death. But the weakness of the system was its intense centralization, which is why in 1532 a few adventurers under Francisco Pizarro could strike in such a deadly way at the heart of the system.

A mushroom-shaped stone from Central America. This may have represented a shaman who was influenced by hallucinogenic mushrooms.

Smallscale Societies in South America

The conditions of existence in South America outside of the Andean region are very varied. Many of the groups in the tropical forest regions of the Amazon and Orinoco basins do not seem to have anything but occasional belief in a High God or Supreme Being. However, such a belief is widespread in the regions of the Pampas and Patagonia. The rituals related to ancestral cults and the preservation of the dead are much more common in the Andes than elsewhere – perhaps because climatically such practices as mummification become feasible, whereas in steaming forests the dead decompose alarmingly fast. Fertility cults and vegetation deities are important in the northwest Amazon region and elsewhere, but not in the Grand Chaco. So we can point to considerable variety, reinforced of course once one begins to look at the content of the various mythologies.

One element, however, is almost universal outside the Andes: shamanism. The shaman was important because by his experience and ritual powers he could project himself into the invisible worlds. He could therefore cure those who might in a sense have died. But he could also enter the worlds of the spirits whose manifestations were in this world – as fish, animals, birds, and so on – and could give guidance to hunters and gatherers (as many of these smaller-scale societies were).

The Pacific Experience

Tabu and Mana

Before we embark on a description of some features of Pacific religion, it is worth noting that it is from its vocabulary that have been drawn two highly important words which have been prominent in the comparative study of religion – *mana* and *tabu* (or taboo). The latter indeed has passed into the stock of ordinary English usage. The term *mana* came to prominence through one of the major theories of the origin of religion formulated by the anthropologist R. R. Marett (1866–1943) in a book published in 1909, *The Threshold of Religion*. He drew upon the reported findings by a fellow anthropologist in a book on the Melanesians published in 1891 that the fundamental concept of their religion was *mana* or power – for instance the power residing in a chief, or a rock, or in some sacralized object. It came to be noticed that similar ideas were to be found in a variety of small-scale cultures across the world. The idea was then taken up by some major theorists, notably Gerardus van der Leeuw (1890–1950), who in his famous *Religion in Essence and Manifestation* made power the central notion in his account of religion.

Tabu reached the West through the account by the famous explorer Captain Cook (1728–79) of his third voyage to the Pacific. He used the Tongan word *tabu* which is equivalent to the more general Polynesian *tapu* and Hawaiian *kapu*. The idea of *tabu* came to be important in writing on the nature of religion and society, referring to interdictions on actions which had a sacred force. Sigmund Freud (1856–1939) gave the term a new psychological force in his famous *Totem and Taboo*.

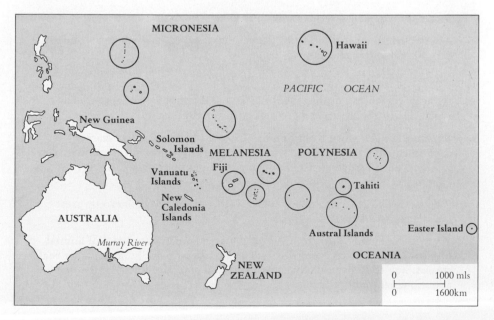

Map 9 Australia and the Pacific Islands.

Smallscale Pacific Island Religions

Polynesian Religion

The most important distinction in Polynesian religion is that between the spiritual or invisible world and the world which we can see and experience. The two are interwoven: the gods are the various forces which lie behind visible events, such as thunder or menstruation, and by their nature they are frequent visitors to the habitations of human beings. There is a distinction often drawn between the heavenly world, the place where the gods are when they are not with us, and the underworld whither the spirits of the dead pass.

Smallscale Religions some key terms

Atua (Polyesian) a god or supernatural being, from the creator Tangaroa to local deities.

Calumet French term now applied to all smoking instruments of Native and South American peoples. Smoking is a ceremonial act, and the pipe is a microcosmic model of the universe.

Corroboree Aboriginal festive occasion with ceremonial rituals and dances, often reenacting myths.

Kachina Masks and other representations of mythic beings used among the Pueblo Indians of the American Southwest.

Mana Sacred and numinous power associated with gods, breach of tabu, holy forces in nature, etc.; used by anthropologists and others as a key notion of religions.

Marae (Polynesian) sacred area with shrine.

Masalai (Melanesian word from Papua New Guinea) animal spirits and demons liable to haunt human beings.

Mizimu (Bantu) the spirits of the dead: ancestors.

Nganga Specialist in dealing with illnesses and various evils: a so-called witch-doctor (Southern and Central African traditions).

Shaman (Tungus word from Siberia) a visionary who can, in sharing experimentally in the vicissitudes of the sick, help to cure them and who can locate resources (such as fish and game) in a hunting society; often experiences death and rebirth.

Tabu or *Tapu* (Polynesian) that which is forbidden and dangerous; great mana generates tapu.

Totem (Algonquin word from North America) a natural species of animal or plant life connected especially with a clan, who do not hunt or gather that species: key concept in many anthropological and psychological theories about the nature of religion.

Most rituals are concerned with attempting some control of the gods. If they are to visit us, then it is best that they do so where and when we want, so it is important to prepare dwellings for them and form incantations to bring them hither, please them, and then (quite as important) send them back to where they came from. Anything that has to do with the gods must be done with great care. The taboos involved are simply a reflection of the fact that gods are dangerous. So indeed is any person with great *mana* or inherent power. The concept of *tabu* pervaded the whole realm of rituals – whether to do with crop-planting or preparing to set out on a voyage – in that it was a general theory of possession and how to encourage and avoid it. The masks and carvings of Polynesian art, for example, represented likenesses of the gods, or things congenial to them. They could thereby be induced to come, regaled with songs and dances, and be safely sent on their way.

Polynesian religions give various accounts of the creation of the world, often by a great God. A moving instance of this is in the following poem from Hawaii about the God Ta'aroa:

He existed, Ta'aroa was his name
In the immensity
   There was no earth, no sky
   There was no sea, there was no human:
Above, Ta'aroa calls.
Existing alone, he became the universe.
Ta'aroa is the origin, the rocks.
Ta'aroa is the sands,
It is thus that he is named.
Ta'aroa is the light;
Ta'aroa is within;
Ta'aroa is the germ.
Ta'aroa is beneath.
   Ta'aroa is form;
   Ta'aroa is wise.
He created the land of Hawaii,
   Hawaii the great and sacred,
   As a body or shell for Ta'aroa …

The mythic dimension: Tangaroa (or Ta'aroa), the god of the ocean, was regarded widely in Polynesia as the great Creator, and here lesser deities are seen coming out of his body, symbolizing their dependence on him.

Maui, Ta'aroa's equivalent from the Society Islands, was often thought of as half god and half human. This half-and-half condition is often the characteristic of crafty people in myth, who thereby confound human categories: it is the hallmark of the recurrent figure known as the Trickster. Maui represents an important motif in Polynesian myth, for though he does not create – which is the prerogative of the gods – he nevertheless may turn what the gods have made into something useful for humans. This is indeed the whole point of ritual, which is not to create power but to direct it, and not to make order but to modify it. Maui, for instance, stole fire from the gods, so that humans could cook and use it in other useful ways. He also fished up various islands with his fishhook, including the North Island of New Zealand, according to Maori myth.

Naturally there are vast resources of myth available in the Polynesian world, and these few examples will suffice for a glimpse into this narrative world. Such stories of the gods, from another angle, help as metaphors of society and social norms, and it is within the ethos of Polynesian religion that morality has its meaning.

Melanesian Religions

If there are variations in the Polynesian world, there are even more so in the whole range of Melanesia. The island of New Guinea, comprising what are now Papua New Guinea, an independent state, and Irian Jaya which is part of Indonesia, contains more than 1000 languages, some spoken by less than 200 people. The islands have diverse cultures, some heavily influenced by Polynesian motifs, as in Fiji. But if one can generalize, then one might say that the Melanesian religions have more confidence in the manipulative power of ritual, and they feel less dependent on the gods. Gods there are,

The ritual dimension: in Papua New Guinea and New Ireland masks and headdresses are ceremonial means of assuming the identity of gods and spirits.

and all kinds of spirits – but they are closer to the earthly realm and not too difficult in many cases to control. The importance of primary power or *mana* can be seen from this perspective, for it is this energy that humans would like to manipulate, and it is the ritual system which manages to do this that is important to Melanesian culture.

Micronesian Religions

The worlds of the Micronesians are varied too. But they have somewhat more concern than the Melanesians with the creation, and the emphasis on female deities is greater. This may be partly because, while males are involved in fishing, navigation, housebuilding, the martial arts, and so on, women are in charge of the gardens and agricultural work. Nevertheless, typically women are thought of as inferior and polluting, because of menstrual blood and giving birth. Sometimes, even so, the High God and Creator is thought of as female, and goddesses are frequently credited with the creation of differing food plants. In the Carolines the Great Goddess, Ligoupup, always existed, and made the world. She is conceived as lying beneath the islands, and when she stirs then there are earthquakes. Her son became god of the underworld and the sea and all that pertains to it; her daughter rose to heaven and wed a deity, by whom she had a son, Aluelap, who is the source of all knowledge. Elsewhere the High God is nominated as Anulap, who is ancient and white-haired, and so very weak that two servants raise his eyelids so that he can see and raise his upper lip so that he can eat. He is a very colorful representation of what historians know as the *Deus otiosus* or "Superfluous God," who is inactive with regard to human affairs (often being so high and spiritual that humans cannot imagine how he could be concerned with the trivial worries of the human race), and is consequently no longer worshiped. Still, he is creator, knows all, and is Supreme Being.

In many ways the Micronesian religious world is like that of the Polynesians, and there has been some Polynesian cultural influence in some of the islands. They are a part of the great mosaic of religions of Oceania, opened up eventually to Westerners from the sixteenth century onward, as navigators from an alien world discovered the often idyllic-seeming islands.

Australia: the Land of the Dreaming

Finally, in our survey of the Pacific religions, we come to the classical culture of Australia before the whites came to settle the land, some two hundred years ago. The societies which inhabit the vast reaches of Australia, from the snowy mountains of the Southeast to the red plains of the West, are varied, but they display some traits in common, which we can look on as classical features of Australian religion and society. The most striking of these is the concept of the Dreaming.

The Dreaming (or Dream Time) is that period long ago (yet still somehow present to us in everyday life) when the deities moved about on the earth, giving shape and substance to the land, generating human beings, and arranging the rules of society. It was in its own way a creative epoch, but it is much more than some generalized period of cosmogony. The Dreaming helps to explain the most particular items in the environment. That environment is – for the most part – a rather harsh one, in which ingenuity is needed to live successfully. It is a hot land, with red deserts and glittering eucalyptus trees, half-dried watercourses and dry gullies, sparse rains and elusive high clouds, grand rounded rocks and strangely contoured hills. It is a land populated sparsely with ingenious animals – the kangaroo and the wallaby, the ant-eating echidna, the lizard goanna – and bright birds, from the small kookaburra to the flamboyant galahs and bright-colored parrots, and many insects, notably the creators of great anthills and the ever-present flies. It is this environment that received its particularities in the phase of the Dreaming.

Important in the cycles of Australian myth are the routes which the protagonists took across the countryside in the Dreaming. These tales indicate places which are sacred, either because of events described in the myths or more intensely because they relate to the fertility of some relevant species. For instance, there is the story of Ngurunderi, in the Murray river region of south Australia. He went down the river in a canoe, after the great Murray Cod, which swished its huge tail to and fro and splashed the water around. It formed the many bends in the river and the swamps which line it here and there. Eventually Cod was caught by his brother-in-law, and he strewed the chopped-up bits into the lower Murray and the lakes at its mouth, to make many species of fish for later humans to gather. Or again, there is a myth from the far north which concerns a famous and widespread mythic figure, the Rainbow Snake. She came from the sea, but at first only found dry – very dry – land. She traveled underneath the earth and came to a waterfall. She went downstream, and when the water disappeared she dug out a large billabong (a pool in a river which is cut off from the flow) and produced an egg, which she set out to harden in the sun, and then slept in a cave. An old man came along and cooked the egg. She grabbed him and dragged him under the water, vomiting up his bones, which hardened. She made two more eggs which hardened there in the pool. She looks after them from the cave above the billabong. This is a highly particular myth, relating to a highly particular sacred site, with its spirit presences, the Rainbow Snake and the old man, frozen as it were into immortality by the tale.

The desert is the great area of mythic tracks where the gods and spirits went on their travels. You cannot know all the stories, and differing tribes characteristically knew different parts of the meaning of the overlapping sacred geography. In such ways the whole land was haunted by divine presences, projected into the Now from the time of the Dreaming. But the Dreaming of course does much more than present us with a sacred cartography. It accounts for social custom, for clan organization, for inventions – in short for the whole of arrangements for living. It explains rituals which in turn are designed to channel the Dreaming to us so that we can benefit from its powers.

Ecopsychism

That organic web of mythic tracks was indeed ruptured by the coming to Australia of people who had very different views of the relation of land to people and of supernaturals to society. But we must first make the imaginative leap to that world which has lasted some 30,000 years or more. We know little of its ancient styles when it first came to the Australian mainland. But we can reach back to view Aboriginal culture before the coming of the Europeans. We see a remarkable experiment in living in which diverse social groups crisscrossed the same land. They managed between them in a segmented way the sacred places and tracks of a unitary landscape, and saw with an inward eye beyond the rocks and trees and leaping animals to the spirits that infused the creation around them and gave sanction and meaning to their customs. Complicated social divisions and initiations and rites meshed in with hunting and gathering, across a changing daily scene. The Aboriginals pioneered a form of ecopsychism, a kind of gently effective way of living in a Nature which was itself conceived as infused with spirits.

It is rather different, this Australian world, from that of Melanesia, Micronesia, and Polynesia, where the sea is often dominant, and the land rich. Here there is a different, drier scene, and one where much more so than elsewhere the diverse social groups are more open to one another, for they

Aboriginal art in Australia: this depicts an episode in a story of Western Arnhem land, with fragile spirits enticing a hunter.

243

share an interwoven system of sacred tracks and places. The Rainbow Snake's eggs have hardened in the sun, and there are unseen persons hovering round, and in, the billabong.

The Configurations of Africa

The traditional religions of Africa before the colonial period divide roughly into four groups. Firstly, there is old Christianity, which in its Coptic form is present in Ethiopia and has had a long history, from at least the fourth century C.E. There has also, secondly, been a community of Jews there. Third, there is Islam, which occupies most of North Africa, though traditionally there are some Christians, including the Coptic Church in Egypt, scattered in among the Muslim majority. Islam has also come south, across the Sahara to much of West Africa, and into the Horn of Africa, the Sudan, and beyond. Then, finally, there are what may be called the classical (traditional) religions of black Africa. It is with these latter, as well as modern Christian/classical hybrids, that we are concerned in the next two sections.

During the period up to 1500 C.E., trans-Saharan trade from the Muslim countries of North Africa stimulated the creation of larger kingdoms to the south – for instance the empire of Ghana in the interior of West Africa, from the eighth to the eleventh centuries, and its successor Mali, at its peak in the fourteenth century. There was also the state of Songhay and important Hausa trading cities in what is now northern Nigeria. In Nigeria and to the west were the forest kingdoms of Oyo, Benin, and Akan. Further east, in the fifteenth century, there was the Funj empire in the Sudan. Various nomadic peoples were filtering south through Africa, among them Bantu-speaking groups. In Zimbabwe, between 1200 and 1500, and in the lower Zaire, in the region of Kongo, were other concentrations of culture and power. Some of these developments were affected by the incoming European influence which had become more marked with Portuguese settlements and expeditions from the fifteenth century. But the dearth of written records means that it is hard to penetrate clearly into the early period.

The creation of kingdoms in the medieval period involved the formation of an ideology of divine kingship, which can still be found in the classical religions of West Africa in particular. This was a natural change, but not of course without conflict, and so we find some traces in ritual of the fight which local cults put up in face of imperial pretensions. As elsewhere in human culture, kings were often associated with the fertility of the land. Generally speaking we are looking at a period after the introduction of settled agricultural practice (often necessary to create the wealth to sustain a widespread monarchy), and this itself tended to breed cults related to the production of riches from the land. These could be grafted on to the kingly ideology. It seems to be the case that the ideal of the sacred king was arrived at in several places in Africa independently, a testimony to the human force of certain ideas with new economic and political developments.

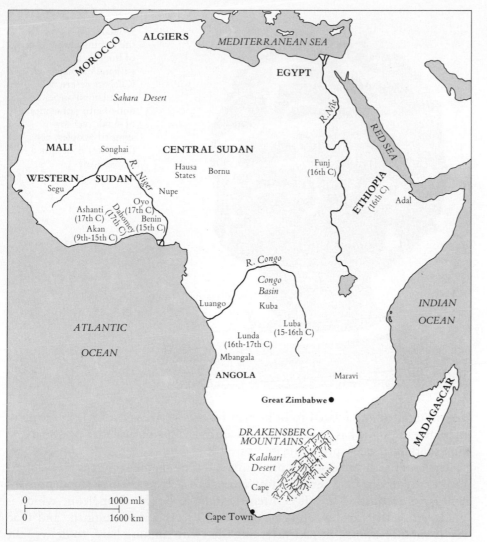

Map 10 Africa, showing locations of tribes between the ninth and seventeenth centuries.

It is, of course, hard to say that there is anything precisely common which we can label as *African* religion – it is only in recent times that African self-consciousness has arisen. Yet there are themes which recur. What we shall do is survey what we can know about religion as it existed when European contacts began. The thematic resonances which we shall explore in the next section are drawn from four different tribes: the Yoruba, from Nigeria, Benin, and Toga; the Nuer from Southern Sudan; the Mbuti of Central Zaire and the Zulu people from the Natal.

Dimensions of African Religion

Mostly, the *doctrinal* content of African religion is anthropomorphic – that is, gods and spirits, those unseen forces which explain and affect human life,

A Bushman or San woman, belonging to the diminishing group of hunters and gatherers around the Kalahari desert, who represent an ancient non-Bantu population of small, yellow-skinned peoples; her face-paint is designed to ward off threatening spirits.

are thought of and related to in human terms. Moreover, much of religion, naturally enough, has to do with human life. This means that personal and this-worldly models predominate in myth.

Myths of death and disorder predominate. One theme concerns messengers of life and death. God sends a slow animal to deliver the news that humans will have everlasting life. It is often thought to be the chameleon, which is made up of the joyous colors of the rainbow. But it is sluggish, and God sends another animal, impatiently, like the swift-running hare, to deliver the news of death. So it turns out that humans are subject to death. God may have wished us eternal life – but it is the result of natural events that we have to die. Themes of disorder in the natural world are typically seen through the figure of the Trickster (which offers interesting parallels with North American religions).

Human shortcomings, such as quarreling and greed, are symbolized in the figure of the sorcerer who plots against the group, acting by night in the bush, naked and incestuous, cannibalistic, and living with wild beasts. The opposite of such characteristics defines a general *ethic*: actions must be harmonious; open and in the light of day. The dead are mostly treated with respect. The procedures of the funeral and mourning become vital social obligations to heal the wound caused in a group by the separation of one of its members.

The Gabon Pygmies on Exile

The night is black, the sky is
   blotted out,
  We have left the village of our
   Fathers,
  The Maker is angry with us ...
The light becomes dark,
   the night and again night,
  The day with hunger
   tomorrow –
  The Maker is angry with us.

The Old Ones have passed away,
  Their homes are far off, below,

Their spirits are wandering –
Where are their spirits wandering?
Perhaps the passing wind knows.
Their bones are far off below.

Are they below, the spirits?
Are they here?
Do they see the offerings set out?
Tomorrow is naked and empty,
  For the Maker is no longer with
   us – there,
  He is no longer the host seated
   with us at our fire.

The most potent *ritual* in sub-Saharan Africa is sacrifice. This may take the form of the offering of plant life, but more characteristically it involves taking life, of sheep, goats, cattle, or chickens. The blood of the animal often is thought to represent its life force, and so it has power, for instance to ward off evil forces. Sacrifice is, as elsewhere in the world, a gesture of communication with the god. It can range in function from healing (by transferring the disease to the animal) to expiating human misdeeds.

Seasonal festivals, changes in the social order (such as the installation of a chief), the marriage ceremonies of individuals (which also often cement family alliances) and the arrival of adulthood – all these are commonly celebrated in ritual sacrifice.

The awareness of the gods in the rivers and the rains, in the forests and in the sky, in lightning and wild animals, is given in *experience* by a sense of spiritual and uncanny power. Very common throughout Africa are those occasions, which can be spontaneous, of the possession of a person by a spirit. In a real way, then, the deities of Africa are really present in society and are commonly experienced.

There is a spectrum of religious specialists in the societies of Africa which range from priests, associated with cults and rituals, through prophets and diviners, to healers. These represent the *institutional* or *organizational* dimension. African traditional ways of curing sickness have developed considerably over the last four centuries or more, and healing cults have during this period taken a more prominent part in the total fabric of African religion. Sickness is tied into religion because a god may make himself known to an individual through the very fact of sickness. A medium is often a person who has been sick, but overcome it. So cured sick people often attach themselves to a shrine to act as a mouthpiece of the god. They may then attract attention, and people may bring the sick to them for treatment.

A common thing in black Africa is to believe in the continued presence of ancestors in society. Here, a previous ruler escorted by his servants is represented at the shrine of the living Oba or ruler of Benin, in West Africa.

Shrines and ritual costumes are the key representatives of the *material* dimension. Many shrines are simply places where spirits reside: a grove in the forest or a fancy-shaped rock in a river. But some shrines are human, or at least involve buildings or markers, such as the palace-like buildings of gods in parts of East Africa. Much of African art is symbolic rather than representational, so you can know from the bits and pieces of a mask what it is (who it is, really) that it represents. Masks and body painting are prominent ways of displaying temporary and ritual possession. Some sculptures, for instance those of kneeling women among the Yoruba, reflect the devotees themselves; this is the human response to divine power rather than a direct representation of divine power itself.

Reflections on Classical African Religion

These brief glimpses of diverse societies provide just a sample of thousands of societies and religions. We have noted some themes from the dimensions of classical religion. Though there is some talk of revival of these ancient ways today, it is likely that their future lies within some larger synthesis, not only between different African societies and conceptions, but also between them and the forces which have been crowding into Africa from outside. African religion is a deeply important facet of human history up to the modern period. It will remain a resource for black Africans, and more widely for humans. But it has never been a single system, or even approximated to a single tradition, which has marked some of the historical world religions.

New Religious Movements in Modern Africa

The Pan-African Worldview

It is notable that much of the African and black theology is based on the sense that there is a common African or black experience. This was scarcely true before the colonial period. The lack of communications in many areas, the divisions of language, the lack of a living "other" to promote a sense of solidarity among blacks – these and many other factors worked against any unitary vision of Africa. It was above all through the colonial experience, and the growing realization of the nature of black history and the sufferings so often meted out to Africans, that such a new sense of identity grew.

The advantage of a pan-African approach is that it combines values in a large enough unit to deal with the influx of such forces as science, capitalism, theories of economic development, Christianity, and so on. And yet an indigenous African worldview has not yet emerged which has quite the edge and complexity needed to embrace modern social and technological change. On the whole, the process of modernization has occurred through conversion to the Christian Churches, and to a lesser extent to Islam.

The Rise of the Independent Churches

By far the most dynamic phenomenon in the modern period has been the growth of independent Churches or new religious movements in a number of regions, which have produced variations chiefly on Christian themes but have tried to adapt religion to the African condition rather than accept the foreign structures of Western missionary religion. They form a bridge between classical African religions and Western thought, and between indigenous values and those of the modern world. Estimates of the number of new religions vary, but probably there are about 10,000, spread over such regions as Nigeria, Ghana, central Kenya, Zaire, and South Africa, but less evident in Uganda and Tanzania. Perhaps fifteen per cent of all Christians in Africa belong to such groups.

There were a number of problems in Africa for blacks in regard to the white religion. One was the general question of control – mission Churches tended to be very paternalistic. Another was the role of ancestor cults, which were important socially in the African scene, but seen as superstitious or idolatrous by the missionaries. Another was the problem of polygamy, which was fairly widespread and built into social structures. There were great injustices caused if a man had to give up all but one wife. Another very potent issue was that of health. In some matters so-called Western medicine was seen to be effective, but in other areas it was much less so, and so a reversion to classical African modes of treatment was reasonable. There were analogies, too, with faith-healing in the Christian context.

In some degree the new religious movements dealt with these problems, by for instance splitting off from mainstream Churches under black leadership; or by focusing on a black Prophet or Messiah figure; or by otherwise establishing black control. They could incorporate methods of faith-healing or more traditional medicine; and they could allow polygamy (with the Bible at their disposal Africans could easily see that polygamy was part of the fabric of ancient Israelite religion). They could reintegrate other features of African society and religious practice.

The first example we will look at is the one founded through the example of the prophet Simon Kimbangu (1889–1951). It is an interesting case, because it was a breakaway movement which, nevertheless, became a member of the World Council of Churches in 1969, thus attaining a kind of ecumenical "respectability." It is a case of Christianity rejoining the mainstream.

The Church of Jesus Christ on Earth Through the Prophet Simon Kimbangu

Simon Kimbangu was born in what was then the Belgian Congo, later renamed Zaire, and was baptized a Baptist after his marriage. He was not able to become a pastor, failing his examinations, though he was trained as a catechist. He received visionary calls to be a healer, and eventually started to heal. He rapidly gained converts, and the colonial administration saw this as a threat. His arrest was ordered in 1921, but he eluded his would-be captors, until later in that year, when he voluntarily surrendered. Though he was sentenced to death for possible/alleged subversion against Belgian rule, the sentence was commuted by the Belgian king. He stayed in prison for the rest of his life and died in 1951. His imprisonment only increased his appeal as a prophet, and the movement continued to spread despite the exile and imprisonment of many of his followers (over two thousand). After his death his Church was reorganized by his youngest son in accordance with his wishes, and eventually came to join the World Council and to be one of the officially recognized Churches of Zaire, with over four million members.

In some ways, of course, Simon Kimbangu's career reminded his followers of the life of Jesus: here too there was a call, a healing ministry, a large following, condemnation to death by a colonial regime. It is notable that the themes of the Bible could reverberate in this way, and cause the Prophet to recognize in his own healing powers the work of the Holy Spirit.

The experiential dimension: the prophetic and shamanistic experiences of this man, Isaiah Shembe, drove him to form the Nazarite Church in Natal province in South Africa. Such independent forms of Christianity are a marked feature of the black African scene.

The Prophet Shembe and South African Zionism

Many of the new religious movements in South Africa have to do with healing. They also emphasize the charismatic powers of their leaders. They were influenced to a greater or lesser degree by an American Church which had some presence in South Africa, the Evangelical Christian Catholic Church of Zion City, Illinois. For this reason these new movements are often classified as Zionist. Since they often look forward to earthly liberation, the name has a deeper significance too.

One of the most notable of these was founded among the Zulu by the Prophet Isaiah Shembe (1870?–1935). At a time when the Zulu people had been deprived of much of its land, and not long after the Zulu rebellion of 1906, Shembe had visionary experiences. In one of these, at the mountain of Inhlangakazi, he underwent twelve days of retreat, temptations, and final victory, through which he got new powers both of casting out evil spirits and of healing. He set up his center at another mountain, Ekuphakameni, outside Durban, which is the scene of a great annual gathering. Shembe's career made many of his followers look on him as Messiah. At any rate, the Nazarite Church which he founded was deeply imbued by his remarkable creativity in composing a body of hymns, which welled up inside him, and which he committed to writing, having learned to read in his early forties

251

Opposite The ritual dimension: Water has played a prominent part in classical African religion and is given new significance in new forms of African Christianity.

for this purpose. This body of hymns was embedded in lovely rituals of solemn dancing and singing, with his followers dressed in the Zulu style. It was a religion of renewal and revival, among a people who had been crushed in war and deprived by colonial rule.

Reflections on Black Africa

The scene in Africa is one of great dynamism. The future will no doubt see the continued spread of Christianity and Islam at the expense of classical African religious forms. The societies in which they are based are on the whole too small to be able to bear the full impact of modern social changes, especially the magnetism of the cities. This last phenomenon will no doubt favor those new movements which can give people a new sense of identity in larger, more impersonal contexts. The struggle over the colonial heritage is by no means complete – the battle in South Africa to get rid of the vestiges and effects of apartheid is still in full flow and probably will last for many years. And Africans still have to put up with the low value placed on their cultural achievements and styles of life by the West. An important ingredient in the attempt to break free from these limitations, and to spell out Africa's distinctive contributions to a world civilization both in the future and from the past, will be the formation of a philosophical framework in which we can view African ideas and institutions. Meanwhile Africa overseas is important, in South America, the Caribbean and North America particularly. There, too, religious dynamism is evident.

Dimensions of African Spirituality

We finish by looking briefly at the dimensions of modern African, and especially Christian, religion. Naturally there is great variety, as we have seen, but some patterns emerge.

First, as to *ritual*: forms of Christianity, both mainstream and new religions, have stressed African forms of worship. This is most notable in the hymns and devotionalism of some of the new movements, in the dance of Shembe's Church, for instance, and in the use of vernacular languages. Impetus to indigenization was given by Vatican II. For many Africans, because of the shortage of priests and pastors among the mainstream Churches, and for other reasons, the Eucharist is not so central. Vital is the imagery of baptism, partly because of the purificatory symbolism of water in the classical African background, and also because of the often spiritual character of streams.

In the *experiential* dimension, there remains an important place for dreams and visions in the formation of new movements – and because of the affinity between African classical religion and Pentecostalism the latter has widespread life. Commitment becomes more important in the shifting choices of urban life and transformations of rural economies, and in these circumstances conversion experiences are important.

As for *ethics*, there is still heartsearching about marriage customs and the role of polygamy in African society. There are also issues about duties toward the ancestors. Very important in the African scene is a sense of solidarity, brotherhood, and sisterhood, which some of the new religious communities wish to express with intensity.

As for the *doctrinal* dimension, there is some way to go in formulating the characteristic African holism in its modern cosmological setting. How can we combine some traditional African views of the interrelation of forces in the universe with a modern scientific worldview? There is also the problem of providing the philosophical basis for religious pluralism in the African setting.

The dimension of *myth* leaves much to reflect on in telling the story of Africa in the perspectives of world history, and the relation of Christianity in Africa to that. It looks as if there is a story emerging which emphasizes the sufferings of blacks, through the slave trade and the colonial era, as providing a parallel with the life of the Israelites in the Old Testament and the role of the Suffering Servant.

In *art*, African carving and painting has already made its first major impact on Western imagination, and is poised to express more deeply the new spiritualities which are flourishing in Africa.

Africa is an exuberant as well as a problem-haunted continent. The dimensions of its religious life match the contributions of other areas, but it may be that deeper creativities also are yet to come.

CHAPTER 12

Conclusion:

Recent Trends in the World of Religions

Toward a New Millennium

The 1990s see profound changes in the world. First, the disintegration of the Marxist states of Eastern Europe, including the old Soviet Union, reveals older forces of nationalism, long suppressed and masked by Communism. These nationalist trends are sometimes entwined with religion. In the former Yugoslavia there is a revival of Islam in Bosnia. Croatia and Serbia are divided less by language than by religion (the first Catholic, the second Orthodox). The Islamic republics of Central Asia are cultivating new relations with neighboring states such as Iran and Turkey. Azerbaijan and Armenia, one Islamic the other Orthodox, are in conflict. Orthodoxy revives in Russia, and Jews have been given new freedoms, including the ability to emigrate.

Second, the center of gravity in Christianity has decisively moved south, though this is not apparently reflected by the Churches' key institutions. Latin America (from Mexico to Patagonia) and Africa (from Ghana to South Africa) will become the main demographic centers of Christian piety and eventually power.

Third, Islam, outside the old Soviet Union, is feeling a new surge of confidence. Its presence in Europe is more apparent, in the old Yugoslavia and in immigrant host countries such as Britain, Germany, and, above all, France.

Fourth, evangelical forms of Christianity are making strong inroads outside more traditional areas, notably in Korea and in Latin America. At the same time new African independent churches and new religious movements are making their presence felt. For instance, they comprise up to a third of the population in South Africa.

Fifth, there are signs that the older Hindu universalism is starting to break down, and a militant revivalism threatens Hindu–Muslim peace in the subcontinent. Meanwhile Buddhism is making a slow recovery from the devastations caused by the Marxist regimes of Asia and the occupation of Tibet.

Sixth, the attraction of secular ideologies has greatly diminished, especially forms of Marxism. However, nationalism, through the lens of ethnic religions, retains great vigor, especially in areas where the lid of totalitarianism has been removed, as in the Balkans and in the former Soviet Union.

These various trends profoundly affect the world as a whole. But they have their varied impacts on the three major faiths of Christianity, Judaism, and Islam.

Modern Christianity: Between Liberalism and Conservatism

Much of mainstream Christianity, and particularly in the North, is a form of liberal or modernist religion in that it takes into account modern scholarship and thinking. So it goes beyond Biblical literalism and pays a lot of attention to social and political concerns which are, broadly speaking, liberal. There is action to help the poor and struggling peoples, and there is worry about environmentalism. Women's causes are much more prominent among Christians, and many Churches and denominations have women priests and ministers. There is a strong drive toward ecumenism, and so the World Council of Churches promotes interchange between the varied members of the Christian family of denominations.

Most of these qualities of liberal Christianity became apparent in Roman Catholicism, notably after Vatican II in the early 1960s. The Church had resisted modernism, but found that it could no longer do so realistically in

The final act of the Second Vatican Council was a procession and mass at St. Peter's on December 8, 1965. Here are seen both Western and Eastern bishops and patriarchs.

face of the forces of the contemporary world. Some brakes have been put on such developments by the more conservative John Paul II, who became Pope in 1978.

A variation on the modernist theme has been Liberation Theology, notably in Latin America, which encourages direct action to deal with social problems and racism. In combating some of these results of colonialism, Catholicism took on a vigorous left-wing flavor in a number of areas in Latin America and elsewhere.

On the other hand, conservative reactions to modernism and liberalism have become evident in the last two decades of the twentieth century. In North America evangelical and fundamentalist Christians found a new role in public politics, reinforcing the political conservatism and patriotism of the Reagan years. For them, the erosion of Biblical authority by liberal scholars and various activists, such as feminists, represented a serious challenge, which seemed to undermine the certainties of faith. Moreover, there grew a nostalgia for older values, perceived to be swallowed up by the wave of social change initiated above all in the 1960s. A new emphasis on family values, in the wake of the development of a high rate of divorce, single-parent families, gay and lesbian rights, and so on, led to right-wing campaigns against easy, or any, rights to abortion. Though this conservatism was strong in America, it had much less impact on Europe. However, under John Paul II, the Roman Catholic Church withdrew somewhat from its more liberal stances in the decade after Vatican II. The right-wing clerical and lay pressure group, Opus Dei, saw a great revival of its influence on Rome.

Evangelical and fundamentalist Christianity also benefited from its flourishing inroads into Latin American life. In addition, it began to get a more meaningful foothold in Eastern Europe and Russia after 1989 and the shriveling of Marxism.

Modernists and conservatives have not become so polarized in the Eastern Orthodox Churches. This is partly because Eastern Churches have such a strong investment in a relatively unchanging ritual dimension, and partly because until its collapse in 1989 they have been greatly preoccupied with the problem of living under the Marxist regime. The new order emerging in the post-Soviet era will no doubt pose to the Churches some of the same issues of modernism which have been faced in the West.

Christianity and Alternatives

In the Western world particularly the recent era has seen an intensification of individualism. This is beginning to spread with the demise of the old collectivism in the former Soviet Union, and in Eastern Europe. As a result there is a growing number of people, who while affirming their spirituality do not belong to any one organization or tradition. A major variety of this type of interest in religion is the New Age movement. We have already noted some of the major motifs which go to make up this somewhat nebulous range of concerns (p. 172). It attests among other things to a shift in attitudes. At

East comes West: a child practicing a form of Indian yoga in America.

one time, the ethos of many Western societies was utilitarian; the worth of an action or institution lay, according to this philosophy, in whether it contributed toward the greatest happiness of the greatest number. Yet the idea of happiness was thought of as worldly and as signifying a fairly superficial kind of wellbeing. The New Agers are dissatisfied with this surface conception and seek wellbeing at deeper levels of the self and in various mystical and religious practices, which range in scope from white witchcraft to aromatherapy.

A rather different slant – though also aimed at a more profound kind of happiness – is taken by those who put their faith in a growing coalescence of major religions, following a theme which dates from the famous World Parliament of Religions in Chicago in 1893. Some writers, notably John Hick (b. 1922), see a kind of Copernican revolution in religious consciousness. The different faiths present diverse paths to salvation or liberation and differing images of reality. But it is useful to think of all these paths and images converging in one Reality – a single "Real" is like the sun, and the varied faiths revolve round it like the planets. There is no doubt that the religions will modify each other during this period of globalization in world culture, both through mutual contacts and more formal dialogue.

The Future of Judaism

Meanwhile, as has already been noted, the future of Judaism will become increasingly tied to that of its two most significant communities – in the United States and in Israel, even if there are often tensions. Recent heavy immigration by Russian Jews into Israel will increase the already considerable pressures to create settlements on the West Bank, occupied in the Six-Day War of 1967. Despite the fact of peace talks in 1992 onward, the peaceful future of Israel is by no means assured. While Islamic militancy, defining itself in part by anti-Israel sentiment, rumbles throughout the Arab world and beyond, there remain severe possibilities of conflict. Moreover some secularist Arab regimes, such as Iraq and Syria, may constitute a threat in the long run. Nevertheless, because of its multifaceted significance, Israel can be expected to be a permanent fixture in the area. First, it constitutes a focus of loyalty for Jews whether they be secular or religious – this helps to cement a community whose religious loyalties are in some decline. Second, it has changed the dynamics of Judaism. No longer is the Eretz a kind of mythic nostalgia, but a concrete geographical place. Jews do not have to be overjoyed at the victories of Judas Maccabaeus and find, amid present troubles, a kind of substitute happiness in events of long ago. There are modern victories and achievements to celebrate.

Third, it represents a huge hostage to fortune in the shifting balances of the new world order (or disorder) coming on top of the end of the Cold War. Fourth, its existence provides a profoundly significant topic for discussion about the status and character of Messianism. It also points out the dilemmas in the whole idea that the Jewish people are called by God to be a "light to the Gentiles" – in other words a moral example to the whole world. It is difficult to combine such ideals with the vicissitudes of statecraft and the military struggles on and beyond the West Bank.

Meanwhile, in the new diaspora (new in the sense that so many parts of the old diaspora – in the Arab lands, Russia, Europe above all – have shrunk and changed), there are sizeable and successful settlements of Jews in South Africa, Argentina, Brazil, and other countries in Latin America. However, these are in immigrant communities, at least from a European point of view. In other words, most Jews have migrated rather recently from the old heartlands of northern, southern and eastern Europe.

The price of integration into mainly white environments has been the drift into merger with the dominant culture, with all its opportunities and challenges. There are perils, especially in North America, for traditional Judaism and even Reform tradition. It is true that there is a conservative revival, which in turn has had its impact on migration into Israel. But one can expect, unless some unforeseen catastrophe revives Jewish solidarity, an increasing shrinkage of Jewish practice, amid increasing Jewish pride in the achievements of the community in the face of the horrors of this century.

The Future of Islam

If the center of gravity of Christianity has moved south, that of Islam has moved east – to South Asia, Malaysia and Indonesia particularly, and, since the demise of the U.S.S.R., to a respiritualized Central Asia. Demographically the Muslim East is overwhelming – more than 300 million in South Asia, and more than 250 million in Southeast Asia, for instance, and another 150 million in Central Asia and China. (The significance of the different forms of Islam is discussed in the sister volume to this one, *Religions of Asia*.) There are bound to be changes wrought by this population balance. One might expect Islam in the republic of India to become more militant, and Hinduism shows similar signs, as shown by the recent destruction of a Muslim mosque in Ayodhya in northern India, allegedly the birthplace of the Hindu god Rāma. Such incidents have created instability and may even cause war in South Asia – a possibility rendered the more perilous by the nuclear arsenals being developed by India and Pakistan.

While the Islamic world is necessarily becoming more and more integrated into the global capitalist economy, it has its reasons to resist the West. It has religious reservations about interest payments in its traditional law or *Sharī'a*, and so various alternatives to charging interest are being developed in Islamic banking. Such problems are difficult to resolve in the modern world. But much more importantly, modernism calls into question the pattern of strict Islamic life. The question can't be answered, as famous Islamic modernists like Muhammad 'Abduh (see p. 209) have demonstrated, and countries such as Egypt still carry on in this compromise tradition. But nationalist backlash, especially among Arabs, has often taken an Islamic form. So-called Islamic fundamentalism is marching forward. Already a number of countries have imposed stricter forms of Islamic law – such as Pakistan, the Sudan, Saudi Arabia and, of course, Iran. But just as vital is the way radical Islamic groups, often suppressed violently by secular regimes, are making headway. The following are a few examples. In Egypt the Muslim Brotherhood, still banned from forming itself into a political party, is highly influential, especially among university students – in alliance with secular parties it has managed to be represented in parliament by thirty-seven seats. Meanwhile, the more radical group the Jihad (or Holy Struggle) works underground. This group was responsible for assassinating President Sadat, for his softness toward Israel. Though he started the nearly successful Yom Kippur War in 1973, Sadat also made peace with Israel through the Camp David Accord (1978) – enough to alienate him from the more militant groups.

In Jordan the fundamentalist bloc is the largest group in the Parliament. In Sudan the National Islamic Front has great influence in the government of Omar Bashir, the general who took power in the 1989 coup. There is a continuing civil war against the Christian and classical-African South that has a greatly religious flavor, though its main motivation is nationalist (that is, the maintenance of meaningless national boundaries inherited from colonial times). In Libya, the regime of Colonel Qaddafi is theoretically Islamic – he is a kind of Qur'anic fundamentalist socialist – but more orthodox believers move underground, challenging the regime. Who knows what the future will bring there? In Tunisia Islamic radicals are severely repressed; while in Algeria, the FIS (or Islamic Salvation Front) won the general election in 1991, but was smothered by the government. In Syria, Islamic fundamentalists are brutally put down. In Afghanistan Islamic movements took over the government in 1992, and may impose an Islamic republic.

All these and other instances imply that there is a militant upsurge which may eventually dominate Middle Eastern politics. More widely, there is a greater sense of Islamic solidarity in the world. Moreover, there is an important Islamic diaspora, in the countries of Northern Europe particularly – notably Germany, Holland and Britain. Despite the split between Sunni and Shi'a Islam, there are obvious developments toward the unification, and thereby increased muscle, of the Islamic world.

Naturally in such countries, though Muslims may increase their earnings and so help with varying causes across the Islamic world, Islam has to live in a minority. With globalization the awareness of this is affecting all religions. Though Christianity is the most populous of all the major religions, ultimately it is a minority in the total world community. The same applies to Islam: both need to adjust to this condition. Islamic law may come to be the norm in a whole host of Islamic countries, but it will still not be the norm in a global community. This poses issues for the way in which Islamic law has to be conceived.

The Future of Secular Ideologies

Meanwhile the world is at a turning-point in philosophy and ideology. Scientific humanism, linked to democratic ideas, remains a powerful intellectual force, reinforced by empiricist and analytic philosophy as practiced widely in English-speaking countries. But darker, more irrational forces are at work: new racism in Europe, and, perhaps fading now, Deconstructionism, as well as the more general slippery slope of post-modernism. These have value in reminding us of the fragility and conditioned nature of human reason and the dangers of too rash claims to objectivity. They link up in some degree with some motifs in Buddhism, and indeed to Marxism. But their subjectivism will not, I suspect, remain satisfying. The human race has so many urgent problems which need new thought. Capitalism has been so far unable really to deal with environmental-ism and the problem of how to accommodate communal spirituality. Marxism proved to be hopeless, and in many cases fraudulent, in dealing with the severe problems of underdevelopment and poverty. Furthermore, it bred a new colonialism. The question of how to reshape formerly communist systems is still unanswered, though part of the answer may well be being worked out, in somewhat repressive circumstances, in China.

It may be that a new history in the tradition of, but beyond, Hegel and Marx, is needed which is humanist but not negative about the spiritual and living needs of people – one which stresses the strength of identity, but within a global structure extending beyond humans to other species. One may also need a recognition that while utter relativism leads to hopelessness, emptiness and weakness, absolute positions are just as deadly – or perhaps more so. There is need for what I call a soft non-relativism, in which people can retain their good reasons for being this or that – Christian or Jewish or Muslim or Buddhist and/or Scottish or American or Australian or Ugandan or Indian or whatever – without viewing other humans as if they belong to different species. For with nuclear weapons looming and spreading, we may run into unparalleled disasters if we fail to understand how human history is driving us inexorably toward a single system and a single human identity. With their transnational character, the traditional religions, as well as a new philosophical humanism, will have an important part to play in softening divisions rather than (as so often) deepening them.

The Importance of the Study of Worldviews

If it were not so often ignored, it would be hard to deny that the study of religion and, more broadly, human worldviews, both modern and traditional, should be a vital ingredient in education. Happily there is a growth of the crosscultural exploration of worldviews in many colleges and universities across the globe. I believe that the vitality and significance of this field will be recognized even more widely as the new global civilization develops.

The virtues which can flow from this study are intrinsic. The exploration of other people of diverse cultures requires empathy – that particular imaginative faculty that carries with it a kind of respect for others' feelings. It means too a suspension of our own point of view, so that we are not hasty in the judgment of others. It breeds the recognition that people can have very different beliefs and yet share elements of spirituality and of ethical concern. Absolute certainty at the public level is therefore not possible, but only inner faith and certitude. From this comes the idea that we have to be tolerant of one another where serious divergences of commitment occur. Historically, it also illuminates ways in which traditions can change, so that there is always hope of convergence of ideas and practices, where desirable, in the future. It suggests too that forces such as nationalism are rather recent in human history, even if ethnic and other differences have always in the past helped to nurture conflict. In all these ways the study of religion nudges us toward a tolerant, informed, empathetic, wise, and rounded view of and attitude toward other human beings.

Because there is so much to learn, it will remind us all that courses, textbooks, and teachers are only the very beginning, if that. Learning about others carries us through our whole life. And its uses will be seen ultimately to be many.

Bibliography

Anthologies of Scriptures
The following collections may be useful in conjunction with the other readings, which are arranged by chapter.

Robert G. Ballou, ed., *The Portable World Bible*, New York, 1976.
Mircea Eliade, ed., *From Primitives to Zen*, New York, 1977.
Ninian Smart and Richard Hecht, eds., *Sacred Texts of the World*, London and New York, 1982.
Andrew Wilson, ed., *World Scriptures*, New York, 1976.

Introduction
Mircea Eliade, ed., *The Encyclopedia of Religion*, 15 vols., New York, 1987.
John R. Hinnells, ed., *Dictionary of Religions*, New York, 1984.
——————— , *A Handbook of Living Religions*, New York, 1985.
——————— , *Who's Who of World Religions*, New York, 1991.
Roger Schmidt, *Exploring Religion*, Belmont, 1988.
Eric J. Sharpe, *Comparative Religion: A History*, London 1976.
——————— , *Understanding Religious Life*, London, 1983.
Ninian Smart, *Worldviews*, New York, 1994.
G. van der Leeuw, *Religion in Essence and Manifestation*, Princeton, 1987.

The Dawn of Western Religions
W. F. Albright, *From the Stone Age to Christianity*, Baltimore, 1958.
Thomas George Allen, ed., *The Book of the Dead*, Chicago, 1974.
J. Gray, *Near Eastern Mythology*, London, 1969.
S. N. Kramer, *History Begins at Sumer*, New York, 1963.
Siegfried Morenz, *Egyptian Religion*, New York, 1973.
Helmer Ringgren, *Religions of the Ancient Near East*, Philadelphia, 1973.

Zoroastrianism and Manichaeism
Mary Boyce, *Zoroastrians: Their Religious Beliefs and Practices*, London, 1979.
——————— , *Textual Sources for the Study of Zoroastrianism*, Manchester, 1982.
John R. Hinnells, *Zoroastrianism and the Parsees*, London, 1981.
Jacques Duchesne–Guillemin, *The Western Response to Zoroaster*, Oxford, 1958.
S. N. C. Lieu, *The Religion of Light*, Hong Kong, 1979.
——————— , *Manichaeism in the Later Roman Empire and China*, Manchester, 1982.
Geo Widengren, *Mani and Manichaeism*, New York, 1965.
R. C. Zaehner, *The Dawn and Twilight of Zoroastrianism*, New York, 1961.

Greek, Roman, and Imperial Religions
Peter Brown, *The Making of Late Antiquity*, Cambridge, Mass., 1979.
Walter Burkert, *Greek Religion*, Cambridge, Mass., 1985.
Hilda Davidson, *Gods and Myths of Northern Europe*, Baltimore, 1964.
G. S. Kirk, *The Nature of Greek Myths*, New York, 1975.
Ramsay MacMullen, *Paganism in the Roman Empire*, New Haven, 1981.
M. P. Nilsson, *A History of Greek Religion*, New York, 1964.
H. J. Rose, *Ancient Roman Religion*, 1948.
Richard T. Wallis, *Neoplatonism*, London, 1972.

The Israelites and Early Judaism
Salo W. Baron, *A Social and Religious History of the Jews*, 18 vols., New York, 1952–80.
I. Epstein, *Judaism*, Harmondsworth, 1968.

Yehezkel Kaufmann, *The Religion of Israel: From Its Beginnings to the Babylonian Exile*, Chicago, 1960.
C. G. Montefiore and Herbert Loewe, ed., *A Rabbinic Anthology*, New York, 1974.
Jacob Neusner, *Judaism: The Evidence of the Mishnah*, Chicago, 1981.
George W. Ramsey, *The Quest for the Historical Israel*, Atlanta, 1981.
G. G. Scholem, *Major Trends in Jewish Mysticism*, New York, 1964.

Late Medieval and Modern Judaism
Joseph Blau, *Modern Varieties of Judaism*, New York, 1966.
Steven T. Katz, *Post-Holocaust Dialogues*, New York, 1983.
E. Kedourie, ed., *The Jewish World*, New York, 1979.
H. Rabinowicz, *The World of Hasidism*, London, 1970.
D. Rudavsky, *Modern Jewish Religious Movements*, New York, 1979.
Alan Unterman, *The Jews: Their Religious Beliefs and Practices*, Boston, 1981.

Early and Medieval Christianity
David B. Barrett, *World Christian Encyclopedia*, Nairobi, 1982.
Peter Brown, *The Cult of the Saints*, Chicago, 1980.
Hilda Davidson, *Pagan Scandinavia*, New York, 1967.
C. H. Dodd, *The Founder of Christianity*, New York, 1970.
W. H. C. Frend, *The Early Church*, Philadelphia, 1966.
M. Gimbutas, *The Slavs*, New York, 1971.
Martin Hengel, *The Son of God*, Philadelphia, 1976.
Paul Johnson, *A History of Christianity*, New York, 1976.
Ramsay MacMullen, *Christianizing the Roman Empire*, New Haven, 1984.
Francis Oakley, *The Medieval Experience*, Cheektowaga, New York, 1988.
A and B. Rees, *Celtic Heritage*, London, 1975.
Timothy Ware, *The Orthodox Church*, Baltimore, 1980.

Christianity in the Modern Era
Ernst Cassirer *The Philosophy of the Enlightenment*, Boston, 1951.
W. Owen Chadwick, *The Reformation*, Baltimore, 1968.
Peter Gay, *The Enlightenment*, New York, 1966.
Kenneth Scott Latourette, *Christianity in a Revolutionary Age*, 3 vols., New York, 1954–61.
——————— , *A History of the Expansion of Christianity*, 7 vols., London, 1971.
E. Molland, *Christendom*, New York, 1959.
R. Dean Patterson, *A Concise History of Christianity*, Belmont, 1993.
George H. Williams, *The Radical Reformation*, Philadelphia, 1962.

The Christianities of North America
Sydney E. Ahlstrom, *A Religious History of the American People*, New Haven, 1973.
Catherine Albanese, *America: Religion and Religions*, Belmont, 1992.
Julia M. Corabett, *Religion in America*, Englewood Cliffs, New Jersey, 1990.
Ann Douglas, *The Feminization of American Culture*, New York, 1977.
J. T. Ellis, *American Catholicism*, Chicago, 1969.
Susannah Heschel, ed., *On Being a Jewish Feminist*, New York, 1983.
Martin Marty, *Righteous Empire*, New York, 1970.
Wade Clark Roof, *A Generation of Seekers*, San Francisco, 1993.
Elizabeth Schüssler–Fiorenza, *In Memory of Her*, New York, 1953.

Early, Classical, and Medieval Islam
A. J. Arberry, *The Koran Interpreted*, New York, 1955.
Thomas F. Glick, *Islamic and Christian Spain in the Early Middle Ages*, Princeton, 1979.
S. Hussain and M. Jagri, *Origins and Early Development of Shi'a Islam*, London, 1979.
Richard C. Martin, *Islam: A Cultural Perspective*, Englewood Cliffs, New Jersey, 1982.
Marmaduke Pickthall, *The Meaning of the Glorious Koran*, New York, 1930.
F. Rahman, *Islam*, Chicago, 1979.
Roger M. Savory, ed., *An Introduction to Islamic Civilization*, New York, 1976.
Joseph Schacht, *An Introduction to Islamic Law*, Oxford, 1974.
H. Montgomery Watt, *Muhammad: Prophet and Statesman*, London, 1974.

Islam in the Modern Era
A. J. Arberry, ed., *Religion in the Middle East: Three Religions in Concord and Conflict*, 2 vols., Cambridge, 1969.
Hichem Djalt, *Europe and Islam*, Berkeley, 1985.
Clifford Geertz, *Islam Observed*, New Haven, 1968.
Y. Haddad *et al.*, eds., *The Islamic Impact*, Syracuse, 1984.
Bernard Lewis, *The Emergence of Modern Turkey*, London, 1963.
M. Perkins and P. Hainsworth, *The Bahā'ī Faith*, London, 1980.
F. Rahman, *Islam and Modernity*, Chicago, 1982.
Wilfred C. Smith, *Islam in Modern History*, Princeton, 1957.

Classical and New Religions in the Americas, the Pacific, and Africa
Burr C. Brundage, *The Fifth Sun: Aztec Gods, Aztec World*, Austin, 1979.
Mircea Eliade, *Australian Religions: An Introduction*, Ithaca, New York, 1973.
Adrian Hastings, *A History of Christianity in Africa, 1950–75*, New York, 1979.
Åke Hultkrantz, *The Religions of the North American Indians*, Berkeley, 1979.
Walter Krickeberg *et al.*, *Pre-Columbian American Religions*, New York, 1968.
Vittorio Lanternari, *Religions of the Oppressed*, New York, 1965.
Luis G. Lumbreras, *The Peoples and Cultures of Ancient Peru*, Washington D.C., 1974.
Roslyn Poignant, *Oceanic Mythology*, London, 1967.
Benjamin C. Ray, *African Religions*, New York, 1976.
J. Eric S. Thompson, *Maya History and Religion*, Norman, Okla., 1970.
H. W. Turner, *Religious Innovations in Africa*, Boston, 1980.
B. R. Wilson, *Magic and the Millennium*, New York, 1978.

Conclusion
David Martin, *A General Theory of Secularization*, San Francisco, 1979.
Peter Merkl and Ninian Smart, eds., *Religion and Politics in the Modern World*, New York, 1984.
Gerald J. Pillay, ed., *Religion and the Future*, Pretoria, 1992.
Wade Clark Roof, ed., *World Order and Religion*, Albany, 1991.

Picture Credits

The author, publishers, and Calmann & King Ltd wish to thank the following institutions and individuals who have provided photographic material for use in this book.

Frontispiece: Barnaby's/Juliet Soester

Introduction
page 12: Topham Picture Source/Associated Press
page 14: Popperfoto
page 15: Barnaby's
page 16: Rex Features
page 17: Harvard University Museum
page 19: John Moss/NHF

Chapter One
page 23: The Mansell Collection
page 26: The Mansell Collection
page 29: W. Forman/Barbara Heller Archive
page 31: Hutchison Picture Library
page 32: The Mansell Collection/Giraudon

Chapter Two
page 36: Edinburgh University Library
page 41: Magnum Photos Ltd/Barbey

Chapter Three
page 48: The Mansell Collection
page 52: Ancient Art and Architecture Collection
page 54: The Mansell Collection/London Museum
page 55: The Mansell Collection/Anderson
page 57: The Mansell Collection/Anderson

Chapter Four
page 58: Ancient Art and Architecture Collection
page 65: The British Library, London
page 68: The Mansell Collection
page 76: The Jewish Museum, New York
page 77: The Mansell Collection

Chapter Five
page 79: Fotomas Index
page 82: Topham Picture Source/The Metropolitan Museum of Art, New York
page 83: The British Library, London
page 86: Topham Picture Source
page 89: Popperfoto
page 90: Popperfoto/Reuters

Chapter Six
page 96: Calmann & King Archives
page 97: Pont Comm di Arch. Sacra, Rome
page 99: The Mansell Collection/Alinari
page 105: Calmann & King Archives
page 107: Victoria & Albert Museum, London
page 110: Calmann & King Archives
page 111: Calmann & King Archives

page 114: The Mansell Collection/The British Library

Chapter Seven
page 119: The Mansell Collection/Anderson
page 121: The Mansell Collection
page 124: Fotomas Index
page 126: Fotomas Index
page 130: The Mansell Collection
page 132: Rijksmuseum, Amsterdam
page 138: Andes Press Agency/Carlos Reyes
page 140: Popperfoto
page 144: The Mansell Collection
page 147: Popperfoto

Chapter Eight
page 153: Fotomas Index
page 155: The Mansell Collection
page 158: Barnaby's
page 164: Topham Picture Source
page 166: Magnum Photos Ltd/McCurry
page 169: Barnaby's

Chapter Nine
page 180: The British Library, London
page 184: The Victoria & Albert Museum
page 189: The Bodleian Library, Oxford
page 191: Rex Features
page 194: Rex Features
page 202: Rex Features

Chapter Ten
page 209: The Victoria & Albert Museum
page 218: Barnaby's
page 219: Robert Hunt Library/Black Star
page 220: Topham Picture Source
page 222: Popperfoto

Chapter Eleven
page 229: Photo James Mooney/Smithsonian Institution, National Anthropological Archives
page 232: Topham Picture Source
page 234: The Mansell Collection/The British Museum, London
page 236: Rietburg Museum, Zurich Collection: von der Heydt
page 239: The Museum of Mankind, London
page 240: Hutchison Picture Library
page 243: Australia News and Information Bureau
page 246: Robert Hunt Library/Black Star
page 248: W. Forman/Barbara Heller Archive
page 251: Popperfoto
page 253: Robert Hunt Library/Black Star

Chapter Twelve
page 256: Rex Features
page 258: Hutchison Picture Library/Highet

Index